水文化汉英翻译教程

C-E WATER CULTURE TRANSLATION COURSEBOOK

顾 翔 主 编

李鲜红 朱 英 副主编

·南京·

图书在版编目(CIP)数据

水文化汉英翻译教程 / 顾翔主编 ; 李鲜红, 朱英副主编. -- 南京 : 河海大学出版社, 2023. 12
ISBN 978-7-5630-8494-4

Ⅰ. ①水… Ⅱ. ①顾… ②李… ③朱… Ⅲ. ①水-文化-中国-英语-翻译-教材 Ⅳ. ①K928. 4

中国国家版本馆 CIP 数据核字(2023)第 212994 号

书　　名　水文化汉英翻译教程
　　　　　SHUIWENHUA HANYING FANYI JIAOCHENG
书　　号　ISBN 978-7-5630-8494-4
责任编辑　周　贤
责任校对　张心怡
装帧设计　有品堂
出版发行　河海大学出版社
地　　址　南京市西康路 1 号(邮编:210098)
电　　话　(025)83737852(总编室)　(025)83722833(营销部)
经　　销　江苏省新华发行集团有限公司
排　　版　南京布克文化发展有限公司
印　　刷　广东虎彩云印刷有限公司
开　　本　718 毫米×1000 毫米　1/16
印　　张　16. 25
字　　数　386 千字
版　　次　2023 年 12 月第 1 版
印　　次　2023 年 12 月第 1 次印刷
定　　价　59. 00 元

主　　编： 顾　翔

副 主 编： 李鲜红　朱　英

参　　编：（按照汉语拼音顺序排列）

冯晓田　高小丽　黄　琪　刘心昊

强逸欣　滕卫东　王　腾　王玉雯

闻　雯　叶雨欣

前言

Preface

根据《大学英语教学指南》，大学英语课程体系主要由通用英语、专门用途英语和跨文化交际三大类课程组成。大学专门用途英语充分体现《大学英语教学指南》的精神，在大学英语教学改革实践的基础上，以培养专业英语能力为目标，将特定学科内容与英语语言学习相结合，着重于语言输入与输出训练相互融通，有助于学生达成英语语境下有效输出专门用途知识与技能的目标。

本教材以河海大学国家双一流高校"水特色"专业建设为契机，为本校及其他相关兄弟院校学生提供从通用英语翻译转向专业英语翻译能力培养的平滑性过渡平台，为他们尽快适应紧随其后的专业英语学习提供强有力的支持。教材依据"以内容为依托"的教学理念编写，具有时代感、知识性和应用性。其内容不仅反映文化翻译学科主线，而且还体现了水文化的基本概念和前沿信息，专业性和可读性相融相通。基于课文内容设计的专业词汇、学术英语词汇、水文化句段篇章翻译，将帮助学生在理解课文的同时掌握文中重要词汇，提高学生活学活用、举一反三的应变能力，并适度拓展其学科外应用能力，特别是水文化汉英翻译能力。

不仅如此，本教材还提供了设计灵活、注重实效的翻译思辨解析和学术技能训练，帮助学生在实践中提高翻译解析能力、习得翻译规范和质检标准、培养学术英语翻译能力，从而得体有效地用英语进行学业学习与学术交流。本教材内容分为八个单元，涵盖了与水文化相关的主要内容、各种必备的翻译策略和技巧、翻译质量标准、机器翻译及后期编辑能力培养，不仅能满足学生水相关专业翻译能力发展的需要，而且还能保证他们在大学期间的英语翻译技能得到持续性提高。丰富的翻译教学内容和多样化的翻译练习内容也为实现分类教学、因材施教提供可能。

本教材酝酿已久，早在2021级研究生入学后，我就一直与他们不断探讨如何编写该教材，原是编写水文化教材，后来转为《水文化汉英翻译教程》。顾翔负责第一单元所有内容的编写，李鲜红负责第二单元中文部分的编写及其英译以及第一单元至第四单元书稿的审稿工作，叶雨欣、黄琪、刘心昊、强逸欣、闻雯、王玉雯分别负责第三、第四、第五、第六、第七、第八单元的中文部分的撰写及其英译。滕卫东、冯晓田负责课程思政内容的收集及编辑，高小丽与王腾主要负责词汇部分和参考译文的审校工作，朱英负责第五单元至第八单元课文汉英翻译的审稿工作。其他部分都由本人负责完成。

本教材中汉英对比研究部分以及部分翻译策略和技巧深受北京大学陈德彰教授《汉英对比语言学》的启迪，沿用了他的部分思路进行编写，在此向他表示衷心的感谢。同时，也衷心感谢本教材参考文献中的所有学者。本书的出版得到“河海大学重点教材出版资金”的资助，谨此表示衷心的谢意。

顾翔

2023年8月于南京月光广场

目录

Contents

第一单元 文化,水文化及水文化建设

Unit 1 Culture, Water Culture and Its Construction

第一节　文化与水文化
Section A　Culture and Water Culture

文化,是一个国家和民族的灵魂和精神家园,是民族凝聚力和创造力的重要源泉,是国家发展和民族振兴的精神支撑,是衡量社会文明和人民生活质量的显著标志。文化是一种软实力,是一个国家或地区凝聚力、生命力、创造力、传播力、感召力和影响力的根基。提高国家文化软实力已成为重要的发展战略。文化的功能不仅取决于其内容形式的独特魅力,还取决于传播能力的强弱。20 世纪人类最大的变化是文化传播对人类社会和人类生产生活的全面渗透。

Culture is the soul and spiritual home of a country or a nation, an important source of national cohesion and creativity, a spiritual support for national development and rejuvenation, and a significant indicator of social civilization and people's quality of life. It is a kind of soft power and the very foundation of the cohesion, vitality, creativity, communication capacity, emotional appeal and influence of a country or a region. Enhancing cultural soft power has also become an important development strategy. The function of culture not only depends on the unique charm of its form and content, but also depends on the strength of communication skills. The biggest change in mankind in the 20th century is the full penetration of cultural dissemination into society and human production and life.

总体而言,水文化,是以水为载体、以人与水的关系为纽带形成的一种独特的文化形态,是中华文化的重要组成部分。水是生命之源、文明之母、生产之要、生态之基。早在 2600 多年前,管仲在《管子 · 水地》篇中说:"水者何也? 万物之本源也,诸生之宗室也。"老子在《道德经》中说:"上善若水。水善利万物而不争,处众人之所恶,故几于道。"孔子在《论语》中说:"智者乐水。"这样的例子不胜枚举,都说明了水具有显著的文化意义。

Generally speaking, water culture is a unique form of culture, with water as its carrier and the relationship between man and water as its link. It is an important component of Chinese culture. Water is the source of life, the mother of civilization, the key to production, and the foundation of ecology. As early as

2,600 years ago, Guan Zhong said in his *Guanzi Chapter of Water and Land*: "What is water? It is the very source of all life forms." Lao Tzu said in *Dao De Jing* (*The Book of the Way and Its Virtues*): "The supreme good is like water. Water benefits everything by giving without taking or contending. It likes the place others dislike, so it follows closely the divine law." In *The Analects*, Confucius said: "The wise find pleasure in water." The list goes on and on, all demonstrating that water is of remarkable cultural significance.

具体而言，水文化是人们在处理人水关系活动中创造的以精神成果为核心，物质、行为和制度等成果的总和。它体现了人与水关系的社会状态，是由全体社会成员共同创造的；水文化的创造既是对水的自然规律的认识，又是改善人水关系的实践行为；是人与水在依赖、依存、发展、升华过程中所形成的精神成果和物质成果；是人们在长期从事水利水事水务活动中对水的深刻感悟和理性思辨；是对"用水、治水、管水、亲水"思想理念和实践行为规律性的认识与把握。

Specifically speaking, water culture is the sum of material, behavioral and institutional achievements created by people in the activities of dealing with the relationship between man and water. It embodies the social state of the relationship between man and water, and is created by all members of the society as a whole. The creation of water culture is not only the product of the understanding of the natural laws of water, but also a practice to improve the relationship between man and water. It is the spiritual and material achievements formed in the process of mutual reliance, interdependence, development and sublimation; it is people's deep understanding and rational thinking of water in the long-term water conservancy and water affairs; it is the understanding and mastery of the idea of "water use, water governance, water management, and water access".

从逻辑上看，水文化是文化的一个子系统。但水为自然之物，本身并不具有文化属性。水文化是在人水关系中形成的文化，是在人与水打交道的过程中创造出来的。水作为一种媒介、载体，只有与人类的物质活动和精神活动相结合，才会产生水文化。水文化产生的关键是人水关系中人的创造性活动。人是水文化的主体，水事活动是产生水文化的源泉。人水关系范围广，涉及生活的各个方面。水文化的历史与人类社会的历史一样久远，而且在不断的发展之中。水文化包括我们熟知的"酒文化""茶文化""畜牧文化""渔业文化""农耕文化""饮食文化""花卉文化"等。从某种意义上说，每个人都与水文化相关。水文化是社会性的文化,具有母体文化的性质,渗透在许多分支文化之中,并对其产生重要影响。

Logically speaking, water culture is a subsystem of culture. But water is a natural thing, and it does not have cultural attributes in itself. Water culture is a culture formed in the process of developing the relationship between man and water, created in the process of dealing with water. As a medium and carrier, water can yield water culture only when it is combined with material and spiritual activities of human beings. The key to the emergence of water culture is the creative activities of people in human-water relations. People are the main body of water culture, and water activities are the source of water culture. The relationship between man and water is broad and involves every aspect of life. The history of water culture is as long as that of human society, and it is constantly developing. Water culture includes the well-known "wine culture", "tea culture", "livestock culture", "fishery culture", "farming culture", "food culture", "flower culture" and so on. In a sense, everyone is related to water culture. Water culture is a social culture, which has the nature of maternal culture, penetrates into many branches of culture and exerts an important influence on them.

水文化不同于水利文化。正如尉天骄教授所言,水文化属于社会性的文化,涉及人类社会的各个方面,与各行各样都有密切联系,是一个"大圆";水利文化属于行业文化,具有鲜明的行业内容和特色,是一个"小圆"。前者的外延比后者要大。但是治水、管水是人水关系中最为重要的部分,因此以治水管水、除害兴利为主要内容的"水利文化"对社会的进步和经济发展影响深远,在"水文化"中居于核心地位。水工程的文化内涵、水环境的文化价值,以及治水文化、管水文化等,属于"水文化"和"水利文化"的共核。

Water culture differs from water conservancy culture. Just as Professor Wei Tianjiao said, water culture is a social culture, which involves all aspects of human society and is closely related to all walks of life. It is a "big circle". Water conservancy culture belongs to industry culture with distinctive content and characteristics of that industry, and it is a "small circle". The connotation of the former is broader than that of the latter. But water governance and water management are the most important part of the human-water relationship. Therefore, the water conservancy culture, whose main content is water governance and water management, and elimination of harms and promotion of benefits, has a profound impact on social progress and economic development, so water conservancy culture is at the core of water culture. The cultural connotation of water engineering, the cultural value of the water environment, as well as the culture of water governance and management etc., are the common core of "water culture" and "water conservancy culture".

水文化的精髓是水的哲学和水的精神。北京大学王岳川教授说："水体现了中华文化精神的极大美德：公正、勇敢、坚韧、洁净；体现出了生命时间的观念。'水的哲学、水的精神'是中国人在人与人、人与自然、人与社会的和谐中把握自己本真精神的集中体现。了解了水文化，就了解了中华文明的根本。"

The essence of water culture is the philosophy and spirit of water. Professor Wang Yuechuan from Peking University said, "Water embodies the great virtues of the Chinese cultural spirit: fairness, bravery, tenacity, and cleanliness; it embodies the concept of life time. The philosophy and spirit of water is the concentrated expression of one's true spirit in the harmonious relationship among people, between man and nature and between man and society. If you understand the water culture, you will understand the fundamentals of Chinese civilization."

水文化，作为文化领域的一个重要方面，逐步成为全国甚至全球关注的热门话题。2006 年，联合国第十四个世界水日确定的主题为"水与文化"。

Water culture, as an important aspect in the cultural field, has gradually become a hot topic, drawing both national and even global attention. In 2006, the theme set by the United Nations on the 14th World Water Day was "Water and Culture".

水文化的主要特性：

Main features of water culture:

第一，水文化是以水和水事活动为载体而形成的文化形态，是人们以水和水事活动为载体创造的一种姓"水"的文化。以水为载体包含两方面意思：一是说，水承载着对人类和社会的伟大贡献，其中包括水对人的生命健康，水对社会政治、经济、军事、科学、技术、文学、艺术、审美等方面的重要联系和伟大贡献；二是说，水承载着人类对水的伟大实践。也就是我们说的水事活动，即人与水发生联系的过程中所从事的一切活动，主要包括人类的饮水、用水、治水、管水、护水、节水、亲水、观水、写水、绘水等重要社会实践活动。这些是水文化形成的基础和发展的动力。两方面相辅相成、相互联系，构建了丰富多彩、博大精深的水文化。因此，水文化的根本特征是“以水和水事活动为载体”的文化。

Firstly, water culture is a cultural form with water and water activities as its carrier, and it is a culture with the surname of "Water" created by taking water and water activities as the carrier. Taking water as the carrier has two meanings: the first meaning is that water makes great contributions to mankind and society, including its contributions to human life and health, society, politics, economy, military, science, technology, and literature, the important connection with and great contributions to the arts, aesthetics, etc. ; the second meaning is that water involves itself in the great practice of mankind. That is to say, the water activities, which refer to all the activities in which people engage themselves in the process of connecting with water, mainly include humans' drinking water, using water, governing water, managing water, protecting water, saving water, accessing water, watching water, writing about and painting water, and other important practice-based social activities. These are the very foundation for the formation of water culture and the driving force for its development. The two aspects complement each other and are interrelated to construct a rich, extensive and profound water culture. Therefore, water culture is the culture with the characteristic of "taking water and water activities as its carrier".

第二，水文化是水在与人和社会生活各方面的联系中形成和发展的文化形态。水与人的生命、生存、健康、生产生活方式，与社会、政治、经济、文化、军事、生态等方面联系紧密，水文化就是在这些联系中形成和发展起来的。没有这种联系就没有水文化形成的基础，也就没有水文化发展的动力。因此，研究水与人类生存和发展各方面的关系，研究水与人类社会文明发展进步各方面的关系应是水文化研究的重要内容。

Secondly, water culture is a cultural form gradually developed in establishing relationships of water with people and all aspects of social life. Water is closely related to human life, survival, health, production and lifestyle, and it is also closely related to society, politics, economy, culture, military, and ecology. Water culture is formed and developed within these relationships, without which there would be no foundation for the formation of water culture, and there would be no driving force for its development. Therefore, the important content of water culture research is to study the relationships between water and various aspects of human survival and development, as well as between water and various aspects of the development and progress of human social civilization.

第三,水文化内涵要素和定义类型与文化基本一致。这是文化与水文化最紧密联系的反映。从水文化的内涵要素讲,水文化具备了人、水、物质财富和精神财富三大要素。从水文化的定义类型讲,从"文化财富型"中可以引申出"水文化是人们以水和水事活动为载体,在与人和社会生活的各方面发生联系过程中创造的物质财富和精神财富的总和"的含义。从"文化方式型"中可以引申出"水文化是人们以水和水事活动为载体,进行生活、生产和思维的方式"的含义。从"文化反映型"中可引申出"水文化是水和水事活动在社会文明和经济发展中地位和作用的反映"的含义。从"文化复合型"中可以引申出"水文化是与水和水事活动有关的知识、信仰、艺术、音乐、风俗、法律以及各种能力的复合体"的含义。

Thirdly, the connotative elements and definition types of water culture are basically consistent with culture, which reflects the closest connection between water culture and culture. In terms of *the connotative elements*, water culture has three major elements: people, water, and material and spiritual wealth. In light of *the definition types* of water culture, what can be derived from *the cultural wealth type* is that "water culture is the sum of the material wealth and spiritual wealth created by people in the process of contacting people and all aspects of social life with water and water activities as the carrier". What can be derived from *the cultural mode type* is that "water culture is the way people take water and water activities as the carrier to live, produce and think". What can be derived from *the cultural reflection type* is that "water culture is a reflection of the status and role of water and water activities in social civilization and economic development". What can be derived from *the cultural complex type* is that "water culture is a complex of knowledge, beliefs, art, music, customs, laws, and various abilities related to water and water activities".

第四,水文化的内容博大精深。既有物质形态的水文化,也有精神形态的水文化。介于物质形态和精神形态之间,还有制度形态的水文化。从这三种水文化形态的相互关系中,我们可以认识到:人类与水的联系作用于自然界,产生了物质形态的水文化;作用于社会,产生了制度形态的水文化;作用于人本身,产生了精神形态的水文化。三者之间,互相联系,各有侧重。

Fourthly, the content of water culture is broad and profound, including both material and spiritual water culture. Between these two forms is institutional water culture. From the interrelationship of these three forms of water culture, we can realize that the relationship between man and water acts on the natural world to produce water culture in material form, acts on society to produce water culture in institutional form and acts on man himself to produce spiritual form. The three are interrelated and each has its own particular emphasis.

第五,水文化具有母体文化的特性。因为没有水,就没有人,也就没有文化。水是生命之源,是文明之源,也是文化之源。水文化渗透到人类文化的各个方面。因此,可以说,水文化是各种文化形态的母体文化,水文化也是女儿文化,但具有母体文化的特性。水具有女儿的形象和母亲的气质。

Fifthly, water culture has the characteristics of maternal culture because without water, there would be no human, hence no culture. Water is the source of life, civilization and culture as well. Water culture permeates into all aspects of human culture. Therefore, it can be said that water culture is the maternal culture of various forms of culture, and it is also a daughter culture with the characteristics of maternal culture as well. Water has the image of a daughter and the temperament of a mother.

New Words, Phrases and Expressions

spiritual [ˈspɪrɪtʃuəl] *a.* 精神的,心灵的;宗教的;(人)高尚的,不为物欲所动的 *n.* (原为美国黑人所唱的)圣歌,灵歌

rejuvenation [rɪˌdʒuːvəˈneɪʃn] *n.* 恢复青春,恢复活力;(组织或体制)恢复活力;(河流、溪流)回春,更生;复兴

indicator [ˈɪndɪkeɪtə(r)] *n.* 标志,迹象;方向灯,转向指示灯;指示器,显示器;指示剂

cohesion [kəʊˈhiːʒ(ə)n] *n.* 凝聚力,团结;内聚力;(句子、文章等在语法或含义方面的)连贯,衔接

vitality [vaɪˈtæləti] *n.* 活力,热情;生机,生命力

inspirational [ˌɪnspəˈreɪʃənl] *a.* 灵感的;启发性的;鼓舞人心的;绝妙的

appeal [əˈpiːl] *n.* 呼吁,恳求;上诉,申诉;吸引力,感染力;(为慈善或正义事业的)募捐;启发,打动 *v.* 呼吁,恳求;上诉,申诉;有吸引力,引起兴趣;启发,打动

enhance [ɪnˈhɑːns] *v.* 增强,提高,改善

strategy [ˈstrætədʒi] *n.* (尤指为获得某物制定长期的)策略,行动计划;战略,战略学

unique [juˈniːk] *a.* 独一无二的,独特的;非常特别的,极不寻常的;(某人、某地或某物)独具的,特有的

charm [tʃɑːm] *n.* 魅力,魔力;护身符,咒语;小挂件,小饰物　*v.* 吸引,迷住;诱使,哄诱;向……施魔法,用魔法控制;有魔力

penetration [ˌpenəˈtreɪʃ(ə)n] *n.* 穿透,渗透,进入;(产品对市场的)渗透度,占有率;(某种信仰在某一社会的)渗透;(为刺探情报对某团体、企业等的)渗入;洞察力

dissemination [dɪˌsemɪˈneɪʃ(ə)n] *n.* 宣传,散播;宣传,散播

supreme [suːˈpriːm; sjuːˈpriːm] *a.* 最高的,至高无上的;(政府、司法或军事机构)拥有最高权力的;极大的,极度的;(处罚、牺牲)涉及死的;杰出的

virtue [ˈvɜːtʃuː] *n.* 高尚的道德,德行;美德,优秀品质;优点,长处

contend [kənˈtend] *v.* 声称,主张;竞争,争夺;处理,对付

divine [dɪˈvaɪn] *a.* 神的,天赐的;绝妙的,极令人愉快的　*v.* (凭直觉)猜测,推测;占卜,预测;(通过探矿术)发现(水源)

analects [ˈænəlekts] *n.* 短论选,短文选 (*The Analects*《论语》)

worthwhile [ˌwɜːθˈwaɪl] *a.* 重要的,有益的,值得做的

demonstrate [ˈdemənstreɪt] *v.* 证明;示范,演示;表露;游行,示威

remarkable [rɪˈmɑːkəb(ə)l] *a.* 引人注目的,非凡的

striking [ˈstraɪkɪŋ] *a.* 惊人的,异常的;妩媚动人的,标致的;罢工的;打击的

sum [sʌm] *n.* 金额,款项;算术,简单计算;总数,总和;全部,一切(尤指数量不大)　*v.* 概括,总结;求……的和

behavioral [bɪˈheɪvjərəl] *a.* 行为的

as a whole 作为整体的(作后置定语)

reliance [rɪˈlaɪəns] *n.* 依赖,依靠

interdependence [ˌɪntədɪˈpendəns] *n.* 相互依赖

sublimation [ˌsʌblɪˈmeɪʃn] *n.* 升华,(心理) 升华作用;高尚化;升华物

rational [ˈræʃ(ə)nəl] *a.* (想法、决定等)合理的,基于理性的;(人)理性的,理智的;富有理性的;(数)有理的,有理数的　*n.* 有理数

mastery [ˈmɑːstəri] *n.* 精通,熟练掌握;控制,驾驭

subsystem [səbˈsɪstəm] *n.* 子系统;分系统

attribute [ˈætrɪbjuːt] *n.* 属性;性质;特征

medium [ˈmiːdiəm] *n.* 媒介,媒体;方法,手段;(艺术创作)材料,素材;灵媒,巫师;培养基;环境;中等,中号;存储(或打印)介质;(颜料)溶剂(如油或水);(品质、状态)中等,中庸　*a.* 中等的,中间的,适中的;五分熟的,半熟的;(程度、强度或数量)平均的;(颜色)不深不浅的,适中的;(投球,投球手)中速的

yield [jiːld] *v.* 产生(收益、效益等),产生(结果);出产(天然产品、农产品、工业产

品);屈服,让步;放弃,让出;给(大路上的车辆)让路;(受压)活动,弯曲,折断;(正式)被……替代 *n.* 产量;收益,利润,红利(或股息)率

emergence [ɪˈmɜːdʒəns] *n.* 出现,显现;崭露头角;摆脱困境

livestock [ˈlaɪvstɒk] *n.* 牲畜,家畜

fishery [ˈfɪʃəri] *n.* 渔业;渔场;水产业

in a sense 从某种意义上讲

maternal [məˈtɜːn(ə)l] *a.* 母性的;母亲的

exert [ɪɡˈzɜːt] *v.* 运用,施加(影响);努力,尽力(exert oneself)

penetrate [ˈpenətreɪt] *v.* 刺入,穿透;打进(某地区或国家的市场);渗入,打入(组织、团体等);洞察,了解;被理解,被领悟;透过……看见,看穿

conservancy [kənˈsɜːvənsi] *n.* 管理;保护;保存

distinctive [dɪˈstɪŋktɪv] *a.* 独特的,与众不同的;区别性的

connotation [ˌkɒnəˈteɪʃ(ə)n] *n.* 内涵意义,隐含意义,联想意义

elimination [ɪˌlɪmɪˈneɪʃn] *n.* 消除,排除;淘汰;消灭,铲除;排泄

profound [prəˈfaʊnd] *a.* (影响)深刻的,极大的;(感情)强烈的,深切的;(思想)深邃的,(见解)深刻的;〈文〉深的,深处的;完全的;艰深的,玄奥的;(疾病、残疾)严重的

at the core [kɔː(r)] **of** 处于……核心

governance [ˈɡʌvənəns] *n.* 统治方式,管理方法

essence [ˈes(ə)ns] *n.* 本质;要素;香精,香料

embody [ɪmˈbɒdi] *v.* 具体表现,体现;收录,包括

tenacity [təˈnæsəti] *n.* 顽强,执着,坚持;黏性

concentrated [ˈkɒnsntreɪtɪd] *a.* 集中的;全神贯注的,全力以赴的;浓缩的

in harmony [ˈhɑːməni] **with** 与……和谐

fundamentals [ˌfʌndəˈmentlz] *n.* 基本面;基本原理(fundamental 的复数)

make great contributions to 为……巨大贡献

involve (**oneself**) **in** 使……参与;使……卷入

engage oneself in 使……参与

complement [ˈkɒmplɪment] *vt.* 补充

connotative [ˈkɒnəˌteɪtɪv] *a.* 内涵的;隐含的;含蓄的

consistent [kənˈsɪstənt] **with** 与……相一致的

be derived [dɪˈraɪvd] **from** *v.* 从……衍生出,源于;(从……中)得到,提取;导出

reflection [rɪˈflekʃ(ə)n] *n.* (光、热或声音的)反射;反射光,反射热,回声;(反射出来的)影像,倒影;深思,反省;(尤指见诸语言的)想法,意见;表现,反映;(数)镜射,反射

institutional [ˌɪnstɪˈtjuːʃənl] *a.* 机构的,慈善机构的;制度的,惯例的;根深蒂固的

act on 根据……行动

emphasis ['emfəsɪs] *n.* 重要性，重点强调；重读，强调；（表达的）强有力

temperament ['temprəmənt] *n.* 气质，性格；（性情）暴躁，喜怒无常；调（音）律

第二节　水文化与水文化建设
Section B　Water Culture and Its Construction

在德国哲学家卡西尔看来，在对宇宙的最早的神话学解释中，人们总是可以发现原始的人类学与原始的宇宙学比肩而立：世界的起源问题与人的起源问题难分难解地交织在一起。这位被西方学术界公认为20世纪以来最重要的学者之一，事实上揭示了一个令人醒目的文化现象：世界与人同源。水，作为自然的元素、生命的依托，以它天然的联系，似乎从一开始便与人类生活乃至文化历史形成了一种不解之缘。纵观世界文化源流，是水势滔滔的尼罗河孕育了灿烂的古埃及文明，幼发拉底河的消长荣枯影响了巴比伦王国的盛衰兴亡，地中海沿岸的自然环境造就了古希腊、罗马文化，流淌在东方的两条大河——黄河与长江，则滋润了蕴藉深厚的中原文化和绚烂多姿的楚文化。

In the eyes of Cassirer, a German philosopher, in the earliest mythological interpretation of the universe, it can always be found that primitive anthropology and primitive cosmology stand side by side: the origin of the world and the origin of man are inextricably intertwined. He is recognized by the Western academia as one of the most important scholars in the 20th century. In fact, he revealed a striking cultural phenomenon that the world shares the same origin as humans. Water, as a natural element and the support of life, with its natural connection, seems to have formed an indissoluble bond with human life and even the cultural history from the very beginning. Looking through the cultural origins of the world, the surging Nile River gave birth to the splendid ancient Egyptian civilization. The ups and downs of the Euphrates River affected the rise and fall of the Kingdom of Babylon. The natural environment along the Mediterranean Sea created the cradle of the ancient Greek and Roman culture. The two great rivers flowing in the Orient, e.g. the Yellow River and the Yangtze River, have nourished the profound Central Plains culture and the splendid Chu culture.

水,以其原始宇宙学的精髓内涵已渗入人类文化思想的意识深层。在漫漫的历史长河中,伴随着人类的进化以及对自然认知的加深,水由物质的层面升华到一种精神的境界。因此,把中华水文化的哲学和精神发扬光大,提升我们对中华文化的自觉、自信和自豪,创新和发展先进的中华文化,对坚定中华民族追求“真善美”的信仰,重振民族精神雄风,践行社会主义核心价值观,铸牢中华文化之魂都具有十分重要的意义。

Water, with its essence and connotation of primitive cosmology, has penetrated into the deep consciousness of human cultural thoughts. In the long history, with the evolution of mankind and human cognition of nature, water has been sublimated from a material level to a spiritual realm. It is therefore of great significance to carry forward the philosophy and spirit of the water culture of China, establish our awareness of, self-confidence and pride in the Chinese culture, innovate and develop the advanced Chinese culture, enforce the belief in the Chinese nation's pursuit of truth, goodness and beauty, revitalize the national spirit, and practice the socialist core values and forge the soul of Chinese culture.

水是人类文明的源泉。中华民族在长期的实践中创造了巨大的物质财富和精神财富,形成了独特而丰富的水文化。弘扬水文化主旋律,颂扬水伟大、水贡献、水精神,提倡人水相亲、人水和谐、人水共荣,有利于形成人人爱水、节水、管水、护水的良好氛围。

Water is the source of human civilization. Chinese nation has created a huge material and spiritual wealth through long-term practice, and formed a unique and rich water culture. It is favorable to carry forward the main theme of water culture, extol the greatness, contribution and spirit of water, promote the mutual friendship, harmony and prosperity between man and water, and thus create a good atmosphere in which everyone loves water, saves water, manages water and protects water.

中国水文化是中华文化和民族精神的重要组成部分,也是引领和推动水事业发展的重要力量。大力推进水文化建设,努力创造无愧于新时代的先进水文化,既是一项紧迫工作,也是一项长期的历史任务。

Chinese water culture is an important part of Chinese culture and national spirit, and it is also an important force to lead and promote the development of water-featured enterprise. Vigorously promoting the construction of water culture and striving to create an advanced water culture worthy of the new era are both an urgent task and a long-term historical mission.

水文化建设是一项社会系统工程,必须按照水利部的规划纲要、各项部署要求,统筹协调好各方力量,充分发挥各方优势,广聚各方智慧,形成共谋水文化发展、共建文化兴水、共享水文化成果的强大合力。

The construction of water culture is a social systems engineering. It is necessary to coordinate all forces involved in accordance with the deployment requirements of the planning outline of the Ministry of Water Resources, give full play to the advantages of all parties, and assimilate the wisdom of all parties, thereby forming a collaborative development and joint construction of water culture, contributing to the powerful synergy by invigorating and enriching water features to develop water culture and sharing its fruits.

水文化建设的重点是培育全社会"人水和谐"的生产生活方式,增强全社会的水意识;弘扬优秀的"水的哲学、水的精神",培育和践行社会主义核心价值观,全面提高人民思想道德素养和科学文化素质;践行"节水优先、空间平衡、系统治理、两手发力"的治水新思路,奋力开创水利事业新局面;不断充实民生水利的文化内涵,使水利工作真正做到保障民生、服务民生、改善民生;加强水生态文明建设,为建设"美丽中国"作出应有的贡献;提高水工程的文化品位,满足人民精神文化需求;繁荣水文化事业,发展水文化产业,增强水文化实力;保护和整理优秀的水文化遗产,服务当代水利建设;加强水文化研究,构建水文化的理论体系;加强水文化教育和传播,扩大水文化在国内及国际上的影响力,为人类文明的进步作出更大的贡献。

The focus of the construction of water culture is cultivating both production styles and lifestyles, promoting the concept of "harmony between human and water" in the whole society and enhancing the water consciousness of the whole society; advocating the excellent "philosophy and spirit of water", cultivating and practicing the core socialist values, and comprehensively improving people's ideological, moral, scientific and cultural qualities; practicing the new water management paradigm of water-saving priority, spatial balance, systemic treatment and two-handed effort, and striving to create a new situation in water conservancy; continuing to enrich the cultural connotation of people's livelihood and water conservancy, and making water conservancy work, really ensuring, serving and bettering people's livelihood; strengthening the construction of water eco-civilization and making due contributions to the development of a Beautiful China;

improving the cultural taste of water engineering and meeting the spiritual and cultural needs of people; making water culture development and water culture industry flourish, enhancing the strength of water culture; protecting and sorting out excellent water cultural heritage, serving contemporary water conservancy construction; intensifying water culture research and building a theoretical system of water culture; strengthening water culture education and dissemination, and expanding water culture domestically and internationally so as to make greater contributions to the progress of human civilization.

文化是民族的血脉和灵魂。习近平总书记明确指出:“一个国家、一个民族的强盛,总是以文化兴盛为支撑的,中华民族伟大复兴需要以中华文化发展繁荣为条件。”水文化建设是社会主义文化建设的重要组成部分,大力加强水文化建设,关系到社会主义文化大发展大繁荣,关系到治水兴水千秋伟业,我们必须认真践行“节水优先、空间平衡、系统治理、两手发力”新时期水利工作方针,不断加大水文化研究发掘和传播普及力度,继承弘扬优秀传统水文化,创新发展现代化特色水文化,努力推出更多高品质、高水平的水文化产品,充分发挥先进水文化的教育启迪和激励凝聚功能,在“立德树人”的教育理念指导下,发挥水文化英语在我校学生英语认知语用能力方面的提升作用。

Culture is the blood and soul of a nation. General Secretary Xi Jinping clearly pointed out, “The prosperity of a country and a nation is always supported by cultural prosperity. The great rejuvenation of the Chinese nation requires the development and prosperity of the Chinese culture as a condition.” Water culture construction is an important part of socialist culture construction. The construction of water culture should be vigorously strengthened, which is related to the great development and prosperity of socialist culture, and the great cause of harnessing water and prospering water resources. We must earnestly implement the water conservancy policy in the new era under the guidance of the philosophy of “water-saving priority, spatial balance, systemic treatment, and two-handed effort”. We must put more efforts into water culture research, discovery and dissemination, inherit excellent traditional water culture, innovate and develop water culture with modern characteristics, strive to introduce more high-quality and high-level water culture products, and give full play to the educational enlightenment and encouragement of advanced water culture. Under the guidance of the educational philosophy of "cultivating virtues and morality", it is good to take maximum advantage of the role of water culture English in improving the cognitive and pragmatic competence of students.

New Words, Phrases and Expressions

mythological [ˌmɪθəˈlɒdʒɪkl] *a.* 神秘的；神话的；神话学的；虚构的

primitive [ˈprɪmətɪv] *a.* 原始的，远古的；（器物等）粗糙的，简陋的；（人、动物或植物发展）早期的；（行为、思想、情感）本能的，自然的；（艺术风格）朴实无华的；原来的，原有的；（语言学）根词的，非派生的；（生）原生的　*n.* 原始派艺术家（或其作品）；词根，原（词）素

anthropology [ˌænθrəˈpɒlədʒi] *n.* 人类学

cosmology [kɒzˈmɒlədʒi] *n.* 宇宙学；宇宙论

inextricably [ˌɪnɪkˈstrɪkəbli] *adv.* 必然地；密不可分地；逃不掉地；解不开地

intertwine [ˌɪntəˈtwaɪn] *vt.* （=interweave）相互交织；纠缠

academia [ˌækəˈdiːmiə] *n.* 学术界；学术生涯

reveal [rɪˈviːl] *vt.* 揭示，透露；表明，证明；展示，显示；（通过神或超自然手段）启示

indissoluble [ˌɪndɪˈsɒljəbl] *a.* 不能分解的；不能溶解的；坚固的；牢固持久的

turbulent [ˈtɜːbjələnt] *a.* 骚乱的，动乱的；（气流）湍流的，（水）湍急的；骚动的，混乱而难以控制的；（技）（与）紊流或湍流（有关）的

Nile [naɪl] **River** 尼罗河

give birth to 产生；孕育

splendid [ˈsplendɪd] *a.* 优秀的；辉煌的；壮丽的，灿烂的；（时光）令人愉快的

ups and downs 上下起伏

the Euphrates River 幼发拉底河

the Mediterranean Sea 地中海

cradle [ˈkreɪd(ə)l] *n.* 摇篮；吊架，吊篮；发源地；（电话的）听筒架　*v.* 轻轻抱着

the Orient [ˈɔːrient] *n.* 东方

nourish [ˈnʌrɪʃ] *vt.* 养育；滋润；滋养；培养，怀有（感情、信念等）

(the) Central Plains 中原

evolution [ˌiːvəˈluːʃ(ə)n] *n.* 进化（论）；演变，发展；（气体的）释放，（热量的）散发；队形变换，位置变换

sublimate [ˈsʌblɪmeɪt] *vt.* 使……升华，使高尚；纯化

carry forward 发扬

innovate [ˈɪnəveɪt] *v.* 创新，革新

revitalize [riːˈvaɪtəlaɪz] *vt.* 使重新充满活力；使复兴

forge [fɔːdʒ] *vt.* 铸造
theme [θiːm] *n.* 主题;主旋律
extol [ɪkˈstəʊl] *vt.* 颂扬;赞美;赞颂
prosperity [prɒˈsperəti] *n.* 繁荣;富强;成功
enterprise [ˈentəpraɪz] *n.* 企业,事业单位;事业心,进取心;事业;创业,企业经营
vigorously [ˈvɪgərəsli] *adv.* 精神旺盛地,有力地,活泼地;坚决地
worthy of 值得……的
era [ˈɪərə] *n.* 时代,年代,纪元
mission [ˈmɪʃ(ə)n] *n.* (尤指赴他国的)使命;职责,天职;(军用飞机或航天火箭的)飞行任务;军事行动;(一个组织的)目的,宗旨;外交使团,代表团;驻外机构,使馆
coordinate [kəʊˈɔːdɪneɪt] *v.* 协调,配合;使身体协调;(使颜色、款式、风格等)搭配,配套;给(原子或分子)配位,与……形成共价键
concerned [kənˈsɜːnd] *a.* 相关的,关于(某个主题)的;担心的,焦急的;关注的,感兴趣的;关心的,挂念的
in accordance [əˈkɔːd(ə)ns] **with** 根据
deployment [dɪˈplɔɪmənt] *n.* 有效运用;部署,调动
outline [ˈaʊtlaɪn] *n.* 大纲;轮廓
(the) Ministry [ˈmɪnɪstri] **of Water Resources** 水利部
give full play to 充分发挥
assimilate [əˈsɪməleɪt] *v.* 融入,(使)同化;吸收,理解;使相似,成为相似
synergy [ˈsɪnədʒi] *n.* (两个或多个组织共同协作后产生的)协同增效作用,协同作用
invigorate [ɪnˈvɪgəreɪt] *vt.* 鼓舞;使充满活力,使精力充沛
cultivate [ˈkʌltɪveɪt] *v.* 开垦,耕作;栽培,培育;陶冶,培养;建立(友谊),结交
comprehensively [ˌkɒmprɪˈhensɪvli] *adv.* 包括地;包括一切地;完全地;彻底地;全面地
ideological [ˌaɪdiəˈlɒdʒɪk(ə)l] *a.* 思想体系的,意识形态的
moral [ˈmɒrəl] *a.* 有关道德的;基于道德的,道义上的;品行端正的,有道德的;伦理的;能辨别是非的 *n.* 道德准则、标准;寓意,道德上的教训
paradigm [ˈpærədaɪm] *n.* 典范,范例;样板,范式;词形变化表;纵聚合关系语言项
prioritize [praɪˈɒrətaɪz] *v.* 按优先顺序列出;优先考虑(处理)
spatial [ˈspeɪʃ(ə)l] *a.* 空间的,与空间有关的;空间理解能力的
livelihood [ˈlaɪvlihʊd] *n.* 生计,营生
ensure [ɪnˈʃʊə(r)] *vt.* 确保,保证;保护,使安全
flourish [ˈflʌrɪʃ] *vi.* 繁荣,昌盛;挥动;(植物或动物)茁壮成长 *n.* 夸张动作;(讲话

或文章的)华丽辞藻,修饰;(手写花体字的)花饰

heritage [ˈherɪtɪdʒ] *n.* 遗产,传统,世袭财产

intensify [ɪnˈtensɪfaɪ] *v.* 加剧,增强;增强(底片)的阻光度,增加(底片)的厚度

earnestly [ˈɜːnɪstli] *adv.* 认真地;热切地;诚挚地

implement [ˈɪmplɪment] *v.* 执行,贯彻;为……提供工具 *n.* [ˈɪmplɪmənt] 工具,器具

integrate [ˈɪntɪgreɪt] *v.* (使)合并,成为一体;(使)加入,融入群体;(使)取消种族隔离;求……的积分;表示(面积、温度等)的总和,表示……的平均值

strive [straɪv] *v.* 努力,力争;斗争,反抗

enlightenment [ɪnˈlaɪt(ə)nmənt] *n.* 启迪,指导,教导; (the Enlightenment)启蒙运动;(佛教)智慧

cognitive [ˈkɒgnətɪv] *a.* 认知的,认识的;记忆的

pragmatic [prægˈmætɪk] *a.* 实用(主义)的;讲求实际的,务实的;(语言学)语用的

C-E Language Disparity 1—Thinking and Language 思维与语言

Translation between Chinese and English is one of the most important translation practices in China. Rapid globalization and deepening opening up of China make such translation increasingly important. Realizing language disparities or differences is the basis of improving translation quality. Understanding the relationship between thinking and language is the first step to decipher or decode language disparities between Chinese and English.

This part is designed to train students' translation skills in such a way that they would know why Chinese and English may sometimes express similar ideas in very different ways and why they should make proper adjustments so as to convey the meaning of the original language in an idiomatic way of the target language. First of all, you should know something about the definition and nature of language.

What is Language?

《辞海》(6th Edition) has this definition:"人类最重要的交际工具。它同思维有密切的联系,是人类形成和表达思想的手段,也是人类社会最基本的

信息载体。人们借助语言保存和传递人类文明的成果。语言是人区别于其他动物的本质性特征之一。共同的语言又常是民族的特征。语言就本身的机制来说,是社会约定俗成的音义结合的符号系统。语言是一种特殊的社会现象,它随着社会的产生而产生的,发展而发展。语言没有阶级性,一视同仁地为社会各个成员服务。但社会各阶段、阶层或社会群体会影响到语言,从而造成语言在使用上的不同特点和差异。"

Language is the most important means of human communication. People think and communicate through language; therefore, language and thinking are closely related. ***In a sense****, language is both the* ***medium*** *and the* ***result*** *of* ***the externalization of thinking****. People retain and transmit human civilization by* ***resorting to*** *language. Language is one of the most fundamental defining features that distinguish man from other animals. Common languages usually have their shared characteristics. In terms of mechanism, language itself is a socially conventionalized system of phonetic and semantic signs or* ***codes****. Language is a special kind of social phenomenon, which comes into being with the emergence of society and develops with social development. Language has no class distinction, equally serving people from all walks of life. But different stages, strata and groups of society can influence language, resulting in different features and disparities in language use.* [《辞海》(6th edition)]

The above is the most comprehensive up-to-date definition of language. In essence, language is a means of human communication, an externalized expression of human thinking and a product of social development. But it is still lacking in some aspects. To compensate for such deficiencies, some other important aspects will be highlighted here.

Firstly, we should attach importance to the relationship between language and psychology. Psychologically speaking, language is a carrier and tool or medium of thinking and reasoning. Cognitively speaking, it is a carrier of culture. All languages reflect the way their users think. Language in a way determines and restricts how one thinks. Thus, it can be concluded that language and thinking are mutually interactive.

The structure of a language, including its vocabulary, idiomatic expressions, sentences, and even the structure of a text, reflects the mode of thinking of the people who speak the language. That way of thinking greatly influences their cognition of the world and thus shapes their own outlook. In this sense, language can be regarded as a world outlook.

Actually, thinking is a kind of mental activity, and language is employed for expressing such mental activity. Then, what is the essence or nature of thinking? Briefly, thinking is man's reflection, deliberation or careful thinking, and viewpoints on the world. It is maintained that language is a system of codes that represents the world. But language reflects the world not as simply as a mirror or a camera. Such reflection has been processed and recreated by man's brain, and in the process subjective elements are inevitably added. People use their sensory organs to sense and experience the objective world and then use language and reasoning to make sense of the world—not the original objective world but the world in the human mind, created by interpreting the objective world. Therefore, to truly and fully understand language, we have to study the relationships or interactions between three different elements: 1) the objective world; 2) language as the medium of cognition about the world; and 3) the subjective perception on the part of people.

As systems of codes established and accepted by social communities, all languages share some universal characteristics, while each language also has its qualities peculiar to itself. As two major languages with long histories, spoken by hundreds of millions of people, both Chinese and English are important languages. Comparison and contrast between them will improve bilingual communication or rather translation in this context.

Characteristics of Language

Virtually all languages have the following most obvious characteristics:

1. Every language is limited while the objective world is infinite. Therefore, any item, whether it should be lexical, syntactic, semantic or pragmatic, is employed to express more than one meaning.

2. Languages are generalized and, in a sense, abstract, but the objective world is concrete, rich and varied, so language is essentially fuzzy or vague. As a result, different people may have different interpretations of the same linguistic

unit.

Languages are of one dimension, that is, linear while the objective world is three-dimensional. Therefore, no language can truly reflect the objective world. A picture is two-dimensional, and thus the effect of reading a novel and that of watching a film are different. The latter is more reflective, which is the reason why film is often more effective and appealing than a novel.

Reasons for Contrastive Studies between Chinese and English

Belonging to different language families and with different histories of development, Chinese and English differ in many ways, ranging from lexical to syntactic and to textual levels, which makes translation between them a daunting task. There are many textbooks teaching translation techniques, such as addition and omission, conversion of parts of speech, rearrangement of word order, breaking-up and combining of sentences, etc., and many other adjustments. These are important techniques, but it is sometimes extremely hard for learners to decide on which technique they should adopt in actual translation. If they are told the reason or motivation behind such techniques, they would become more conscious to adopt appropriate techniques. A fairly good understanding of the similarities and differences between the two languages will play a decisive role here.

Chinese and English do share many similarities, but it is the disparities or differences that pose as obstacles in translation, so contrastive studies between these two languages seem more important than mere comparison. People growing up in specific languages and cultural traditions look at the world in ways different from those growing up in other languages and cultural traditions. So, as a reflection of their cognition and expression, one language used by one people is different from another used by another people. That is, the root reasons that cause the differences between the two languages are the different ways of thinking and different world outlooks. Translation theories do not offer much help to practitioners. Some outstanding differences between Chinese and English based on large numbers of cases, especially those of current usage, will be given to illustrate some tentative conclusions.

There are at least the following differences between Chinese and English:

1. Chinese people are more inclined to think in terms of images while English speakers are good at abstract thinking. As a result, there are more imagery words in Chinese, and more explanatory words in English. For example, Chinese has rich measure words or classifiers; English contains more abstract nouns, some of which have no equivalents in Chinese. We can thus say that Chinese has a lower degree of lexicalization than English. Verbs have a higher frequency and freer usage in Chinese while nouns and prepositions are used more frequently in English; therefore, Chinese is more **dynamic** while English is more **stative**. The basic motivation behind this phenomenon is that the East stresses the "acting" while the West emphasizes the "existing".

2. The Chinese prefer **comprehensive thinking** while English speakers prefer **analytical thinking**. Consequently, it can be found that the ways of expressing time and space are different in the two languages. Chinese sentences and English sentences have a different focus and word order: the Chinese sentence first deals with background and conditions before giving out the most important information while the English sentence puts important information straightly, such as an assessment or a conclusion, at the beginning. We can also see a remarkably different order of attributes and adverbials in the two languages.

3. The Chinese think more or less in a **curving** way while English speakers think more in a **linear** way. That is why Chinese paragraphs are more likely to be a typical **spiral** structure while most English paragraphs are a **linear** structure. In typical Confucian philosophy, people are far more important than objects, while Western philosophy stresses objectification and externalization. That is, English-speaking people often attach more importance to the influence of the objective world on human beings. This difference in subjective and objective consciousness results in the fact that Chinese sentences use **personal subjects** more frequently while English sentences more often use **impersonal subjects**. Another result of this is that the Chinese language uses far fewer **passive sentences** than the English language. This distinction in emphasis between **subjectivity** and **objectivity** is shown in many ways in the two languages.

4. Since ancient times, China had the theory of "five elements" and Yin and

Yang, stressing the harmonious relationship between man and nature. Traditional Chinese aesthetics stresses perceptional comprehension. As a result, the Chinese language is often a flow of seemingly diffusive thoughts with covert grammar rules and few connectives, hence it is a typical **paratactic** language. On the contrary, Western aesthetics has always stressed logical, rational thinking and formal demonstration, hence it is a **hypotactic** language. For such reasons, the English language is very compact with strict rules, making it more linear and straightforward. Chinese uses far fewer conjunctions and similar connectives than English.

1）水文化是什么？What is water culture?

2）——你还好吗？—Are you all right as ever?

3）——你看起来相当疲惫。—You look rather weary.

4）最近我一直为儿子工作的事儿烦着呢。Recently I have been worried about my son's job.

5）——他是谁？来这里干什么？—Who is he? What is he here for?

——我怎么会知道？—How can I know?

6）——你好吗？饿不饿？我给你弄点吃的来吧。—Are you all right? Feeling hungry? Shall I get you something to eat?

——我还行。倒是真饿了，能吃他五六根油条。—I'm OK, though quite hungry. I can do with five to six **deep-fried dough sticks**.

First of all, we can see all English sentences begin with a **capital** letter. There is no **capitalization** in Chinese, as **Chinese characters** do not have any **morphological change**.

Second, the word order of the questions is different. "水文化是什么?" is translated into "What is water culture?" rather than "Water culture is what?". "你还好吗?" is translated into "Are you all right as ever?" The English version does not retain the interrogative word "吗". And the single character "还" is translated into two words "as ever" and "好" is translated into two words "all right".

Third, the English translation of "我怎么会知道?" has a different word order of the adverb "怎么" and "how". "饿不饿?" is translated as "Feeling hungry?"—both are **elliptical** sentences but different parts are omitted. "饿" is an adjective and can serve as the predicate of the sentence such as "我饿" while in English, one has to say "I am/feel hungry" because only verbs can function as the predicate. English verbs have different **morphological** changes to form different tenses ("feeling" in the second dialogue is the elliptical of "are you feeling").

Fourth, "能吃他五六根油条" and its English version "I can do with five to six deep-fried dough sticks" has a number of differences: 1) the subject "I" is added; 2) "五六根油条" is translated as "five to six deep-fried dough sticks"; 3) the preposition "to" is added but there is no measure word equaling to "根" in English; 4) "deep-fried dough sticks" has the marker "-s" for the plural; 5) "油条" is a culturally-loaded expression, so a new term "deep-fried dough stick" is coined, though now it is also transliterated as "youtiao"; 6) "(我)能吃" literally means "I can eat" but here it is liberally translated as "I can do with", an idiomatic expression, so as to faithfully convey the pragmatic meaning of the original. This example illustrates that a meaning in one language is often expressed in the other language in diametrically different ways.

The above four aspects reveal some basic differences between Chinese and English.

In a way the Chinese lays stress on **dialectical thinking** while English speakers pay more attention to **formal logic**. That is why the Chinese sentence develops gradually in the sequence of logic or time order, like the sections of a bamboo, and the English sentence is of a more closely-knit logical structure like a bunch of grapes. The Chinese language employs lexical means to express these notions, but English verbs have rich morphological changes to express the tense, voice, and mood. In long sentences or paragraphs, Chinese clauses or sentences are like very loose chains whose links seem sporadic. You can hardly find any level of structure.

Most people agree that Chinese is essentially a **semantic** language, its grammar being implicit, with much **flexibility** and **elasticity**. As a written language with a history of over five thousand years, many Chinese words contain abundant **cultural accumulation**. As a result, the meanings of some words may be abstract and sometimes subtle.

Please appreciate the following C-E translations with the differences in language and thinking in mind:

Source Language 源语原文	English Version 英语译文	Comments 点评	Notes 备注
雾笼罩着江面，气象森严。十二时，“江津”号起碇顺流而下了。在长江与嘉陵江汇合后，江面**突然开阔**，天穹顿觉低垂。浓浓的黄雾，渐渐把重庆隐去。一刻钟后，船又在两面碧森森的悬崖陡壁之间的狭窄的江面上行驶了。（刘白羽《长江三日》节选）	Mist **wraps** the river, **lending majesty to the scene**. At noon the S. S. Jiangjin starts downstream. Once the Jialing River **merges with** the Yangtze River, the river **fans out abruptly** and the sky subsequently seems to **hang low**. Chongqing gradually disappears into the thick **yellowish mist**. A quarter of an hour later, the boat is steaming along a narrow stretch of river again between sheer darkly green **precipice**s and **cliff**s. (*Three Days on the Yangtze River* by Liu Baiyu)	lending majesty to the scene，现在分词短语作结果状语	**majesty** *n.* 威严 **merge** *v.* 汇合 **fan out** 呈扇形展开 **hang low** 低垂 **yellowish** *a.* 淡黄色的；微黄色的 **precipice** *n.* 悬崖；绝壁；险境 **cliff** *n.* 悬崖；峭壁 Please refer to: https://www.vrrw.net/wx/8783.html and read more original context and comments.

(continued)

Source Language 源语原文	English Version 英语译文	Comments 点评	Notes 备注
曲曲折折的荷塘上面,**弥望的**是田田的叶子。叶子出水很高,像**亭亭的**舞女的裙。层层的叶子中间,零星地**点缀着**些白花,有**袅娜地**开着的,有**羞涩地**打着朵儿的;正如一粒粒的明珠,又如碧天里的星星,又如刚出浴的美人。微风过处,送来**缕缕**清香,仿佛远处高楼上渺茫的歌声似的。这时候叶子与花也有一些的颤动,像闪电般,霎时传过荷塘的那边去了。叶子本是**肩并肩密密地**挨着,这便宛然有了一道凝碧的波痕。叶子底下是**脉脉的**流水,遮住了,不能见一些颜色;而叶子却更见风致了。(朱自清《荷塘月色》节选)	All over this **winding** stretch of water, **what meets the eye** is a **silken** field of leaves, reaching rather high above the surface, like the skirts of dancing girls **in all their grace**. Here and there, layers of leaves are **dotted with** white lotus blossoms, some in **demure** bloom, others **in shy bud**, **like scattering pearls**, or **twinkling** stars, or beauties just **out of the bath**. A breeze stirs, sending over breaths of fragrance, **like faint singing drifting from a distant building**. At this moment, a tiny thrill shoots through the leaves and flowers, like a streak of **lightning**, straight across the forest of **lotus**es. The leaves, which have been standing **shoulder to shoulder**, are caught trembling in an **emerald** heave of the pond. Underneath, the **exquisite** water is covered from view, and none can tell its color; yet the leaves on top **project themselves all the more attractively**. (Translated by Zhu Chunshen)	"弥望的"译成"what meets the eye"相当传神,让人想起"catch one's eye";"亭亭的"译为"in all their grace"处理得非常老道;"袅娜地"译为"in demure bloom","羞涩地打着朵儿"译为"in shy bud",都译得活灵活现	**winding** *a.* 曲曲折折的 **silken** *a.* 柔然的 **in one's grace** 婷婷的 **demure** *a.* 羞涩的 **bud** *n.* 花朵 **lightning** *n.* 闪电 **lotus** *n.* 荷花 **emerald** *a.* 鲜绿色的;翠绿色的;翠绿色;翡翠 **exquisite** *a.* 精致的;精美的;细致的 **project** *vt.* 表现;展现;投射 Please refer to the following website: https://zhuanlan.zhihu.com/p/330364942, which can help readers deeply understand the beauty of this version.

(continued)

Source Language 源语原文	English Version 英语译文	Comments 点评	Notes 备注
若夫淫雨霏霏,连月不开;阴风怒号,浊浪排空;日星隐曜,山岳潜形;商旅不行,樯倾楫摧;薄暮冥冥,虎啸猿啼。登斯楼也,则有去国怀乡,忧谗畏讥,满目萧然,感极而悲者矣。(范仲淹《岳阳楼记》节选)	In the rainy season, an unbroken **spell** of wet weather lasts for months. Chilly winds howl and **turbid** waves **surge** sky high. The sun and the stars lose their **lustre**, and the mountain ranges are scarcely visible. Merchants and travelers have to put off their voyage, for the **masts** of the ships have collapsed and their **oars** broken. It is dark towards evening, the roaring of tigers and the cry of monkeys can be heard. On **ascending** the Tower at such a time (At such a time anyone ascending the Tower) anyone will be filled with **nostalgia** for the imperial court and his home as well as fears of **calumny** and **derision** against him. With a scene of desolation around him, he will feel pain and despair at heart.		**spell** *n.* 一段时间 **turbid** *a.* 浑浊的;雾重的 **surge** *v.* 涌现 **mast** *n.* 桅杆 **ascend** *vt.* 攀登 **desolation** *n.* 孤寂;悲哀;忧伤 **well up** *vp.* 涌出;流露;喷发
至若春和景明,波澜不惊;上下天光,一碧万顷;沙鸥翔集,锦鳞游泳;岸芷汀兰,郁郁青青。而或长烟一空,皓月千里;浮光跃金,静影沉璧;渔歌互答,此乐何极!登斯楼也,则有心旷神怡,宠辱偕忘,把酒临风,其喜洋洋者矣。(范仲淹《岳阳楼记》节选)	In springtime it is warm and the sun is bright. The lake is **tranquil** and it merges with the **azure** sky into a vast expanse of blue. The water-birds are playing, some **fluttering** in the sky, some gathering together on the sandbars. Fishes of **varied hues** are swimming merrily in the water. The sweet-smelling grass by the banks and the faintly scented **orchids** on the sandy beaches are **lush** and green. Sometimes, when the mist over the lake vanishes, the glorious moon shines over the vast land, its brightness glistening with golden light on the lake. The reflection of the moon is like a piece of jade in the depths of the water. The fishermen's songs chime in with each other. How delightful they are! On ascending the Tower at such a time, one will feel a spiritual uplift, caring for neither glory nor shame. With a cup of wine in the gentle breeze, he will enjoy the greatest happiness in life.		**tranquil** *a.* 平静的;宁静的 **azure** *a.* 蔚蓝的;天蓝色的 **flutter** *vi.* 拍打翅膀 **hue** *n.* 颜色;色调 **orchid** *n.* 兰花;淡蓝色 **lush** *a.* 茂盛的;郁郁葱葱的

(continued)

Source Language 源语原文	English Version 英语译文	Comments 点评	Notes 备注
嗟夫！予尝求古仁人之心，或异二者之为，何哉？不以物喜，不以己悲。居庙堂之高，则忧其民；处江湖之远，则忧其君。是进亦忧，退亦忧。然则何时而乐耶？其必曰："先天下之忧而忧，后天下之乐而乐"欤？噫！微斯人，吾谁与归？（范仲淹《岳阳楼记》节选）	Ah! I have tried to study the minds of people of **lofty** ideals in ancient times. Perhaps they were different from the people I mentioned above. Why is this? The reason is that they were not thrown into **ecstasies** over their success(es), nor felt depressed over their failures. When they were in high positions at court, they were concerned about the people. When they were in remote places, they were concerned about their emperor. They worried when they were sent into exile. Then, when were they happy? They would say, "Always to be the first in the country to worry about the affairs of the State and the last in the country to enjoy oneself." Alas! Who else should I seek company with **save** him? (Translated by Luo Jingguo)		**lofty** *a.* 崇高的 **ideal** *n.* 理想 **ecstasy** *n.* 狂喜；陶醉
上善若水， 水善利万物 而不争， 处众人之所恶， 故几于道。 居善地， 心善渊， 与善仁， 言善信， 政善治， 事善能， 动善时。 夫唯不争， 故无尤。 （老子《道德经》第八章）	The **highest good** is like water. Water benefits everything by giving without taking or **contending**. It likes the place others dislike, so it follows closely the **divine** law. The place should be low, the mind broad, the gifts kind, the speech **trustworthy**, the rule sound, the deed well done, the action timely. Without **contention**, a man is **blameless**. (Translated by Xu Yuanchong)	"上善"有多种不同的译本，如 the greatest virtue/good; the supreme good 等 "道"也有不同的译法，如 Tao, Taoism 等	**contend** *vi.* 竞争；争夺 **divine** *a.* 神的；天赋的；绝妙的 **contention** *n.* 争夺；竞争 **blameless** *a.* 清白的；无懈责备的无过失的 《道德经》有100种左右的英译本，如有兴趣，请仔细对比研究。

From the above examples, we can see the disparities between Chinese and English in their **wording**, **rhythm**, **use of images**, **sentence structure**,

language flow, and even **punctuation marks**. Chinese is generally considered an "isolating language", for its words do not **undergo** any morphological change when serving different grammatical functions. There is no **tense**, **aspect**, **voice**, **mood**, **gender**, **number** or **case**.

Chinese is an **analytical language**, mainly using lexical means rather than morphological changes to describe and express various ideas while English is a **comprehensive language** that requires grammatical means and morphological changes.

Most scholars have now reached the consensus that the Chinese language has the following four grammatical characteristics:

1) Chinese has rich function words, which in great part express grammatical meaning.

2) Word order is very important to the Chinese sentence. A shift in word order will correspondingly cause much change in meaning.

3) The part of speech of a word does not correspond to its function in the sentence.

4) Compound words, phrases, and sentences have similar structures.

C-E Translation Strategies and Skills 1—Foreignization and Domestication 异化与归化

Generally, there are two strategies in dealing with cultural elements in translation: **foreignization** and **domestication**. The changeability and fun of translation often consists in the different translation strategies, skills, or methods. This part will focus on the introduction of the concepts of "domestication" and "foreignization" (put forward by Lawrence Venuti, a famous American translation theorist, in his book *The Translator's Invisibility* in 1995) and their illustrations with specific examples.

Domestication aims to localize the source language and take the target language or target readers as the end-result, so that the content of the original text is conveyed in a way that target language readers are accustomed to. **Naturalized translation** requires that the translator should approach the readers of the target language and that translators should express like the native author. The translators must change the translation into the native language if they want to talk to their readers directly. Naturalized translation helps readers to better understand the translated text and enhance its readability and appreciation.

Foreignization means that translators try their best not to disturb the original author, so that readers can get closer to him/her. In translating, it is to accommodate the linguistic characteristics of foreign cultures, absorb foreign expressions, and require translators to get closer to the original author and adopt the expressions of the source language to convey the content of the original text, that is, it is to turn the source language into the destination. The purpose of using the foreignization strategy is to take into account the differences in national cultures, preserve and reflect the features of exotic nationalities and language styles, and keep the exotic flavor for target readers.

Please appreciate the following Foreignized and Domesticated Versions:

Source language	Foreignized Version	Domesticated Version
The drive back to my home in Edmonton was an endless journey of destructive emotions and thoughts. In a truck-stop restaurant, I sat staring at a glass of cheap red wine. **Of all the gin joints in all the towns in all the world, she walks out of mine.**	在我开车回到埃德蒙顿的路上,我陷入了无尽的悲伤之中。随后,我来到一家汽车旅馆,端着一杯廉价红酒出神,**觉着这世上有那么多家旅馆,她终究还是走出了我的那一家**。	在我开车回到埃德蒙顿的路上,我陷入了无尽的悲伤之中。随后,我来到一家汽车旅馆,端着一杯廉价红酒出神,**弱水三千,终究我已不是她的那一瓢水了**。
You say that you love rain, but you open your umbrella when it rains... You say that you love the sun, but you find a shadow spot when the sun shines... You say that you love the wind, But you close your windows when wind blows... This is why I am afraid; You say that you love me too... (Written by William Shakespeare)	你说你喜欢雨, 但是下雨的时候,你却撑开了伞; 你说你喜欢阳光, 但当阳光播撒的时候,你却躲在阴凉之地; 你说你喜欢风, 但清风扑面的时候,你却关上了窗户。 那是因为我害怕, 你对我的爱也是如此。	你说烟雨微芒,兰亭远望;后来轻揽婆娑,深遮霓裳。 你说春光烂漫,绿袖红香;后来内掩西楼,静立卿旁。 你说软风轻拂,醉卧思量;后来紧掩门窗,漫帐成殇。 你说情丝柔肠,如何相忘;我却眼波微转,兀自成霜。 Please refer to the following webpage and appreciate more versions: http://news. sohu. com/a/505621631_121124407

C-E Guided Translation Practice 1

水文化是文化体系中的重要组成部分，是一种客观存在的文化新形态。它是人类历史文明进程中人们在处理人水关系活动中创造的以精神成果为核心的物质、行为和制度成果的总和，集中体现了人与水关系的一种社会状态。水文化的本质是人水关系的文化。水文化的产生、形成和发展有其深刻的历史渊源、自然因素、社会环境、文化元素乃至水利行业背景，源于人类在与水打交道的过程中，对人水关系不断从感性到理性认识的结晶和升华。对“水”的认识已上升至“生命之源、生态之基、生产之要”，水利在国民经济和社会发展中的地位和文明进步中的作用愈显重要，而水文化正是凝聚人与水的重要源泉和支撑。因此，加强水文化建设是经济社会发展的时代需要，是繁荣社会主义先进文化的重要内容。

第二单元　水与文学

Unit 2　Water and Literature

“水生民，民生文，文生万象”，水与中华文化的孕育十分密切。华夏先民把对水的崇拜与幻想写进了文学作品中，从《山海经》中记载的“女娲补天”“精卫填海”“大禹治水”的故事，到《诗经》里脍炙人口的《关雎》《汉广》《蒹葭》，其后的《庄子》、《楚辞》、汉代的乐府民歌、唐诗宋词、明清小说等，无不表现出寓情于水、以水传情的文化取向。自然之水经过人类的再创造，已升华为一种情感寄托，对水的描写、吟诵、歌咏，使水具有了显著的文化意义，可以说，被赋予了丰富内涵的水，从一开始就体现出特有的文学情怀。

“Water gives birth to people; people give birth to culture; culture gives birth to everything”, showing the close relationship between water and the birth of Chinese culture. Chinese ancestors expressed their water worship and fantasy in literary works. The origin of water novels and poetry can be traced back to the stories of “Goddess Nv Wa Patches up the Sky”, “Jingwei Fills up the Sea” and “Emperor Yu Tames the Flood” in *The Classic of Mountains and Seas*, and to the popular poems of *Guan Jv*, *Han Guang*, and *Reeds* in *The Book of Songs*. The subsequent *Zhuangzi*, *Odes of Chu*, folk songs and ballads in the Han Dynasty, Tang Poetry and Song Lyrics, Ming and Qing novels, all demonstrate the cultural orientation of embodying love in water and conveying love through water. Water in nature has been sublimated into a kind of emotional sustenance through the re-creation of human beings. The description, chanting, and singing of water gives water itself cultural significance. It can be said that water has been endowed with a rich connotation and reflected the unique literary sentiment since its existence.

水既是文学艺术表现的对象，又是启迪文心和艺术匠心的源泉。细读中国的经典文学作品，几乎无水不写，写则涉水。本章将从诗歌和小说两个方面来阐释水与文学的不解之缘。

Water is not only the object of literary and artistic expression, but also the source of inspiration and artistic ingenuity. A close reading of classic Chinese literature reveals that every form of water is written about and every piece of writing involves water. This chapter will explain the inextricable relationship between water and literature from two aspects: poetry and novels.

第一节 水与诗歌
Section A Water and Poetry

文学用形象反映生活，表达情感。水形态的多样化，为诗词的创作增添了生机和光彩，成为诗人们表情达意的媒介。“无水花不开，无水花不艳”，在自然界众多的意象中，水成为诗人最喜爱的意象符号之一。咏颂水的诗句可谓如织似绣，不可胜数。据统计，现存李白的近千首诗中，有近半涉及“水”；杜甫留给后人1400首诗，有370余处与水相关；白居易创作的2900余首诗中，也有760余处情系水景。诗人笔下的水，或呈黄河巨浪，或化溪泉淙淙，或变豪气于云，或现柔情绵绵。水在诗歌的天空中幻化出一道道奇异的彩虹，令人目不暇接、击节叹赏。“水诗歌”的创作也为中国文学增添了无限生机和绚丽光彩，成为我们最为宝贵的文化财产之一。

Literature reflects life and expresses emotions through images. The diversity of water forms adds vitality and brilliance to the creation of poetry and becomes a medium for poets to express their emotions. “A flower does not bloom without water, and a flower cannot be beautiful without water.” Among many images in nature, water has become one of the poets' favorite imagery symbols. There are countless poems in which water is celebrated. According to statistics, among about 1,000 existing poems by Li Bai, nearly half of them involve water; among 1,400 poems by Du Fu, more than 370 are related to water; and among 2,900 poems by Bai Juyi, more than 760 have references to water. The water under the poets' pen is either in the form of the huge waves of the Yellow River, or in the form of the murmur of a stream, or in the form of boldness in the clouds, or in the form of tenderness. In the sky of poetry, the water is transformed into strange rainbows, which are dazzling and admiring. The creation of water poetry has also added infinite vitality and splendor to Chinese literature, and has become one of our most valuable cultural assets.

1. 淡淡流水，泛泛柏舟——咏流水

1. Chanting flowing water

水一旦进入诗人的想象，就渗入了诗人的千般感情，在他们的笔下便生出了优美的诗行。骆宾王的《咏水》是历代咏水诗的代表作，水的地位、水的价值、水的作用、水的动态、水的静态、水的一切都饱含在全诗八句四十个字之中。《咏水》一诗不仅具有极高的文学价值，而且亦具有深远的社会意义。它赋予水很深的价值意义，融诗趣哲理于一体，透露的是对水的描写和歌颂，蕴含的是诗人自身所推崇的儒风与道骨。

Once the water captures the poets' imagination, it permeates into a plurality of types of emotions. In their writings, inspiring lines flash out. Luo Binwang's *Chanting Flowing Water* is a masterpiece of poems that chant water through the ages. The status of water, the value of water, the role of water, the dynamics of water, the stillness of water, and actually all about water are contained in the eight lines and forty words of the poem. The poem is not only of great literary value, but also of profound social significance. It endows water with a deep value and meaning, integrating poetic taste with philosophy, revealing the water description and eulogy, and implicating the Confucianism and sage-like temperament that the poet himself espouses.

2. 万古江河，百川东流——赞江河

2. Praising rivers

江河是一首首流动的诗，是一幅幅流动的画。华夏的众多江河都流淌着中华文明的印迹，许多江河都被称为"诗河""史河""文化河"。中华民族热爱江河，不仅用画笔描绘江河，用音乐讴歌江河，还用诗文赞美江河。

比如唐朝诗人张若虚笔下的长江："春江潮水连海平，海上明月共潮生。滟滟随波千万里，何处春江无月明。……"在《春江花月夜》中，诗人凭借对春江花月夜的描绘，始终围绕"江"和"月"两个主题，尽情讴歌大自然的奇丽景色，赞美人间纯洁的爱情，巧妙地将游子思妇的同情心、对人生哲理的追求、对宇宙奥秘的探索结合起来，从而产生一种情、景、理水乳交融的幽美而邈远的意境。

再如唐朝诗人薛能笔下的黄河："何处发昆仑，连乾复浸坤……九曲终柔胜，常流可暗吞。……"写出了黄河内在的神韵和柔胜的气质。

Rivers are flowing poems and paintings. Many rivers in China have witnessed traces and footprints of Chinese civilization, many of which are called "rivers of poetry", "rivers of history", and "rivers of culture". Chinese people love rivers, not only painting them with their brushes or eulogizing them with music, but also praising them with poetry.

For example, the poet Zhang Ruoxu of the Tang Dynasty wrote about the

Yangtze River in his famous poem *The Moon over the River on a Spring Night*:

In spring the river rises as high as the sea;
And with the river's tide up rises the moon bright.
She follows the rolling waves for ten thousand li;
Wherever the river flows, there overflows her light.
…

(Translated by Xu Yuanchong)

In this poem, the poet, with his depiction of the moon over the river on a spring night, always focuses on the two themes of "the river" and "the moon", eulogizing the wondrous scenery of nature and praising the pure love on earth. He cleverly combines the compassion of wanderers and their wives' yearning to see them, the pursuit of philosophy of life with the exploration of the mysteries of the universe. This combination results in a beautiful and distant artistic conception that blends love, scenery and reason.

Another example is the Yellow River described by the poet Xue Neng of the Tang Dynasty. The Yellow River's intrinsic charm and its soft temperament are captured in his poem *The Yellow River*.

3. 水光潋滟，潭面无风——观湖泊

3. Watching lakes

我国古代的文人墨客大多喜欢追寻湖泊美的足迹，行吟泽畔，留下难以数计的诗文辞赋。孟浩然的"气蒸云梦泽，波撼岳阳城"及杜甫的"吴楚东南坼，乾坤日夜浮"都是写洞庭湖的名句；王勃在传世名文《滕王阁序》中有"落霞与孤鹜齐飞，秋水共长天一色"的句子，写的是鄱阳湖上的景色；美轮美奂、堪称"诗湖"的西子湖令一代又一代的游人为之魂牵梦萦、倾倒不已，最著名的当属苏轼的《饮湖上初晴后雨》，诗云："水光潋滟晴方好，山色空蒙雨亦奇。欲把西湖比西子，淡妆浓抹总相宜。"

Most of the ancient Chinese literati and writers liked to walk along the banks of the beautiful lakes, and left countless poems and verses about lakes. "Over Dongting Lake hangs thin mist; The waves surge up to Yueyang town" by Meng Haoran, and "Wu and Chu slope off to south and east; Heaven and Earth day and night float on these waters" by Du Fu are famous lines about the Dongting Lake. In his famous parallel prose *A Tribute to King Teng's Tower*, Wang Bo wrote the wonderful line "The sunlight shoots through the rosy clouds, and the autumn water is merged with the boundless sky into one hue", which is about the scenery of the Poyang Lake. The beautiful West Lake, which can be called a "poetic lake", has made generations of travelers fall in love with it. The most famous poem about West Lake is Su Shi's *Drinking at the Lake, First in Sunny, then in Rainy Weather*, which reads:

The brimming waves delight the eye on sunny days;
The dimming hills present rare view in rainy haze.
West Lake may be compared to Lady of the West,
Whether she is richly adorned or plainly dressed.
(Translated by Xu Yuanchong)

4. 大海广阔，涤心扩怀——颂大海

4. Singing to the sea

中国古代的咏海诗歌就像中国文化浩瀚海洋里的一颗明珠，熠熠闪光。最早对大海进行写实性描绘的是三国时期的曹操，他留下了大气磅礴的《观沧海》，诗文极力描绘大海的雄浑壮阔，勾勒出大海吞吐日月、包容天地的雄伟气象，歌颂壮丽的山河，透露出作者一统山河的强烈愿望。

《观沧海》

东临碣石，以观沧海。
水何澹澹，山岛竦峙。
树木丛生，百草丰茂。
秋风萧瑟，洪波涌起。
日月之行，若出其中。
星汉灿烂，若出其里。
幸甚至哉，歌以咏志。

The ancient Chinese poetry of chanting the sea is like a pearl in the vast ocean of Chinese culture, shining brightly. The earliest realistic depiction of the sea was attributed to Cao Cao during the Three Kingdoms Period. He left behind the majestic *The Sea*, a poem that portrays the majesty of the sea, outlining the majestic scene of the sea as it swallows the sun and the moon and accommodates the heaven and the earth. In fact, the magnificent mountains and rivers of the motherland are celebrated in this poem, revealing the author's sincere love for the rivers and mountains and his strong desire to unify the rivers and mountains. The following is the poem:

I come to view the boundless ocean
From Stony Hill on eastern shore.
Its water rolls in rhythmic motion
And islands stand amid its roar.
Tree on tree grows from peak to peak;
Grass on grass looks lush far and nigh.
The autumn wind blows drear and bleak;
The monstrous billows surge up high.
The sun by day, the moon by night
Appear to rise up from the deep.
The Milky Way with stars so bright
Sinks down into the sea in sleep.
How happy I feel at this sight!
I croon this poem in delight.
(Translated by Xu Yuanchong)

5. 潮来怒卷,汐自东西——叹潮汐

5. Admiring the tide

钱塘江潮作为一种自然奇观,让无数的文人墨客为其痴迷,历代观潮诗人、词家对其吟咏不绝。"八月十八潮,壮观天下无。"这是苏轼咏赞钱塘秋潮的千古名句。再如孟浩然的《与颜钱塘登樟亭望潮作》,这首诗写出了大潮澎湃动荡的伟力,鲜明生动,有声有色,情在景中,情景交融,为咏潮诗景物形象的塑造提供了优秀的范例。

The tide of the Qiantang River, as a natural wonder, has fascinated countless literati and writers, and has been intoned by poets and lyricists throughout the ages. "The eighteenth tide of August is as spectacular as any in the world", which is a famous line from Su Shi's poem in praise of the autumn tide in Qiantang River. Another example is Meng Haoran's poem titled *Composed after Climbing the Zhangting Pavilion and Watching the Tide with Magistrate Yan of Qiantang*. This poem, which is a blend of emotions and scenes, expresses the turbulent power of the tide. It's vivid, colorful and impressive, serving as an excellent example of how to create the image of a tidal wave.

6. 声喧石乱,色静深松——歌婉溪

6. Eulogizing streams

很多文人雅士对溪水可谓情有独钟,很多与溪水相关而又流传至今的诗歌,蜚声千古。比如王维的《青溪》描绘了青溪的蜿蜒多姿,诗人笔下的青溪是喧闹与沉郁的统一,活泼与安详的糅合,幽深与素静的融合,吟之令人羡慕向往。诗人自己更是心已恬静无欲,如清溪之水,以洁净淡泊的态度,保持着无声的沉默。

附全诗:

言入黄花川,每逐青溪水。随山将万转,趣途无百里。
声喧乱石中,色静深松里。漾漾泛菱荇,澄澄映葭苇。
我心素已闲,清川澹如此。请留磐石上,垂钓将已矣。

Many literati and scholars have a fondness for streams, and many poems related to them have been passed down through the ages. For example, *A Green Stream* by Wang Wei depicts the meandering beauty of the stream, which is a unity of noise and melancholy, a blend of liveliness and tranquility, and a fusion of depth and quietness. The green stream is enviable and desirable. The poet is already peaceful in mind and rids himself of desire, just as the clean, silent and indifferent water in that stream. The following is the poem:

To view the Yellow-flower Stream, always
I follow the course of Blue Brook's flow
Which curls through the hills in a myriad of ways
With barely thirty miles to go.
Sometime it roars 'mid a riot of stones,
But then calms down in the thick of pines.
The duckweeds dance, in easeful tones,
While the image of reeds in the limpid shines.
My mind has long been free from care.
This clear, leisured brook, O it's just what I wish!
As well I might stay on that huge rock o'er there,
With tackle to fish as long as I wish.

(Translated by Wang Baotong)

7. 夜来风雨，润物无声——品雨韵

7. Appreciating the rain

自古以来，诗人们大都喜欢以雨入诗。几千年来，淅淅沥沥的雨落在诗里，造就了无数的咏雨佳作，也吟就了不少传世之作。比如杜甫的《春夜喜雨》，字字扣喜意，句句蕴喜情，喜始喜终，一喜贯穿。不仅切夜、切春，而且写出了典型的春雨也就是"好雨"的高尚品格。诗人一喜春雨知时节，二喜万物可滋润，三喜灾荒可消除，四喜百姓有救济，五喜自家有指望，六喜一朵朵红艳艳的花汇成花的海洋。诗人情系民生的高尚情怀和期盼雨水能润泽民生的狂喜之情跃然眼前，情真意切，栩栩如生。

附全诗：

好雨知时节，当春乃发生。
随风潜入夜，润物细无声。
野径云俱黑，江船火独明。
晓看红湿处，花重锦官城。

Since ancient times, most poets like to describe the rain in their poems. For thousands of years, the rain has fallen on the poems. Countless masterpieces of rain chanting have been composed and many of them have been handed down from generation to generation. For example, in *Happy Rain on a Spring Night* by Du Fu, every word conjures up the meaning of joy, and each sentence contains joy. It begins and ends with joy. Joy runs through the whole poem. The poet is happy that the typical spring rain, the good rain, is timely, that everything can be nourished, that disasters can be eliminated, that the people can count on it and receive a relief, and that the world changes into a sea of bright red flowers. The poet's noble sentiments for the people's livelihood and his ecstasy of expecting the rain to nourish everything are vivid and sincere. The following is the poem:

Good rain knows its time right;
It will fall when comes spring.
With wind it steals in night;
Mute, it moistens each thing.
O'er wild lanes dark cloud spreads;
In boat a lantern looms.
Dawn sees saturated reds;
The town's heavy with blooms.
(Translated by Xu Yuanchong)

New Words, Phrases and Expressions

diversity [daɪˈvɜːsəti] *n.* 多样性,多样化;不同,差异

brilliance [ˈbrɪliəns] *n.* 才华,聪慧;光亮,光辉

bloom [bluːm] *n.* 花,花朵;花期;青春焕发,风华正茂;(肤色的)红润;(一些水果和植物的)粉衣,粉霜 *v.* 开花,绽放;繁荣,兴旺;精神焕发

imagery [ˈɪmɪdʒəri] *n.* 意象,比喻,形象化描述;一组图片;(艺术作品中的)像,画面

symbol [ˈsɪmb(ə)l] *n.* 象征,标志;符号;代表性的人(物)

statistics [stəˈtɪstɪks] *n.* (statistic 的复数形式) 统计学;统计数字

under the poets' pen 在诗人的笔下

murmur [ˈmɜːmə(r)] *n.* 低语声,轻柔的谈话声;持续轻柔的声音;私下的抱怨,咕哝;(医)(心脏的)杂音 *v.* 低语,轻声地说;私下抱怨,发牢骚;发出持续轻柔的声音

in the form of 以……形式

transform [trænsˈfɔːm] *v.* 使改观,使变形,使转化;变换(电流)的电压;(数)变换(数学实体)

dazzling [ˈdæz(ə)lɪŋ] *a.* 令人赞叹的,给人深刻印象的;耀眼的,炫目的

infinite [ˈɪnfɪnət] *a.* 无限的,无穷尽的;(数量或程度上)极大的,无穷大的;非限定的 *n.* (空间或数量的)无穷大(the infinite);上帝(the infinite)

splendor [ˈsplendə(r)] *n.* 壮丽,壮观;美景;让人印象深刻的事物 (splendors)

asset [ˈæset] *n.* 有利条件,有价值的人或物;资产,财产

chant [tʃɑːnt] *v.* 反复唱,反复呼喊;唱圣歌,诵经文 *n.* 反复喊的话,唱的调子;圣歌,颂歌

capture [ˈkæptʃə(r)] *v.* 俘获,捕获;夺取,占领;吸引,引起;记录,体现;拍摄,录制;使(数据)保存于电脑中;(河流)袭夺 *n.* 捕获;被捕获;被捕获的人(或物);占领,攻占;夺取,抢占;(数据)存储

permeate [ˈpɜːmieɪt] *v.* 渗透,弥漫;(观点、信念、感情等)充满,充斥

plurality [plʊəˈræləti] *n.* 多数;复数;兼职;胜出票数

a plurality of =a large number of

nourish [ˈnʌrɪʃ] *v.* 养育,滋养;培养,怀有(感情、信念等)

flash [flæʃ] *v.* 闪光,闪亮;(快速)出示,显示;飞驰,掠过;闪现;迅速播出或传送(信息);突然显露(强烈情感);(尤指用无线电或光波)通信,联络 *n.* 闪光;闪光灯;闪现;突然理解,顿悟;(感情的)突发;(产品包装上用来吸引顾客眼光的)色带,突显区域;(尤指为帮助行船而从堰闸里放出的)水流;飞快一瞥 *a.* 阔气的,爱显摆的;突然而短暂的

endow [ɪnˈdaʊ] *v.* (with) 向(人、机构)捐赠,资助;赋予

integrate [ˈɪntɪɡreɪt] A with B *v.* (使)合并,成为一体;(使)加入,融入群体;(使)取消种族隔离;求……的积分;表示(面积、温度等)的总和,表示……的平均值

eulogy [ˈjuːlədʒi] *n.* 悼词,颂词,赞词;颂扬

implicate [ˈɪmplɪkeɪt] *v.* 使牵连其中,涉及;表明或意指……是起因;暗指,暗示

Confucianism [kənˈfjuːʃənɪzəm] *n.* 孔子学说;儒家思想

sage [seɪdʒ] *n.* (正式)智者,圣贤;鼠尾草(叶子用于烹饪);浅灰绿色 *a.* 睿智的,贤明的

espouse [ɪˈspaʊz] *vt.* 支持;赞成;信奉;嫁娶

witness [ˈwɪtnəs] *n.* (尤指犯罪或事故的)目击者;(法庭等的)证人;(签署正式文件的)见证人,连署人;见证人;证据,证言;证明标志 *v.* 目击,目睹;见证,经历(事件、变化等);做见证;证明,表明;为……作证;做证人

footprint [ˈfʊtprɪnt] *n.* 脚印,足迹;占用空间;覆盖区

eulogize [ˈjuːlədʒaɪz] *vt.* 颂扬;称赞

depiction [dɪˈpɪkʃn] *n.* 描述,描绘

wondrous [ˈwʌndrəs] *a.* 奇妙的;令人惊奇的;非常的

compassion [kəmˈpæʃ(ə)n] *n.* 同情,怜悯

yearning [ˈjɜːnɪŋ] *n.* 渴望,向往 *a.* 渴望的

blend [blend] *v.* (使)混合,调和;(使)协调,融合;调制,配制 *n.* 混合物;交融,融合;混合词

intrinsic [ɪnˈtrɪnzɪk] *a.* 内在的,固有的

literati [ˌlɪtəˈrɑːti] *n.* (literatus 的复数)文人;文学界

surge [sɜːdʒ] *n.* 激增,猛增;(风、水等的)奔涌,汹涌;(情感的)涌起,翻涌;(人群的)蜂拥;电流急冲,电涌;增兵,增援 *v.* 急剧上升,激增;(人群、自然力)汹涌,奔腾;(感情)涌起,涌现;(电压、电流)猛增,浪涌

slope [sləʊp] *n.* 斜坡,斜面;山坡;滑雪斜坡;斜度,坡度;扛枪姿势 *v.* 倾斜,成斜坡;歪斜;悄悄地溜走

parallel [ˈpærəlel] *a.* 平行的;相似的,同时发生的;(计算机)并行的;并联的 *n.* 相似手法,共同点;相似的人(或物);(地球的)纬线,纬圈;(印刷)平行符号 *v.* 与……相似;与……同时发生;与……并行;与……相当

shoot [ʃuːt] *v.* 开(枪或其他武器);射杀,射伤;发射(子弹等);狩猎;投(球),射门;玩,打(某种游戏);拍摄(电影、照片等);(使)急速移动;将(目光、问题或话语)转向;(朝特定方向)急速延伸;一举(成功或成名);猛长,激增 (shoot up);(疼痛)穿刺;闩(门闩),拔出(门闩);(船只)急速穿过(急流、瀑布或桥);(植物、种子)发芽

merge [mɜːdʒ] *v.* (尤指商业结构)合并;(使)融合,逐渐消失;平稳并线

boundless [ˈbaʊndləs] *a.* 无限的;无边无际的

hue [hjuː] *n.* 颜色,色调,色度;种类,派别;叫声 (hue and cry)

brim [brɪm] *n.* 帽檐,帽边;(容器的)口,边沿 *v.* (brimmed; brimmed; brimming) (使)满,盛满;充满

dim [dɪm] *a.* (dimmer; dimmest) 暗淡的,昏暗的;模糊的,看不清的;(非正式)愚笨的,迟钝的;前景暗淡的,不乐观的 *v.* (dimmed; dimmed; dimming)(使)变暗;变淡漠,失去光泽;(使)变模糊

haze [heɪz] *n.* 霾,烟雾;懵懂,迷糊 *v.* 变朦胧;(美)戏弄(大学新生,作为入学或入会仪式的一部分);变糊涂

adorn [əˈdɔːn] *v.* 装饰;使生色

pearl [pɜːl] *n.* 珍珠;珍珠母;珠状物;极其优秀的人;珍贵的东西;人造珍珠;珠灰色;珍珠项链,珍珠首饰 (pearls) *v.* 〈文〉呈珠状滴;使呈珠灰色或蓝灰色;(潜水)采珍珠;用珍珠装饰 *a.* 珍珠般的;镶珍珠的

realistic [ˌriːəˈlɪstɪk] *a.* 务实的,实事求是的;实际的,现实可行的;写实的,逼真的

attribute [əˈtrɪbjuːt] *v.* 把……归因于;认为是……所作;认为……具有某种特质 [ˈætrɪbjuːt] *n.* 属性;性质;特征

majestic [məˈdʒestɪk] *a.* 雄伟的;威严的;壮观的

portray [pɔːˈtreɪ] *v.* 描绘,描写;(在艺术或文学作品中)描述,刻画;(在电影、戏剧等中)扮演

majesty [ˈmædʒəsti] *n.* 雄伟,壮丽,威严;陛下(对国王或女王的称呼);君权,王权

outline [ˈaʊtlaɪn] *n.* 轮廓,外形;轮廓图,草图;提纲,大纲;梗概,要点;(词的)速记形式 *v.* 概述,略述;勾勒,描画……的轮廓

meteorology [ˌmiːtiəˈrɒlədʒi] *n.* 气象状态;气象学

swallow [ˈswɒləʊ] *v.* 吞下,咽下;(由于紧张等)做吞咽动作,咽口水;吞没,淹没;耗尽(金钱、资源);完全相信,信以为真;抑制(感情、言语);默默忍受(侮辱、批评等) *n.* 吞,一口;燕子

accommodate [əˈkɒmədeɪt] *v.* 为……提供住宿;容纳,提供空间;考虑到,顾及;顺应,适应;帮助(某人),向……施以援手;迎合,迁就;调解

unify [ˈjuːnɪfaɪ] *v.* (使)联合;(使)统一;使协调

fascinate [ˈfæsɪneɪt] *v.* 使无法动弹;深深吸引,迷住

intone [ɪnˈtəʊn] *v.* 吟诵;吟咏

lyricist [ˈlɪrɪsɪst] *n.* 抒情诗人;(流行歌曲等的)歌词作者

spectacular [spekˈtækjələ(r)] *a.* 壮观的,令人惊叹的;惊人的,突如其来的 *n.* 壮观场面,盛大演出

in praise of 表扬;赞美

pavilion [pəˈvɪliən] *n.* （英）（运动场边的）运动员席，看台，更衣室；（临时的）大帐篷，临时建筑；大型文体馆；凉亭，阁；分馆式病房，分馆　*v.* 搭帐篷；置……于亭中；笼罩

impressive [ɪmˈpresɪv] *a.* 给人印象深刻的，令人钦佩的

tidal [ˈtaɪd(ə)l] *a.* 潮汐的；受潮汐影响的

depict [dɪˈpɪkt] *v.* 描述，描绘

meandering [miːˈændərɪŋ] *a.* 曲折的；聊天的；漫步的　*n.* 漫步；漫谈；（建筑）曲径

unity [ˈjuːnəti] *n.* 团结，统一；整体性，统一性；三一律（指戏剧在时间、地点和情节三点上的统一性）；统一体；（数目或数字）一

melancholy [ˈmelənkəli] *a.* （令人）悲哀的，（令人）沮丧的　*n.* 抑郁，忧郁；精神病（= melancholia）

tranquility [træŋˈkwɪləti] *n.* 宁静，安宁

fusion [ˈfjuːʒ(ə)n] *n.* 融合，结合；核聚变；混合音乐；融合菜肴；熔化；融合物

enviable [ˈenviəb(ə)l] *a.* 值得羡慕的，引起忌妒的

rid oneself of 摆脱

indifferent [ɪnˈdɪfrənt] *a.* （to）冷淡的，不关心的；中等的，平庸的；一般的，相当差的；中立的；不分化的

curl [kɜːl] *v.* （使）弯曲，卷曲；（使）盘绕，（使）弯弯曲曲移动；边缘翘起；撇（嘴）　*n.* 鬈发，卷发；（头发的）卷曲；卷曲物，螺旋状物；（锻炼肌肉的）弯曲运动

a myriad of [ˈmɪriəd] *n.* 〈文〉无数，大量；（古典历史剧中）一万　*a.* 无数的，大量的

duckweed [ˈdʌkwiːd] *n.* 浮萍；水萍

limpid [ˈlɪmpɪd] *a.* 透明的；平静的，无忧虑的

tackle [ˈtæk(ə)l] *v.* 应付，解决（难题或局面）；与……交涉；擒获；对付（尤指罪犯）；质问，责问

appreciate [əˈpriːʃieɪt] *v.* 欣赏，鉴赏；理解，明白；感谢，感激；升值，增值

conjure [ˈkʌndʒə(r)] *v.* 变魔术，使……变戏法般地出现或消失；想象出，设想出；使浮现于脑海

eliminate [ɪˈlɪmɪneɪt] *v.* 剔除，根除；对……不予考虑，把……排除在外；（比赛中）淘汰；铲除，杀害；（生理）排除，排泄；消去

sentiment [ˈsentɪmənt] *n.* 观点，看法，情绪；多愁善感，伤感情绪

livelihood [ˈlaɪvlihʊd] *n.* 生计，营生

ecstasy [ˈekstəsi] *n.* 狂喜，陶醉；摇头丸（Ecstasy）；（情绪或宗教原因引起的）疯狂，出神

mute [mjuːt] *a.* 缄默的，沉默的；哑的，不会说话的；无声的，宁静的；（猎犬）追猎时不吠叫的；（字母）哑音的，无音的　*n.* 弱音器；哑巴；闭锁音　*v.* 消音，减音；减弱，缓和；关闭声音

moisten [ˈmɔɪsn] *vt.* 弄湿;使……湿润 *vi.* 潮湿;变潮湿
lantern [ˈlæntən] *n.* 灯笼,提灯;(灯塔上的)灯室;天窗
loom [luːm] *v.* (尤指阴森森地)隐约出现,赫然耸现;逼近,临近 *n.* 织布机;(尤指海上物体在黑暗或浓雾中的)隐隐显现
saturate [ˈsætʃəreɪt] *v.* 使湿透,浸透;使充满,使饱和;充斥(市场),使(市场)供大于求

第二节 水与小说
Section B Water and Novel

不仅是古代的诗词歌赋中频频出现与水有关的意象,古代小说的内容更是离不开水。代表着中国古代小说最高峰的四大古典名著,无一不是提到了水,无一不是将水置于整个小说的情节发展和叙事脉络中。

Water-related imagery appears frequently not only in ancient poems and verses, but also in ancient novels. The four great classic Chinese novels, which represent the pinnacle of ancient fiction, all refer to water and place it in the plot development and narrative of the entire novel.

神魔小说杰作《西游记》中的师徒四人都跟水有很深的渊源。唐僧出生后被母亲放置在江中木板之上,顺水漂流,被金山寺长老救起,取名江流儿,长大后其虔诚向佛,法名玄奘。江流儿的身世是融合了中国古代神话、唐宋小说、宋元戏剧及民间传说的相关内容而潜心创造的一个文学故事。孙悟空的出身更是与水有关,他出生于海上仙山——花果山,花果山位于大海之中,四面环水。孙悟空不仅出生于水世界,他使用的兵器——金箍棒也是借于龙宫水世界,而金箍棒是大禹治水遗下的定海神针,这又与治水神话发生了关联。猪八戒的身世也同样与水有关,先民视猪为水中动物,加之猪的浴身习性和降雨有某些联系,古代误以为降雨与猪有关,便以猪为水畜,奉为水神,水神河伯的形象为猪。猪八戒被贬前在天河做天蓬元帅,天蓬元帅即是掌管天河水兵的水神。再看沙僧,他在流沙河做水怪,观音菩萨为沙僧取的法名"悟净"就与水有关。沙僧他自己曾道:"弟子向蒙菩萨教化,指河为姓,与我起了法名,唤作沙悟净。"

Journey to the West, Monk Tang and his three disciples all have a deep connection with water. After being born and placed on a wooden plank in the river by his mother, Monk Tang drifted downstream and was rescued by the elder of the

Jinshan Temple, where he was named Jiangliu'er, and grew up to devote himself to Buddhism with the Dharma name Xuanzang. The birth of Jiangliu'er (literally means "Son of the River") is a literary story created by integrating ancient Chinese mythology, novels of Tang and Song, plays and folklore of Song and Yuan. The origin of the immortal monkey Sun Wukong is even more related to water, as he was born on Mount Huaguo, a mountain of immortals on the sea, surrounded by water on all sides. Not only was Sun Wukong born in the water world, but the weapon "The Compliant Golden-Hooped Rod" he used was also borrowed from the water world of the Dragon Palace, and this magic rod was left behind by Yu the Great to control flood, which in turn has a connection with the myth of flood controlling. The origin of Zhu Bajie (Monk Pig) is related to water as well. The ancestors regarded pigs as aquatic animals. In addition, the bathing habits of pigs were related to rainfall. In ancient times, the ancestors mistakenly believed that rainfall had something to do with pigs, so they took pigs as water animals and worshiped them as water gods. Before he was deported, Zhu Bajie served as the Heavenly Marshal in the Heavenly River, and the Heavenly Marshal was the water god who was in charge of the water soldiers in the Heavenly River. As for Monk Sha, he was a water monster in the River Liusha, and his Dharma name Wujing, which Guanyin Bodhisattva took for him, is related to water. Monk Sha once said, "I had been taught by the Bodhisattva to refer to the river as my surname, thus I was given the Dharma name of Sha Wujing."

英雄传奇小说《水浒传》就更不用说了，仅仅是小说的题目就能够显示出水的地位来。

There is no need to mention the heroic legendary novel *Outlaws of the Marsh*. The title of the novel alone shows the status of water.

小说的核心是塑造人物，因此，人物性格的描写是关键。而不少小说中的人物都带有水质，柔情似水是描摹温柔的女性。不仅是女性，男性人物性格的塑造也与水密切相关，如《三国演义》中的刘备。曹操评价刘备的一段话亦是以水喻人。“操曰：刘备，人中之龙也，生平未尝得水。今得荆州，是困龙入大海矣。孤安得不动心哉！”曹操把刘备比喻成龙，只不过没有得到有利于其的环境而无法大展手脚。曹操一生把刘备视作最强劲的竞争对手，但刘备在早期一直没有自己的根据地，得荆州后，如龙入大海，故曹操也要夺取荆州。

The core of the novel is to portray the characters. Therefore, characterization is its key. Many of the characters in the novels are related to water. Water-like tenderness is a description of women who are as gentle as water. Not only female characters but also male characters are closely related to water, such as Liu Bei in *Romance of the Three Kingdoms*. A comment by Cao Cao on Liu Bei is about a metaphor of water. Cao Cao said, "Liu Bei is a dragon among men, but he has never had access to water in his life. Now that he has gained Jingzhou, it seems that a trapped dragon has entered the sea. How can I not be impressed?" Cao Cao compared Liu Bei to a dragon, but initially Liu Bei had not been given a conducive environment in which he could make his mark. Cao Cao regarded Liu Bei as his strongest rival throughout his life, but Liu Bei had never had a base of his own in his earlier days. So when he gained Jingzhou, it was like a dragon entering the sea, and Cao Cao wanted to take Jingzhou too.

带着浓厚的社会人情小说色调的古典文学巨著《红楼梦》也与水密不可分。大观园的世界是女子的世界。"女人是水做的骨肉,男人是泥做的骨肉,我见了女儿便清爽,见了男子便觉浊臭。"曹雪芹将女性的世界和水的世界在无形中勾连在了一起,从而更为小说增添了神韵,增添了一种空明的美感。

A Dream of Red Mansions, a masterpiece of classical literature with strong tones of social and humanistic fiction, is also inseparable from water. The world of the Grand View Garden is a world of women. Jia Baoyu said, "Women are flesh and blood made of water, while men are made of clay; I am refreshed when I see a girl, but I feel stinky when I see a man." Cao Xueqin connects the world of women and the world of water in an invisible way, thus adding to the novel a divine charm and a sense of crystal beauty.

在现代文学中,知识分子对水的描述和思索仍在继续,而且呈现出了新的文化向度。周氏二兄弟的作品中存在着大量关于水的文字,他们的家乡在浙江绍兴,天然的水文化培育了他们对水的喜爱与敏感。鲁迅有很多关于童年宝贵记忆的描写都与水有关,可以参看他的《故乡》和《社戏》。周作人的文字中也涉及大量和水有关的内容,可以参看他的《乌篷船》和《水乡怀旧》。他在《水里的东西》一文中说道:"我是在水乡生长的,所以对于水未免有点情分。学者们说,人类曾经做过水族,小儿喜欢弄水,便是这个缘故。我的原因大约没有这样远,恐怕这只是一种习惯罢了。"沈从文也自小与水结下了不解之缘,当他以"乡下人"的主体视角身份构造着他心目中的"湘西世界"时,水更是他笔下时时出现的亲密对象。即使他远离了家乡的活水,他的心中也会有一片关于水的天地,那仿佛是他创作力的不竭源泉。“我虽离开了那条河流,我所写的故事,却多数是水边的故事。故事中我所最满意的文章,常用船上水上作为背景。我故事中人物的性格,全为我在水边船上所见到的人物性格。我文字中一点忧郁气氛,便因为被过去十五年前南方的阴雨天气影响而来。我文字的风格,假若还有些值得注意处,那只是因为我记得水上人的言语太多了。”

In modern literature, descriptions and musings on water by intellectuals persist and take on new cultural orientations. There is a great deal of writings about water in the works of the two brothers of Zhou family, whose hometown is in Shaoxing, Zhejiang province. The natural water culture cultivated their love and sensitivity to water. Many of Lu Xun's descriptions of his precious childhood memories are related to water. You can refer to his *My Old Home* and *Village Opera*. Zhou Zuoren's writings are also invested with a great deal of water-related stuff. You can refer to his *Wupeng Boats* and *Nostalgia for the Canal Town*. He said in his essay *Something in the Water*: "I grew up in a canal town, so I have some affection for water. Scholars say that humans were once aquatics, and that children like to play with water for this reason. But for me, I am afraid it is just a habit." Shen Congwen has also forged an indissoluble bond with water since he was a child. When he was constructing the Western Hunan world in his mind from the perspective of a "countryman", water was an intimate object in his writing. Even when he was away from the living water of his hometown, there was still a world of water in his mind, as if it were the inexhaustible source of his creativity. He said, "Although I have been away from that river, most of the stories I write are waterfront stories. The most satisfying parts of my stories are often set on the water or on a boat. The characters in my stories are the very people that I have seen on the boats by the water. The melancholic atmosphere in my writing is the consequence of the rainy weather in the south fifteen years ago. If there is something noteworthy about the style of my writing, it is only because I remember so much of the words of the people on the water."

水文化在当代文学中更焕发出其夺目的生机来。张承志的《北方的河》,王安忆的《黄河故道人》《流水三十章》,迟子建的《额尔古纳河右岸》《清水洗尘》,李杭育的《流浪的土地》,残雪的《黄泥街》《污水上的肥皂泡》,余华的《河边的错误》,格非的《迷舟》《山河入梦》,莫言的《酒国》等作品都在不同层面上与水文化发生着或隐或显的关系。

Water culture has taken on an even more dazzling vibrancy in contemporary literature. *The River in the North* by Zhang Chengzhi, *The People of the Old Yellow River* and *Thirty Chapters of Flowing Water* by Wang Anyi, *The Right Bank of the Erguna River* and *Cleaning the Dust with Clear Water* by Chi Zijian, *The Wandering Land* by Li Hangyu, *Yellow Mud Street* and *Soap Bubbles on Sewage* by Can Xue, *The Mistake by the River* by Yu Hua, *The Lost Boat* and *Mountains and Rivers into a Dream* by Ge Fei, and *The Republic of Wine* by Mo Yan are all implicitly or explicitly related to water culture at different levels.

New Words, Phrases and Expressions

pinnacle [ˈpɪnək(ə)l] *n.* 高峰;小尖塔;尖峰;极点

narrative [ˈnærətɪv] *n.* 记叙文,叙述;叙事技巧 *a.* 叙述的;叙事体的

disciple [dɪˈsaɪp(ə)l] *n.* 耶稣的十二门徒之一(=the Disciples);追随者,门徒

plank [plæŋk] *n.* 木板,板条;(政党等的)政策准则,(政策或纲领的)要点;(成败的)关键

Dharma [ˈdɑːmə] *n.* (佛教中的)达摩(指佛的教法、佛法、一切事物和现象);(印度教的)法则

literally [ˈlɪtərəli] *adv.* 按照字面意义地,逐字地;真正地,确实地;(用于夸张强调)简直

mythology [mɪˈθɒlədʒi] *n.* 神话(学),神话故事;错误信念,谬误

immortal [ɪˈmɔːt(ə)l] *a.* 不死的,永存的;不朽的,流芳百世的,永垂千古的 *n.* 神,永生不灭者;永垂不朽的人物

compliant [kəmˈplaɪənt] *a.* 服从的,顺从的;(与规定或标准)符合的,一致的;(物理、医学)有可塑性的

hoop [huːp] *n.* (金属、木或类似材料制成的)箍,环(尤指用于箍桶或制框架);圈形耳环(hoop earring);滚圈;呼啦圈(hula hoop 简称) *v.* (用环或似用环)绑,箍

rod [rɒd] *n.* 棒,杆;钓鱼竿;钓鱼者;权力,权杖;枝条,柳条;(责打人用的)棍棒;杖责,惩罚(the rod)

aquatic [əˈkwætɪk] *a.* 水生的,水栖的;与水生动植物有关的;水(上)的 *n.* (尤指适于在水塘或水族馆中生活的)水生植物(或动物);水上运动(aquatics)

worship [ˈwɜːʃɪp] *v.* 敬奉(神);爱慕,崇拜 *n.* 敬神,拜神;崇拜,爱慕;(英)阁下(对地位高的人的尊称)

deport [dɪˈpɔːt] *v.* 驱逐(非本国居民)出境

Marshal [ˈmɑːʃ(ə)l] *n.* (英国)陆军元帅,空军元帅;司仪,典礼官;(尤指体育赛事的)总指挥;(美国法院的)执行官;(一些美国城市的)警察或消防局长

monster [ˈmɒnstə(r)] *n.* 怪兽,怪物;残忍的人,恶魔;小恶棍,捣蛋鬼;庞然大物;难以驾驭之人,难以掌控之事;畸形动植物　*a.* 很受欢迎的;庞大的,巨大的

legendary [ˈledʒəndri] *a.* 非常著名的;享有盛名的;传奇的;传说的

Outlaws [ˈaʊtlɔːz] *n.* 执法悍将(游戏名);不法之徒(电影名)

Marsh [mɑːʃ] *n.* 沼泽,湿地

humanistic [ˌhjuːməˈnɪstɪk] *a.* 人文主义的;人道主义的

inseparable [ɪnˈseprəbl] *a.* (人)形影不离的;(东西)分不开的,不可分离的;(前缀)不可单独成词的　*n.* 不能分开的人(或事物)

refresh [rɪˈfreʃ] *v.* 使恢复精神,使消除疲劳;使记起,提醒;翻新;刷新,更新(网页);(美)再斟满(饮料);浸入冷水冷却或保鲜;恢复精神;喝饮料;吃点心;补充给养

stinky [ˈstɪŋki] *a.* (stinkier; stinkiest) 发恶臭的,十分难闻的;令人厌恶的;糟糕透顶的

spokesperson [ˈspəʊkspɜːsn] *n.* 发言人;代言人

invisible [ɪnˈvɪzəb(ə)l] *a.* 看不见的,隐形的;无形的;不为人注意的　*n.* 无形进出口

orientation [ˌɔːriənˈteɪʃ(ə)n] *n.* 目标,定位;方向,朝向;(基本的)态度,倾向;(岗前、学前、课前等的)情况介绍,培训;适应,熟悉

cultivate [ˈkʌltɪveɪt] *v.* 开垦,耕作;栽培,培育;陶冶,培养;建立(友谊),结交

sensitivity [ˌsensəˈtɪvəti] *n.* (对细节或质量的)感知,觉察;(对新情况的)灵敏度;敏感,易生气;多愁善感;体贴;小心谨慎;过敏;敏感性;悟性,敏锐性;表现力;机密性

nostalgia [nɒˈstældʒə] *n.* 怀旧,念旧

affection [əˈfekʃn] *n.* 喜爱,关爱;爱恋,爱慕之情;精神状况;疾病;影响

forge [fɔːdʒ] *v.* 形成,缔造;锻造;伪造;稳步前进;假冒　*n.* 锻铁炉;锻造车间

indissoluble [ˌɪndɪˈsɒljəbl] *a.* 不能分解的;不能溶解的;坚固的;牢固持久的

bond [bɒnd] *n.* 纽带,联系;公债,债券;结合,黏合;承诺,契约;枷锁,桎梏　*v.* (使)建立亲密关系;与……粘合、连接

construct [kənˈstrʌkt] *v.* 建造,修建;组成,创立,构思;绘制,作图　*n.* [ˈkɒnstrʌkt] 构想,观念,概念;(短语的)结构成分,结构体;建造物;构筑物;制成物

intimate [ˈɪntɪmət] *a.* 亲密的;密切的; 个人隐私的(常指性方面的);宜于密切关系的;温馨的;便于有性关系的

inexhaustible [ˌɪnɪɡˈzɔːstəb(ə)l] *a.* 用之不竭的;无穷无尽的

waterfront [ˈwɔːtəfrʌnt] *n.* 滨水路;滨水区;码头区

melancholic [ˌmelənˈkɒlɪk] *a.* 忧郁(症)的

noteworthy [ˈnəʊtwɜːði] *a.* 值得注意的;显著的;重要的

vibrancy [ˈvaɪbrənsi] *n.* 振动;活力
soap [səʊp] *n.* 肥皂;(非正式)肥皂剧 *v.* 擦肥皂;(俚)对……拍马屁
bubble [ˈbʌb(ə)l] *n.* 气泡,泡沫;经济泡沫;泡状物;安全的地方或位置 *v.* 冒泡,沸腾;发出冒泡声;忙碌,活跃;兴奋,激动;(情绪、感情等)涌动
sewage [ˈsuːɪdʒ] *n.* 污水,污物
implicitly [ɪmˈplɪsɪtli] *adv.* 含蓄地,暗中地;绝对地
explicitly [ɪkˈsplɪsɪtli] *adv.* 清楚明确地;直截了当地;详述地;坦率地;露骨地

C-E Language Disparity 2—Conception and Terminology 概念与术语

Belonging to two different language families, Chinese and English are different in many respects, such as lexical gap, which may cause much difficulty in C-E or E-C translation. Gaps in translation concern not just the lexical level but also the levels of phrases and sentences. Besides, there are other gaps, including "semantic/meaning gap", and "usage gap". The concept of "lexical gap" can be found in the comparison of different languages, especially when people find no equivalent in the target language. However, when there is a "semantic gap", a synonymous word or phrase, sometimes even a clause, could be employed to convey the intended meaning in the target language, which is a method lying somewhere between literal and liberal translation. The "usage gap" requires translators to have deeper understandings of Chinese characters/words to be translated, which sometimes involve not only their extended meaning and implied meaning but also their cultural implications and pragmatic function, hence high demands on translators.

Different Motivations behind Terminology

When characters or words first come into being, they usually refer to specific or definite objects or phenomena. Over time, people classify objects into one kind or another and use a single word to denote them, showing that the meanings of characters or words are not just entities but also reflect the process of generalization, a step forward in people's perception. Though the process is virtually the same for speakers of different languages, the meanings of characters or words are not only references to things in the objective world, but also the result of the perceptions in communication. Living in different environments with different habits and customs, different nations may have different ways of classifying things. A concept represented by a word in one language may not form a concept/kind in another. Therefore, lexical gaps emerge. Look at the following table and study both Chinese expressions with 手 and their English versions, which would be inducive to decode the motivation behind such terms.

序号	中文	英文	序号	中文	英文
1	手势	(hand) gesture	13	手足之情	brotherly love
2	手语	sign language	14	手巧的	nimble fingered
3	手笔	handwriting	15	手松的	free-handed
4	手杖	walking stick	16	手痒的	itching
5	手段	means	17	手脚不干净	sticky-fingered
6	手法	skill	18	手无寸铁(的)	bare-handed
7	手感	feel	19	眼疾手快(的)	be quick of eye and deft of hand
8	手气	luck	20	心狠手辣(的)	be merciless and vicious
9	手册	handbook	21	手忙脚乱(的)	in a frantic rush; in a great fluster
10	手车	handcart	22	手勤脚快(的)	hard-working
11	手工	handwork	23	心慈手软(的)	be kind and lack the courage to do something
12	手工艺	handicrafts	24	心灵手巧(的)	be clever and deft

Different nations may have different motivations in creating compound words because of seeing different features of things from different perspectives. Therefore, the same object may have different names in different languages. For example, what is called "黑茶" in Chinese is called *dark green tea* in English, because the former refers to the color of the tea while the latter refers to the color of the processed tea leaves.

Owing to different ways of classifying things, certain morphemes in Chinese may have no exact equivalents in English. For instance, in Chinese 大 may mean *big*, *large*, *grand*, *heavy*, *much*, *thorough*, *total*, *strong*, *old*, *general*, *major*, *enormous*, *immense*, *gigantic*, *colossal*, etc. Please study the following Chinese terms, expressions or idioms with 大 and their English versions:

Chinese	English	Chinese	English
大舌头	thick-tongued person; one who lisps	大老粗	an uncouth fellow; an uneducated person; a rough hand
大块头	fat persons	大好友	great friendship
大集体	large/big collectives	大作	masterpiece; your celebrated work/book/article
大清早	early in the morning	大杂烩	hodgepodge; hotchpotch
大团圆	happy reunion	大方向	general orientation
大牲口	draught animal	大手笔	the work or writing of a great author or calligrapher
大姑子	husband's elder sister; sister-in-law	大伙儿	we all; you all; everybody
大陆架	a continental shelf	大练兵	big-scale training
大老爷们	masters of tact and subtlety	大排档	open-air food stall; street food vendor; sidewalk snack booth
大规模	large-scale; big/ massive scale	大路货	popular goods of reliable quality
大环境	political and economic environment	大风大浪	strong wind and big waves; violent storms and waves
大吃一惊	be aghast; be taken aback	大发雷霆	be furious; fly into a rage; scream at sb. angrily
大手大脚	extravagant; wasteful; free-handed; spend extravagantly	大模大样	in an ostentatious manner
万事大吉	Everything is just fine.	大功告成	be accomplished; be crowned with success; be highly successful
大快人心	affording general satisfaction; most satisfying to the people; to the immense satisfaction of the people	大醇小疵	fine on the whole despite a few defects
大刀阔斧	make snap and bold decisions	大材小用	large resources put to small use; one's talent wasted on petty things; not do justice to one's talent
大公无私	selfless; fair-minded; give no thought to self	大大咧咧	careless; casual

(continued)

Chinese	English	Chinese	English
大红大紫	in the limelight	大动干戈	go to war; go into a fight; do sth. in a big way
大男大女	Single men or women above the average age for marriage	大放厥词	talk a lot of nonsense; let loose a torrent of empty rhetoric
大而无当	large but impractical; unwieldy	大喜过望	overjoyed; delighted that things are even better than expected
宽宏大量	magnanimous; large-minded; generous	大谬不然	downright wrong; grossly mistaken
大步流星	with vigorous strides; at a stride	大气磅礴	of great momentum; powerful; grand and magnificent
大风大浪	a lot of social turbulence; vast changes	大显身手	display one's skills to the full; give full play to one's ability
大大落落	natural and poised	大言不惭	unshamedly brag; talk big; braggart
大器晚成	Great vessels take years to produce. /Great minds mature slowly.	大张旗鼓	on a grand scale; with a great fanfare
大同小异	Much the same with only minor differences	大有可为	being worth doing; having good prospects

Different Ways of Classifying Things

All peoples all over the world share more or less similar desires and feelings or emotions, which is the very reason why most people can find equivalents in another language in their mother tongue. Things must be classified as similar kinds of things or things of the same or similar usage. The terms for such groups stand for a much wider range of things than the words for the basic kinds, which are collections of many similar images. Different standards and references may be used to form such groups, so things belonging to one group from one people's perspectives may belong to another from another people's perspectives and result in levels of conceptualization, which is academically termed "hyperonymic lexical gap". In Chinese the expression 帽子 includes the English words *hat*, *cap*, *headgear*, *bonnet*, *helmet*, etc., and its metaphorical usage label. The English word *grain* may refer to 谷物,谷粒;颗粒;纹理;质地;显影颗粒;固体推进剂 in Chinese. 笔,车,and 牛 each stands for a group of things, but to English speakers the things referred to by these Chinese characters do not form types at all. All these are common **lexeme**（词位）**gaps** between Chinese and English. Please study the following table carefully：

G1	Chinese	English	G2	Chinese	English
1	汽车	*automobile*	1	铅笔	*pencil*
2	小汽车	*car*	2	钢笔	*pen/fountain pen*
3	轿车	*sedan*	3	毛笔	*ink brush*；*writing brush*
4	大客车	*bus*	4	蜡笔	（*wax*）*crayon*
5	卡车	*truck*，*lorry*	5	粉笔	*chalk*
6	翻斗卡车	*tipper*	6	画笔	*paintbrush*
7	面包车	*van/minibus*	7	鸭嘴笔、绘画笔	*drawing pen/ruling pen*
8	出租车	*taxi*	8	圆珠笔	*ball-point pen*
9	车	词位空缺	9	笔	词位空缺

Look at G2 carefully. It is very difficult for Chinese people to translate such a sentence as“楼下有大约 20 辆车”or“我笔盒里有 10 支笔”into English just because there is not one single word in English corresponding to the Chinese word 车 or 笔.

Group 3，4，5 and 6 show different kinds of *hair*，*dog*，*meat* and *doctor* respectively. Please try your best to keep them in mind.

G3	Chinese	English	G4	Chinese	English
1	毛发	*hair*	1	狗	*dog*
2	胡子	*facial hair*	2	猎犬	*hound*
3	大胡子	*beaver*	3	西班牙猎犬	*spaniel*
4	嘴唇上的胡子	*mustache*	4	赛特种猎犬	*setter*
5	络腮胡子	*whiskers*	5	训练后能找回猎物的猎犬	*retriever*
6	下巴上的胡子	*beard*	6	一种活泼的小狗	*terrier*
7	山羊胡子	*goatee*	7	小狗	*puppy*
8	汗毛	*fine hair growing in every pore*	8	老虎犬	*bulldog*

G5	Chinese	English	G6	Chinese	English
1	肉	*meat*	1	医生/大夫	*doctor*
2	猪肉	*pork*	2	内科医生	*physician*
3	鸡肉	*chicken*	3	外科医生	*surgeon*
4	羊肉	*mutton*	4	儿科医生	*pediatrician*
5	羔羊肉	*lamb*	5	妇科医生	*gynecologist*
6	牛肉	*beef*	6	牙科医生	*dentist*
7	鹿肉	*venison*	7	皮肤科医生	*dermatologist*
8	鱼肉	*fish*	8	眼科医生	*oculist/ophthalmologist*
9	果肉	*flesh*	9	骨科医生	*orthopedist*
10	肌肉	*muscle*	10	执业医生	*practitioner*

Group 7, 8, 9 and 10 are more examples of this kind. The Chinese word 树枝 has its corresponding word *branch* in English, but more English words may refer to the same thing 树枝, though different in size: *branch*, *bough*, *spray*, *twig* and *sprig*. There are three words for the Chinese word 雾: *fog*, *mist* and *haze*. The Chinese word 草 covers the scope of several words in English: *grass*; *hay*; *straw*; *weed*; *herb*, *thatch and aquatic or water plants*, etc.; 书 includes *book*, *certificate*, *report*, *agreement*, etc.

G7	Chinese	English	G8	Chinese	English
1	树枝	*branch*	1	很浓的雾	*fog*
2	大树枝	*bough*	2	浓度中等的雾	*mist*
3	小树枝	*spray*, *twig*; *sprig*	3	浓度小的雾	*haze*

G9	Chinese	English	G10	Chinese	English
1	草	*grass*, *straw*	1	书	*book*
2	青草	*grass*	2	国书	*a letter of credence*, *credentials*
3	干草	*hay*	3	家书	*a letter from home*
4	稻草	*straw*	4	证书	*a certificate*

(continued)

G9	Chinese	English	G10	Chinese	English
5	野草	*weed*	5	申请书	*a letter of application*
6	药草	*herb*	6	报告书	*a report*
7	茅草、杂草	*thatch*	7	协议书	*an agreement*
8	水草	*aquatic/water plants*	8	白皮书	*the white book*
9	草鸡	*hen*	9	畅销书	*the best seller*
10	草屋	*thatched hut*	10	委托书	*a letter of appointment*
11	草稿	(*rough*) *draft*	11	百科全书	*an encyclopedia*
12	草场	*grazing ground*; *grassland*	12	使用说明书	*directions*
13	草包	*straw bag*	13	成绩通知书	*a grade report*
14	草民	*common people*	14	成交确认书	*sales confirmation*

As Chinese and English belong to different cultures and have undergone different historical developments, the number of words in a specific semantic field is often different.

Differences among Synonyms or Synonymous Expresssions

English is abundant in synonyms or synonymous expressions to express and describe subtle or delicate differences and variations in meanings in terms of degree, level, tone, register, or style, and commendation or derogation because of its wealth of sources, including Greek, Roman, Latin, French, German, even Chinese, etc. The Chinese language has undergone thousands of years of development, and thus ancient words and modern words coexist. Vast areas of China have produced various dialects all based on the same writing system, many of which have been accepted by the standard Putonghua. The English language has enormous etymologies and introduced enormous numbers of words into its own vocabulary from almost every language of the world.

Large numbers of synonyms or synonymous expressions also cause many translation difficulties. Translators are required to exercise discretion in understanding nuances or subtle or delicate differences among synonyms, or words with the same or similar meanings in the wording of the source text to find most proper equivalents in the target language. Should they fail to find any at all, translators have to take appropriate adjustments to translate specific meanings of the original, always keeping it in mind that context is the only criterion in judging the quality of all translations. Please look at G11 and G12 with 笑 and 走 as the cover words:

G11	Chinese	English	G12	Chinese	English
1	高兴地笑	*laugh*	1	走	*go*
2	微笑	*smile*	2	散步;走过	*walk*
3	露齿而笑	*grin*	3	从容漫步	*amble*
4	得意地笑	*smirk*	4	大踏步走过	*stride*
5	轻声地暗笑	*chuckle*	5	步履艰难地走	*trudge*
6	咯咯出声笑	*chuckle*	6	用脚尖走	*tiptoe*
7	哈哈大笑	*chortle*	7	蹒跚地走	*stagger*
8	(捧腹)大笑	*guffaw*	8	重步行走	*plod*
9	暗笑;忍笑(通常有不敬之意)	*snigger*; *snicker*	9	踱步	*pace*
10	冷笑	*sneer*	10	游荡	*loiter*
11	开怀大笑;眉开眼笑	*beam*	11	昂首阔步走	*strut*
12	开玩笑	*joke*	12	漫步	*ramble*
13	说俏皮话;说妙语	*quip*	13	潜行	*lurk*
14	(因紧张)窃笑;傻笑	*titter*	14	爬行	*creep*, *crawl*
15	假笑;痴笑,傻笑	*simper*	15	绊倒	*stumble*
16	哄笑;大笑	*roar*	16	攀爬	*scramble*
17	讥笑	*deride*	17	摇摆不定	*lurch*
18	嘲笑	*taunt*	18	一瘸一拐地走	*limp*
19	纵声大笑	*horselaugh*	19	迈进	*march*
20	讥笑并辱骂	*deride and upbraid*	20	快步走	*rush*
21	笑逐颜开	*beam with smiles*	21	跑步	*run*

As carriers of culture, all languages have peculiar cultural characteristics, which is another important cause of semantic gap between Chinese and English. Lexical gaps are therefore representative of cultural gaps. Culturally unique things require special words for reference and such words are "culturally unique words", e. g. 阴阳,红包,匾 in Chinese, for which there are no equivalents in English. In translating, descriptive or explanatory phrases or notes are more frequently required. Chinese 文房四宝 can be translated as "the four treasures of the study, including writing brush, inkstick, inkstone and paper"; 大锅饭 as "getting an equal share regardless of the work done"; 儒学 as "Confuciannism"; 八卦 as "trigram"; 阴 as "the soft inactive female principle or force in the world in Chinese thought"; 阳 as "the strong active male principle or force in the world in Chinese thought"; 单职工家庭 as "one-earner family" or "a single-income family"; 合乎国情,顺乎民意 as "to conform with the national conditions and the will of the people".

Semantic Gap

Corresponding words in any two languages do not have exactly the same meaning. The so-called equivalents in different languages correspond only within certain scopes of meaning. As far as translation is concerned, such semantic gaps cause more problems than lexical gaps, especially for translation beginners. The result would be dead translation or mistranslation.

Semantic gap first manifests itself in the lack of certain referential meanings (also known as denotative or designative meaning) of corresponding words between source and target languages. Such corresponding words may have different ranges or scopes of reference. Take the Chinese word 天 for example and its English equivalent *sky* have very different reference ranges. 天 also contains meanings in the words *weather*, *heaven*, *god*, etc.

Traditional Chinese philosophy emphasizes 天人合一. "Heaven and man combine into one." is an obvious mistranslation, which should be translated as "the harmony between man and nature". 改天换地 can be properly translated as "transform nature", 人定胜天 as "Man can conquer nature" and 天伦之乐 can be translated as "the happiness of family reunion" or "family happiness".

Different Extended Meanings

The meanings of a word extend and develop through usage and over time, thus acquiring extended meanings, such as shifted or metaphorical meanings (also known as associated meanings, implied meanings, or connotative meanings). Different languages have different ways and directions of such extensions. As a result, even corresponding words in Chinese and English with the same or similar denotative meanings may often be endowed with different extended meanings. For example, in Chinese 狗 usually contains very derogatory associated meanings while the associated meanings of the word *dog* in English are basically either neutral or commendatory. 你是走狗（"You are a running dog."）or "Every dog has his day."（凡人皆有得意日。）are cases in point.

Different Directions of Meanings

A good sense of direction is an important issue in people's lives. There are many words and terms in every language denoting directions. Some entail single directions, such as 上/下 *up/down*, but not 高/低 *tall/short* or 长/短 *long/short* as they only refer to height without directional reference. Some others such as 在……之前/之后 *after/before*, 左/右 *left/right*, 进/出 *in/out*, 南/北 *south/north*, 过去/将来 *past/future*, 来/往 *come/go*, often go along with adverbials such as 来这里/去那里 *come here/go there*, 进来/出去 *come in/go out*, 进/退 *advance/retreat*, 离开/到达 *leave/reach*, 接近/避开 *approach/shun*, *give/receive* 给予/接受, 带来/取走 *bring/take*. Chinese characters 带 and 取 do not distinguish direction, as we can say 带来,带去; 取走,取来 and that is why many people often confuse *bring* and *take*. 攻/守 *attack/defend*, 涨/缩 *expand/contract*, 吸/呼 *inhale/exhale*, 吃/吐 *eat/vomit*, 吸引/排斥 *attract/repel* at the beginning of learning English. Translators are consequently required to have a good sense of direction in terms of words.

But it has to be pointed out that not every pair of antonyms have directional meanings or implications, such as 好/坏 *good/bad*, 爱/恨 *love/hate*, 加/减 *add/subtract*, 拒绝/接受 *refuse/accept*, 记得/忘记 *remember/forget*, 相信/不信 *believe/disbelieve*, etc.

Most corresponding words between Chinese and English denote the same directions, but they sometimes do signify different directions, which deserves special attention as it sometimes also leads to translation difficulties. "Direction" here refers not only to space (such as *upper/lower*, *up/down*, *front/back*, *in/out*), time (such as 前/后 *before/after*, 早/晚 *early/late*), but also to logical and emotional directions (such as 对/错 *right/wrong*, 主动/被动 *active/passive*, 同义词/反义词 *synonym/antonym*, and other opposed viewpoints or aspects of looking at things). As English has a comparatively higher degree of abstraction, many English words, especially verbs, denote either direction, while their corresponding words in Chinese are mono-directional, such as *breathe*, *commute*, *marry*, *rent*, etc. Of course, every rule has its exception, and there are cases where the opposite is true. For example, 怀疑 is equivalent to a pair of antonyms in English: *doubt* (怀疑极有可能是假的) and *suspect* (怀疑极有可能是真的). The meaning of 带 is expressed by either *bring* or *take*. Chinese distinguishes 买进 *buy* from 卖出 *sell*, but does not distinguish 借进 *borrow* from 借出 *lend*. Systematic studies on the directional meanings of words are recommended to further people's understanding of antonyms.

Usage Gaps—Transitivity

Transitivity refers to the characteristic that certain verbs have of exerting action onto a direct object. According to systemic grammar, there are mainly three process types of transitivity: 1) material process; 2) mental process; and 3) relational process. This distinction applies to most languages. But some so-called lexical equivalents in Chinese and English differ in their usage in the transitivity of verbs and thus their specific sentence patterns. For instance, *salute* is a transitive verb, but 致敬 is intransitive; "*salute* somebody" translated into Chinese should be 向某人致敬. The intransitive verb *object* is an opposite case, as 反对某事 should be "*object* to something" in English.

Differences Caused by Word Formation

Affixation is one of the most important ways of forming new words in English. Affixes like *-en*, *en-/em-*, *-ize*, etc., can easily turn nouns, adjectives, etc., into verbs to express a concept in terms of motion or action. Because there is no such affixation in Chinese, very often grammatical means should be used to express such motions and actions, for example, *embitter* 使变苦, *lighten* 使变轻, *globalize* 使全球化, *clarify* 澄清, etc. Their meanings have to be expressed in Chinese by causative structures. Another example is that many adverbs formed by suffix *-ly* such as *admittedly*, (*un*)*fortunately*, (*un*)*luckily*, are used to modify the whole sentence instead of modifying a verb, etc., thus called disjunctive adverbs or sentence modifiers, whose meanings can hardly be expressed by single words in Chinese.

Differences Caused by Flexible Usage—Conversion

Chinese has a lower degree of **lexicalization**, but in English using nouns or adjectives as verbs is a common phenomenon and an important trend. Look at the following examples:

1. 他*读的是*生活这所大学。He was *schooled* by life itself.（school 从名词转为动词）

2. 看到自己喜欢的食品，她*舔了舔*自己的双唇。She *wetted* her lips at the sight of her favorite food.（wet 从形容词转为动词）

3. 他们*开派对*玩到深夜。They *partied* till the late night.（party 从名词转为动词）

4. 由于*定价*不合适，苏珊被挤出市场。Susan has *priced* herself out of the market.（price 从名词转为动词）

5. 最后，他从怒气冲冲*转变成*毅然决然。His anger finally *blossomed* into determination.（blossom 从名词转为动词）

6. 看到又红又大的苹果时，他竟然*流口水*了。His mouth *watered* at the big red apples.（water 从名词转为动词）

From the English translation provided we can see **syntacticalization** is adopted to express the notions expressed in English by single words, because Chinese has no usage like this.

Another similar phenomenon in English is the **nominalization**, turning adjectives, link verbs, etc. directly into nouns. This includes turning adjectives with the use of articles:

1. 他是这家高尔夫俱乐部的*常客*。He is a *regular* of this Golf Club.

2. *不到*长城非好汉。The Great Wall is a *must* for any tourist to China.

3. 他们正努力*缩小*贫富差距. They are trying to *narrow* the gap between

the rich and *the poor*.

The process of **coding** in Chinese is based on images by using simplified pictures, but in English the basis is sound, which is often arbitrary. **Generalization** is based on people's perception of things of the same kind. **Categorization** is the process of grouping things with family resemblance and giving them a common name. In this respect, Chinese seems to form more systematic series of different strata, and words referring to objects of the same group often have similar elements, such as the various 杯 mentioned above. English seems to be more developed in regard to the process of **abstraction** and thus has many more abstract nouns, as a result of more developed traditional logical or analytical thinking. The last stage of **concretization** seems to be something unique in English, as Chinese does not have this process.

Please appreciate the following translation：

女性是贾宝玉的精神信仰，也是《红楼梦》倾心赞美的对象。为什么曹雪芹要通过贾宝玉的这句话对水德极力赞美呢？其实，水，在中华文化当中具有重要的地位。水是生命之源，“上善若水，水善利万物而不争”。杜甫赞美春雨“润物细无声”，秦观说“柔情似水，佳期如梦”，《诗经》里有名句“所谓伊人，在水一方”。水具有滋润万物的力量。而且，水是灵动的，具有无穷的生命力。正如张若虚写下的“春江潮水连海平，海上明月共潮生”。《红楼梦》里的女性，真的具有中华文化赋予水的美好特质。

Girls are not only Jia Baoyu's spiritual belief, but also what the author of *A Dream of Red Mansions* has highly praised. Why does Cao Xueqin want to highly praise the water's virtues through Jia Baoyu's words? In fact, water plays an important role in Chinese culture. Water is the source of life. "The supreme virtue is like water; it benefits all things without contention." Du Fu praised the spring rain for its nourishing things silently; Qin Guan said, "Tender feelings are as gentle as water; happy days are as beautiful as a dream." In *The Book of Songs* there is a famous line which reads "The fair lady I think resides on the other side of the water." Water has the power to nourish all things. Moreover, water is agile and has infinite vitality. As Zhang Ruoxu wrote, "The tide of the spring river is even with the sea; the moon over the sea rises with the tide." (In spring the river rises as high as the sea, /And with the river's rise the moon up rises bright.) The girls in *A Dream of Red Mansions* really have the beautiful characteristics given to water by Chinese culture.

《红楼梦》里不仅是在贾宝玉赞美女性的时候赞美水,《红楼梦》写水,可以说是写得出神入化。林黛玉的前世是西方灵河岸边的绛珠仙草,是神瑛侍者的甘露让它可以久延岁月。绛珠仙子为了报恩,愿意把一生的泪水都还给贾宝玉。大观园里有沁芳溪,这条河具有"绕堤柳借三篙翠,隔岸花分一脉香"的美。大观园里的水是纯净的,代表着青春的美好。贾宝玉和林黛玉共读《会真记》也是在沁芳溪畔。连警幻仙姑都会吟咏"飞花逐水流"。可以说,在《红楼梦》里,水具有美好的特质。

In *A Dream of Red Mansions*, Jia Baoyu not only praises water when praising girls, but the description of water in *A Dream of Red Mansions* can be said to have reached the acme. Lin Daiyu's previous life is the Crimson Pearl Herb on the bank of the Western River of Souls. It is the nectar of the Deity Shenying waiter that makes it last for years. In order to repay her kindness, Fairy Crimson Pearl is willing to return all her tears to Jia Baoyu. In the Grand View Garden there is a river named The River of Seeping Fragrance, with the beauty of "Willows on the dyke lend their verdancy to three punts;/Flowers on the further shore spare a breath of fragrance." The water in the Grand View Garden is pure, representing the beauty of youth. It is just nearby Seeping Fragrance Lock Bridge under the peach blossom that Jia Baoyu and Lin Daiyu read *The Western Chamber*. Even the Goddess of Enchantment will chant "flying flowers chase water". It can be said that in *A Dream of Red Mansions*, water has been endowed with beautiful characteristics.

C-E Translation Strategies and Skills 2—Literal Translation and Free Translation 直译与意译

Literal Translation, or direct translation, is the rendering of text from one language to another, word-for-word, rather than conveying the whole sense of the original. It is the way to maintain the content and the form of the source language in accordance with the culture, emphasizing similarity in form and the uniformity between source text and target text in terms of lexis, syntax and style. It doesn't mean completely word-for-word translation. Superficially speaking, it means not to alter the original words and sentences. Strictly speaking, it strives to keep the sentiments and style of the original. It takes sentences as its basic units and the whole text into consideration at the same time in translating, strives to reproduce both the ideological content and the style of the original works, and retains as much as possible the figures of speech.

Free Translation is a supplementary means to convey the meaning and spirit of source text without trying to reproduce its sentence patterns or figures of speech. It doesn't emphasize the original form, including words, syntax, structure, metaphor and other rhetorics. It requires the correct expression of original content but doesn't stick to the original form; it changes the original work's figures of speech, sentence structures or patterns, but retains the original meaning. It stresses the target language's smoothness and the communicative effect of the translated version. This approach is most frequently adopted when it is really impossible for translators to translate the original meaning merely literally.

Please study and appreciate the following typical examples:

Source Language	Literal Translation	Free Translation
丢脸	lose face	be disgraced; bring shame on oneself
铁饭碗	the iron rice-bowl	a secure job; a lifelong job
城门失火,殃及池鱼。	A fire on the city walls brings disaster to the fish in the moat.	Make the innocent bystanders get into trouble in a disturbance
初生牛犊不怕虎。	Newborn calves make little of tigers. / Newborn calves are not afraid of tigers.	Young people are fearless.
他很会写文章。	He writes very well.	He is a very good writer.
儿童不宜。	Not decent enough for children.	Adults only.
你不要班门弄斧了。	Don't show your axe before Lu Ban's door. /Don't display your axe at Lu Ban's door.	Remain modest before an authority. / Don't teach a fish how to swim. / Don't teach a spider how to spin. / Don't teach your grandmother how to suck eggs.
他当上了海员。	He became a sailor.	He followed the sea.
巧妇难为无米之炊。	Even the cleverest housewife cannot cook a meal without rice.	One cannot make bricks without straw.

(continued)

Source Language	Literal Translation	Free Translation
打开窗户说亮话。	to open the window and say bright words	to put all cards on the table (摊牌)
她怕碰一鼻子灰,话到了嘴边,又把它吞了下去。		She was afraid of being snubbed. So she swallowed the words that came to her tips.
她一个单身人,无亲无故。	She is single, with no parent or relative.	This girl was all by herself and far from home, without a single relative or friend to help her.
生命诚可贵,爱情价更高,若为自由故,二者皆可抛。		Life is precious and love is even more valuable, yet for the sake of freedom both can be sacrificed.
处理人民内部的矛盾必须坚持和风细雨的方法,坚持"团结—批评—团结"的方法。	It is essential to persist in using methods as mild as a drizzle and asgentle as a breeze, and adhere to the formula of "unity-criticism-unity" in dealing with contradictions among the people.	

The difference and connection between "domestication and foreignization" and "literal translation and free translation".

Historically, foreignization and domestication can be regarded as the conceptual extension of literal translation and free translation, but they are not completely equivalent to **literal translation** and **free translation**. The core issue of literal translation and free translation is how to deal with form and meaning at the linguistic level, while **foreignization** and **domestication** break through the limitations of language factors and extend their horizons to language, culture and aesthetics. Domestication brings the original author into the culture of the target language, while foreignization brings the reader into a foreign situation by accepting the linguistic and cultural differences of the foreign text. It can be seen that literal translation and free translation are mainly value orientations limited to the language level, while foreignization and domestication are value orientations based on the cultural context. The differences between them are obvious and should not be confused.

C-E Guided Translation Practice 2

山水诗鼻祖是东晋的谢灵运。谢灵运所开创的山水诗,把自然界的美景引进诗中,使山水诗成为独立的审美对象。他的创作,不仅把诗歌从"淡乎寡味"的玄理中解放了出来,而且加强了诗歌的艺术技巧和表现力,并影响了一代诗风。山水诗的出现,不仅使山水成为独立的审美对象,为中国诗歌增加了一种题材,而且开启了南朝一代新的诗歌风貌。继陶渊明的田园诗之后,山水诗标志着人与自然进一步的沟通与和谐,标志着一种新的自然审美观念和审美趣味的产生。东晋出现大量的山水诗,主要是纷乱的国情使然。

第三单元　水与艺术

Unit 3　Water and the Arts

水是艺术之魂。

Water is the soul of the arts.

水文化，乃是有关人水关系的文化，其产生、形成和发展有其深刻的历史渊源、自然因素、社会环境、文化元素乃至水利行业背景，源于人类与水相处过程中对人水关系认识的总结和升华。中国水文化，是一种客观存在的，历史十分悠久，又具勃勃生机的文化形态。"仁者乐山，智者乐水"，自古以来，"水"就被赋予了丰富的文化内涵，从人的性情到对世界的认知，皆可以水为载体来阐释。水文化艺术是水文化发展的重要表现形式，是精神文明建设的重要内容。

Water culture is a culture related to the relationship between human and water. Its generation, formation and development have profound historical origins, depending on natural factors, social environment, cultural elements and even the background of the water conservancy industry. It originates from the summary and sublimation of the cognition of the relationship between human and water in the process of getting along with water. Chinese water culture is an objective cultural form with a long history and vitality. "The virtuous find pleasure in hills; the wise find pleasure in water (translated by Paul White)." Since ancient times, water has been endowed with rich cultural connotations. From human temperament to cognition of the world, water can be used as a carrier to interpret the world. Water culture and art is an important manifestation of the development of water culture and an important content of spiritual civilization construction.

艺术作为人类精神灵魂的家园，取法自然、依托自然，从自然中汲取灵感。水在大自然中无处不在，它激发了艺术家的壮志，抚慰了艺术家的心灵，净化了艺术家的情感，而艺术家则赋予它以不同的情感和不朽的灵魂。本单元将从音乐和绘画两个方面来阐释水与艺术之间的点滴关系。

Art, as the home of human spiritual soul, follows nature, relies on nature and draws on inspiration from nature. Water is ubiquitous in nature. It stimulates the artists' aspirations, soothes their soul, and purifies their emotions. The artists give it different emotions and an immortal soul. This chapter will explain the relationship between water and the arts from two aspects, music and painting.

第一节　水与音乐
Section A　Water and Music

水文化是人在与水打交道的过程中形成的，这种文化深深地根植于民族文化和人类文化之中，是一种客观存在的文化形态。

Water culture is formed in the process of humans dealing with water. This kind of culture is deeply rooted in national culture and human culture, and it is an objective cultural form.

音乐追随文化而发展，文化通过音乐而弘扬。音乐形象生动地体现了文化特色，使文化广泛流传，并随时代变迁永远流传下去，使文化更加充分地发展与弘扬。

Music evolves with culture, and culture is promoted through music. Music vividly embodies the cultural characteristics, making culture widely spread, and at the same time, it will be passed on forever over time so that the culture can be developed and promoted more fully.

音乐作为中国水文化的重要组成部分，体现了中国人民对水的情感、意志、力量、幻想和追求。“凡音之起，由人心生也。人心之动，物使之然也。感于物而动，故形于声。”中国传统的世界观，即“天人合一”“天人感应”，崇仰创造万物的大自然，又重视人的内心体验，而音乐的产生正是源于人心对大自然的感悟。不同的水形态、水精神有着不同的特色，不同的特色体现了不同的水文化，不同的水文化产生了风格不同的音乐。中国丰富多彩的音乐折射出水文化的方方面面，同时它又以其独特的功能作用于中国水文化之中。

As an important part of Chinese water culture, music embodies Chinese people's emotion, will, strength, fantasy and pursuit of water. "All the modulations of the voice arise from the mind, and the various affections of the mind are produced by things (external to it). The affections thus produced are manifested in the sounds that are uttered" (translated by James Legge). The traditional Chinese worldviews, namely harmony between humanity and nature and interaction between heaven and man, admire the nature that creates all things and attach importance to the inner experience of human beings. The production of music is derived from humans' perception of nature. Different water forms and water spirits have different characteristics. Different characteristics reflect different water cultures, and different water cultures produce different styles of music. China's colorful music reflects all aspects of Chinese water culture, and at the same time it plays an important role in Chinese water culture with its unique function.

水与音乐的关系主要体现在以下几个方面：

The relationship between water and music is mainly reflected in the following aspects:

1. 音乐可以表现水的特性

1. Music can express the characteristics of water

水乃万物之源。《管子·水地》篇中有："水者，何也？万物之本源也，诸生之宗室也。"音乐在表现水作为万物之源时，诞生了"小时候，妈妈对我讲，大海，就是我故乡……""遥远的东方有一条江，它的名字就叫长江。遥远的东方有一条河，它的名字就叫黄河……"以及"洪湖水呀，浪呀嘛浪打浪啊，洪湖岸边是呀嘛是家乡啊"这些熟悉的歌词。这些歌曲通俗易懂，格调高雅，优美动听，感情真挚，通过这些歌词可以很直观地感受到人们对水的亲切，对水的依恋，以及对水作为万物之源的喜爱。

Water is the source of all things. In *Guanzi*: *Chapter of Water and Land*, there is a question: "What is the water? The origin of things and the ancestral clan of all living things." When music expresses water as the source of all things, a series of familiar lyrics were born, such as "When I was young, my mother told me that the sea is my hometown..." "There is a river in the far east, and its name is the Yangtze River. There is a river in the far east, and its name is the Yellow River..." and "The waves of Honghu Lake are rolling, and the shores of Honghu Lake are my hometown." These songs are easy in content, elegant in style, beautiful in sound and sincere in emotion. Through these lyrics, we can intuitively feel people's kindness to water, attachment to water, and love for water as the source of all things.

水也有汹涌澎湃的一面。在抗战时期，音乐家冼星海回国后痛感国家苦难深重，深知民众的苦痛。在民族危亡的紧急关头，他站在民族斗争的前列，为抗战发出怒吼，执笔谱写歌曲。《保卫黄河》就是其代表作，他通过描述黄河之水奔腾的一面来表达中华民族在困境中怒吼的力量。音乐在表现水的奔腾咆哮时，体现了中国人民不屈不挠，永远压不垮、打不倒的精神。

Water can be turbulent. During the War of Resistance Against Japan, the musician Xian Xinghai returned to China and felt the nation's overwhelming peril and the suffering of the people. At the critical moment of national peril, he stood at the forefront of the national struggle, roaring and composing songs. *Defending the Yellow River* is his representative work. He expresses the power of the Chinese nation in a difficult situation by describing the surging and roaring side of the Yellow River. When music expresses the surge and roar of the water, it has also become a symbol of the Chinese people's invincibility.

2. 水可以作为音乐的灵感

2. Water can inspire music

水为音乐提供了灵感。很多音乐创作取材于自然,来源于水。人类自诞生以来,每个时期都会产生许多脍炙人口、影响深远的以"水"为代表的歌曲。在诸多音乐艺术作品中,水是一个重要的意象母题。所谓母题,就是在音乐行为中经常出现的主题或题材。例如,没有太湖就没有《太湖美》,没有黄河就没有冼星海的《黄河大合唱》;国外也是如此。有人说,历史是歌的书写,歌是历史的凝结。

Water provides inspiration for music composition. Many pieces of music come from nature and water. Since the early times of human history, many popular and influential songs represented by "water" have been produced in every period. In many musical works, water is an important image motif. The so-called motif is a theme or subject that often appears in musical behavior. For example, without the Taihu Lake, there would be no song of *The Beautiful Taihu Lake*, and without the Yellow River, there would be no *Yellow River Cantata* by Xian Xinghai; the same is true abroad. Some people say that history is the writing of songs, and songs are the condensation of history.

水不仅能作为音乐的主题,还能充当音乐元素。"水乐",即是著名音乐家谭盾先生将水元素用作音色,以直接或间接(制作的水的响器)的水声,通过创造性的发展,形成"光(色)谱模型"的演绎,构成一系列五光十色的、似有形又无形的水之神奇交响。其中,《永恒的水》诠释了最自然的天籁之声,乐声透着一种空灵和悠远。

Water can be used not only as the theme of music, but also as a musical element. Water Music refers to the famous musician Mr. Tan Dun's use of water element as timbre to form the deduction of light (color) spectrum model through creative development with direct or indirect water sound (produced by water loudspeakers), forming a series of colorful, tangible and intangible magical symphonies of water. Among them, *Eternal Water* interprets the most natural sound, and the music reveals a sense of ethereality and distance.

3. 人水相处过程中诞生了不少音乐佳作

3. Many music masterpieces were born in the process of humans getting along with water

纵观古今,人与水的相处过程不乏考验与灾难。古有"黄河夺淮",泗州城惨遭灭顶之灾,淮剧《水漫泗州》即取材于此;今有水利工作者献身水利工作,将重大水利事迹、重要水利传记和水利精神谱写成歌,弘扬水利人勇于探索、开拓创新、不辞辛劳、团结协作的新风正气,如淮安市的《淮安水利之歌》、无锡市的《无锡水韵》和盐城市的《守潮人之歌》。它们唱出了水利人的理想和追求,更激励着后来者不忘责任、坚守情操,不断追求卓越。

Throughout the ages, there is no lack of trials and tribulations in the process of humans getting along with water. In ancient times, there was the disaster of "the Yellow River capturing the Huai River", and Sizhou City was destroyed. The Huai drama *The Flooding of Sizhou* was based on this. Today, water conservancy workers have dedicated themselves to water conservancy work, and they compose songs of important water conservancy deeds, biographies and spirits to promote the new style of workers who are brave, innovative, painstaking, and cooperative, such as the *Song of Huai'an Water Conservancy* of Huai'an City, *Wuxi Water Rhyme* of Wuxi City, and *Song of Tide Watchers* of Yancheng City. They sing out the ideals and pursuits of water conservancy workers, and inspire the latecomers to register their responsibilities in their minds, stick to their sentiments, and constantly strive for excellence.

New Words, Phrases and Expressions

generation [ˌdʒenəˈreɪʃ(ə)n] *n.* 一代(人);一代人的时间;(产品发展的)代;产生

formation [fɔːˈmeɪʃ(ə)n] *n.* 组成物;构成;形成,产生;编队,队形;(社会、政治等的)形态

originate [əˈrɪdʒɪneɪt] *v.* 起源,产生;创始,开创

summary [ˈsʌməri] *n.* 总结,概要 *a.* 总结性的,概括的;(司法程序)即决的,简易的

cognition [kɒgˈnɪʃ(ə)n] *n.* 认识,认知;认识(或认知)的结果

benevolent [bəˈnevələnt] *a.* 仁慈的,乐善好施的;(用于慈善机构名称)慈善的,救济的

temperament [ˈtemprəmənt] *n.* 气质，性格；（性情）暴躁，喜怒无常；调（音）律（在平均律中，8 度音阶包含有 12 个均等的半音程）

manifestation [ˌmænɪfeˈsteɪʃ(ə)n] *n.* 表现，显现；表现形式；（鬼魂或神灵）出现，显灵；示威运动

ubiquitous [juːˈbɪkwɪtəs] *a.* 普遍存在的，无所不在的

stimulate [ˈstɪmjuleɪt] *v.* 促进，激发（某事物）；激发，鼓励；使（身体、生物系统）兴奋，刺激；起刺激作用

aspiration [ˌæspəˈreɪʃ(ə)n] *n.* 渴望，抱负，志向；送气音；吸引术，抽吸

soothe [suːð] *v.* 使平静，安抚；减轻，缓和（疼痛）

purify [ˈpjʊərɪfaɪ] *v.* 使（某物）洁净，净化；变纯净；洗涤（思想），净化（心灵）；提纯，精炼

immortal [ɪˈmɔːt(ə)l] *a.* 不死的，永存的；不朽的，流芳百世的，永垂千古的　*n.* 神，永生不灭者；永垂不朽的人物

vividly [ˈvɪvɪdli] *adv.* 生动地；强烈地；历历在目地；栩栩如生地

embody [ɪmˈbɒdi] *v.* 具体表现，体现；收录，包括

fantasy [ˈfæntəsi] *n.* 幻想，想象；想象产物，幻想作品；虚拟比赛（游戏）；幻想曲，集成曲；期望

ancestral [ænˈsestrəl] *a.* 祖先的；祖传的

clan [klæn] *n.* 宗族，氏族；（非正式）大家庭，大家族；（非正式）集团，帮派

intuitively [ɪnˈtjuːɪtɪvli] *adv.* 凭直觉地

attachment [əˈtætʃmənt] *n.* 附加设备，附属物；（邮件）附件；文件附件；喜欢，依恋；（临时的）隶属，委派；信念，拥护；连接，连接物；扣押

turbulent [ˈtɜːbjələnt] *a.* 骚乱的，动乱的；（气流）湍流的，（水）湍急的；骚动的，混乱而难以控制的；（技）（与）紊流（有关）的，（与）湍流（有关）的

resistance [rɪˈzɪstəns] *n.* 反对，抵制；抵抗，反抗；抵抗力，免疫力；阻力；电阻；（敌占区的）秘密抵抗组织

overwhelming [ˌəʊvəˈwelmɪŋ] *a.* 难以抗拒的，令人不知所措的；巨大的，压倒性的

peril [ˈperəl] *n.* 巨大的危险，危难；（某活动或行为的）危险，问题

critical [ˈkrɪtɪk(ə)] *a.* 批判的，爱挑剔的；极其重要的，关键的；严重的，危急的；病重的，重伤的；评论性的，评论家的；临界的

roar [rɔː(r)] *v.* 吼叫，咆哮；（人群）用欢呼声激励，为……喝彩，为……加油；哄笑，大笑；（尤指车辆）轰鸣着疾驶，呼啸而过；果断行事，迅速发生；熊熊燃烧　*n.* 吼叫声，咆哮声；（风或海的）呼啸声，（机器的）隆隆声；（狮等的）吼叫声；爆笑声

invincibility [ɪnˌvɪnsəˈbɪləti] *n.* 无敌；不可战胜

composition [ˌkɒmpəˈzɪʃ(ə)n] *n.* 成分构成，成分；（音乐、艺术、诗歌的）作品；创作，

作曲;构图;作文

influential [ˌɪnfluˈenʃ(ə)] *a.* 有影响力的,有势力的 *n.* 有影响力的人

motif [məʊˈtiːf] *n.* 主题;主旨;图形;意念;基序,模体

cantata [kænˈtɑːtə] *n.* 大合唱;(意)清唱剧;康塔塔(一种声乐套曲)

condensation [ˌkɒndenˈseɪʃ(ə)n] *n.* 冷凝,凝结;凝结的水珠;(书等的)简缩;凝聚反应,缩合反应;精神凝缩(作用)

timbre [ˈtæmbə(r)] *n.* [声] 音色;音质;音品

deduction [dɪˈdʌkʃn] *n.* 演绎,推论;扣除,扣除额

spectrum [ˈspektrəm] *n.* 范围,幅度;光谱;波谱,频谱;余象

loudspeaker [ˌlaʊdˈspiːkə(r)] *n.* 扩音器,喇叭;(收音机或乐器的)扬声器,喇叭

tangible [ˈtændʒəb(ə)l] *a.* 明确的,真实的;可触摸的,可感知的 *n.* 可触知的东西

intangible [ɪnˈtændʒəb(ə)l] *a.* 不可捉摸的,难以确定的;(资产、利益)无形的 *n.* 无形的东西

symphony [ˈsɪmfəni] *n.* 交响乐;(美)交响乐团(symphony orchestra 的简称);和谐的东西;(史)大型声乐作品中的过门

eternal [ɪˈtɜːn(ə)l] *a.* 永恒的,永存的;似乎无休无止的,没完没了的

masterpiece [ˈmɑːstəpiːs] *n.* 代表作,杰作;极好的例证;手艺人为取得大师资格并进入行会而制作的作品

trial [ˈtraɪəl] *n.* 审判,审理;试验,试用;(对人的忍耐、自制力的)考验,磨炼;烦人的事,惹麻烦的人;预赛,选拔赛;(检验车手技能的)摩托车障碍检验赛;(动物的)比赛,表演

tribulation [ˌtrɪbjuˈleɪʃ(ə)n] *n.* 苦难;磨难;忧患

dedicate [ˈdedɪkeɪt] *v.* 致力于,献身于;把(书、戏剧、音乐作品等)献给;为(建筑物或教堂)举行奉献(或落成)典礼

biography [baɪˈɒgrəfi] *n.* 传记,传记文学;生平

innovative [ˈɪnəveɪtɪv] *a.* 革新的,新颖的;富有革新精神的

painstaking [ˈpeɪnzteɪkɪŋ] *a.* 刻苦的,下苦功的 *n.* 辛苦,勤勉

cooperative [kəʊˈɒpərətɪv] *a.* 合作的,协作的;乐于配合的;(企业或其他组织)合作性的

latecomer [ˈleɪtkʌmə(r)] *n.* 迟到者;新来者

register [ˈredʒistə] *v.* 登记,注册;(正式地或公开地)发表意见,提出主张;流露、表达出;注意到,受到注意;(仪器上)显出,显示;把……挂号邮寄;取得(结果),得(分) *n.* 登记表,注册簿;注册员;(适合特定场合使用的)语体风格,语域;(美)现金出纳机;(电子设备的)寄存器

第二节 水与绘画
Section B Water and Paintings

“天地之气,各以方殊,而人亦因之。”水,是地球地理与人类生命中不可缺少的元素,而它对绘画艺术的影响,也正体现了客观物质条件对主观艺术精神所发挥的作用。

“The *Qi* of heaven and earth is unique, and it is also true of people.” Water is an indispensable element in geography and human life, and its influence on the art of painting also reflects the effect of objective material conditions on the subjective artistic spirit.

中国绘画艺术源远流长,独具一格。水在中国绘画中扮演着至关重要的角色,除了能以水作画,成为绘画的工具材料之外,还可作为绘画的题材。

Chinese painting has a long history and its own unique style. Water plays a vital role in Chinese paintings. Water can be used as a tool and material for painting, and it can also be used as the subject of painting.

1. 中国造纸业高度发达,纸和绢成为中国绘画的主要载体

1. China’s paper industry is highly developed, and paper and silk have become the main carriers of Chinese painting

纸和绢吸水性强,本身柔软,极其适合水媒介颜料。水媒介绘画成为中国人的审美欣赏主体对象,逐渐培养了中国人对水媒介绘画的深厚趣味,加之笔墨也是文人日常必备的工具,中国人书写和绘画的工具都是毛笔,没有本质区别,所以文人画家凭借自己对笔墨的感情和绘画的趣味,发展出水墨画,这逐渐也成为中国画的一大表现形式。水墨画,是中国绘画的代表,也被称为国画。作为中国封建知识分子阶层的语言表达方式,水墨画法在初唐时已初步形成。水墨画具有水乳交融、酣畅淋漓的艺术效果。具体地说,就是将水、墨和宣纸的属性很好地体现出来,如水墨相调,出现干湿浓淡的层次;将水墨和宣纸相融,可以产生洇湿渗透的特殊效果。唐代张彦远在《历代名画记》中说:“运墨而五色具。”只有水才可以让墨生动、活跃、丰富。从王维、张璪的破墨山水到王洽等人的泼墨山水,这种精致、敏感的水墨体验方式已延续千余年历史。

Paper and silk are highly **water-absorbent** and soft, which is extremely suitable for **water-based pigments**. Painting with water as the **medium** has become the main object of Chinese people's **aesthetic appreciation**, and gradually cultivated Chinese people's deep interest in it. In addition, pen and ink are also essential tools for literati in daily life. Chinese writing and painting tools are all brushes, and there is no essential difference. Therefore, literati painters have developed the form of ink painting based on their feelings for pen and ink and their interest in painting, which has gradually become a major form of Chinese painting. Ink painting is the representative of Chinese painting and is also called traditional Chinese painting. Ink painting, as the expression of the Chinese feudal intellectual class, had initially **taken shape** in the early Tang Dynasty, which has the artistic effect of blending water and milk. **Specifically**, the **attributes** of water, ink and rice paper are well reflected, such as the blending of ink and water, which shows a **gradation** of dry and wet **density**; and the combination of ink and rice paper produces a special effect of **moisture penetration**. *Famous Paintings in Past Dynasties* by Zhang Yanyuan of the Tang Dynasty reads, "Even if only a single ink color is used, the picture can produce color changes." Only water can make ink vivid, active and rich. From the landscape ink-painting of Wang Wei and Zhang Zao to splash-ink landscapes of Wang Qia and others, this delicate and sensitive way of ink and wash has continued for more than a thousand years.

2. 以自然山水为题材进行绘画创作的山水画是中国人情思中最为厚重的沉淀

2. Landscape paintings with natural mountains and waters as the theme are the heaviest and thickest precipitation of Chinese people's feelings and thoughts

中国山水画出现在战国之前,滋育于东晋,确立于南北朝,兴盛于隋唐。而山水画中,以表现水景为主要内容的占有相当大的比重,滚滚奔流的江河、碧波万顷的湖泊以及灵动的飞瀑、溪涧和流泉等,都是山水画家们乐于表现的对象。作为中国传统绘画中的一科,山水画的本质体现为人与自然的审美关系,即人以绘画艺术形式再现自然山水的审美追求。《云舒浪卷》《湖光潋滟》《黄河逆流》,这些是南宋时期著名山水画家马远画的《十二水图》中的几幅。这十二幅水图对水的不同形态、环境气候带来的各种变化描摹得细致入微。

Chinese landscape painting appeared before the Warring States period, nurtured in the Eastern Jin Dynasty, established in the Southern and Northern Dynasties, and flourished in the Sui and Tang Dynasties. In Chinese landscape paintings, the main content of waterscape occupies a considerable proportion. The rolling rivers, the lakes with blue waves, and the smart waterfalls, streams and springs are all objects that landscape painters are willing to portray. As a subject of traditional Chinese painting, the essence of landscape painting is embodied in the aesthetic relationship between man and nature, that is, man's aesthetic pursuit of reproducing natural mountains and waters in the form of painting art. *Twelve Views of Water*, painted by the famous landscape painter Ma Yuan during the Southern Song Dynasty, depicts the different forms of water and the various changes brought about by the environment and climate in detail, such as *Hu Guang Lian Yan* (*The Brimming Waves*), *Huanghe Ni Liu* (*The Yellow River Breaches Its Course*), and *Yun Shu Lang Juan* (*Rolling Clouds and Rippling Waves*).

请仔细欣赏马远的《十二水图》。

Please carefully appreciate the following *Twelve Views of Water* by Ma Yuan.

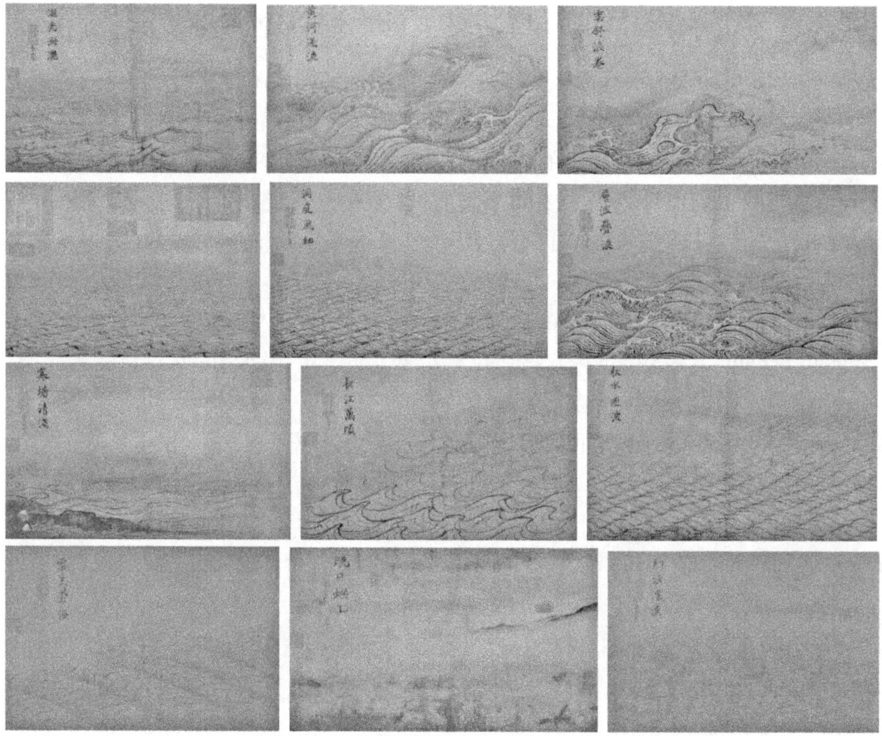

《十二水图》,南宋,马远,绢本设色,纵向 26.8 厘米,横向第一段 20.7 厘米,第二段至第十二段 41.6 厘米,北京故宫博物院藏。《十二水图》是一部由 12 幅画合裱为一卷的长卷。除第一幅外,其余 11 幅的画面上都写有图名。《十二水图》生动地描绘出湖水烟波浩渺、江涛汹涌奔腾、沧海咆哮怒吼等多种情势,真可谓曲尽其态,同时还表现了浮云掠过水面的阴影感和阳光照射水浪造成的光感,追求光影感在中国古代绘画中并不多见。

The **Scroll** of *Twelve Views of Water*, drawn by Ma Yuan in the Southern Song Dynasty, of silk color, 26.8 cm in length, the first section 20.7 cm in breadth, the second to the twelfth sections 41.6 cm, collected by the Palace Museum in Beijing. The Scroll of *Twelve Views of Water* is a long scroll composed of twelve paintings **mounted in a volume**. Except for the first, the other eleven pictures have their names written. The Scroll of *Twelve Views of Water* vividly **depict**s a variety of states of water, such as the vast lake, the surging river and the roaring sea. At the same time, it also shows the shadow of the floating clouds over the water and the light caused by the sun on the waves. This sense of light and shadow is rare in ancient Chinese paintings.

New Words, Phrases and Expressions

indispensable [ˌɪndɪ'spensəb(ə)l] *a.* 不可或缺的,必需的;不能撇开的,责无旁贷的 *n.* 不可缺少之物,必不可少的人

objective [əb'dʒektɪv] *a.* 客观的,不带个人情感的;客观存在的;宾格的;目标的 *n.* 目的,目标;出击目标(尤指在军事攻击中);(语法)宾格

subjective [səb'dʒektɪv] *a.* 出自(或涉及)个人感情的,个人的;主观的(非现实世界的);(语法)主语的;自觉的 *n.* (语法)主格 (the subjective)

vial ['vaɪəl] *n.* (装香水、药水等的)小瓶(同 **phial**) *vt.* 装入小瓶

water-absorbent [əb'zɔːbənt; əb'sɔːbənt] *a.* 吸水的 *n.* 吸水剂

water-based ['wɔtəbest] *a.* 以水为基的

pigment ['pɪgmənt] *n.* 色素;颜料 *v.* 给……染色;呈现颜色

aesthetic [iːs'θetɪ] *a.* 审美的,美学的;美的,艺术的 *n.* 美感,审美观;(aesthetics) 美学;美术理论

appreciation [əˌpriːʃi'eɪʃn] *n.* 欣赏,鉴赏;感激,感谢;理解,领会;升值,增值;(赞赏性的)演讲,文字

initially [ɪ'nɪʃəli] *adv.* 开始,最初

take shape 成形;形成

specifically [spəˈsɪfɪkli] *adv.* 特意,专门地;明确地,具体地;具体来说,确切地说;局限性地;专门

gradation [ɡrəˈdeɪʃn] *n.* 逐渐的变化;层次;阶段;等级;刻度

density [ˈdensəti] *n.* 密集;稠密;密度(固体、液体或气体单位体积的质量)

moisture [ˈmɔɪstʃə(r)] *n.* 潮气;水汽;水分

penetration [ˌpenəˈtreɪʃ(ə)n] *n.* 穿透;渗透;进入

splash-ink *n.* 泼墨

delicate [ˈdelɪkət] *a.* 易损的;易碎的;脆弱的;虚弱的;纤弱的

sensitive [ˈsensətɪv] *a.* 体贴的;体恤的;善解人意的;感觉敏锐的;艺术感觉好的;有悟性的

precipitation [prɪˌsɪpɪˈteɪʃ(ə)n] *n.* 降水,降水量(包括雨、雪、冰等);沉淀;淀析

nurture [ˈnɜːtʃə(r)] *v.* 养育;养护;培养;扶持;帮助;支持;滋长;助长

flourish [ˈflʌrɪʃ] *vi.* 繁荣;昌盛;兴旺;茁壮成长;健康幸福

proportion [prəˈpɔːʃ(ə)n] *n.* 部分;份额;比例;倍数关系

rolling [ˈrəʊlɪŋ] *a.* 起伏的,绵延的;规则的,周而复始的;(走路)左右摇晃的,摇摆的;(水面)汹涌澎湃的;旋转的 *n.* 旋转,动摇,轰响

philosophy [fəˈlɒsəfi] *n.* 哲学;哲学体系,思想体系;人生哲学,生活(工作)准则;(某一知识或经验领域的)理论基础研究,基本原理

peak [piːk] *n.* 巅峰,顶点;山顶;有尖峰的山;尖端,尖顶;帽檐,帽舌;极值,峰值;(艏或艉的)尖舱;(帆的)后上角 *v.* 达到高峰,达到最大值 *a.* 巅峰状态的,最高的;高峰时期的

integration [ˌɪntɪˈɡreɪʃ(ə)n] *n.* 结合,融合;取消种族隔离;(数)积分法,求积分;(心理分析)整合

calligraphy [kəˈlɪɡrəfi] *n.* 书法,书法艺术

brushwork [ˈbrʌʃwɜːk] *n.* 绘画;笔法;画法;书法

faction [ˈfækʃ(ə)n] *n.* 派系,宗派;派系之争,内讧;纪实与虚构相结合的电影(或书等)

variable [ˈveəriəb(ə)l] *a.* 易变的,多变的;时好时坏的;可变的,可调节的;(数)(数字)变量的;(植、动)变异的;(齿轮)变速的 *n.* 可变性,可变因素

C-E Language Disparity 3—Concretization vs. Abstraction 具体化与抽象化

Words of different languages came into being in different ways, but the formation of the meanings of words follows a similar process of abstraction, including generalization, categorization, conceptualization, and abstraction.

The meanings of words are not innate in their own form (whether spoken or written) but come from subjective perceptions about the objective world, and result from the process of cognition or the interaction between signs, meanings, and the communicator's purpose.

Cognition begins with categorization to form concepts, the system of which is organized through categories. Therefore, categorization is the very foundation of the forming of categories and concepts. Human beings would naturally show the results of such categorization and conceptualization in words ever since human language emerged, which is the lexicalization of categories or concepts. What kinds of things belong to the same category? The category is formed through the subjective relation between prototypes, family resemblance, and the members within the same category. It is very important to keep in mind that things belonging to the same category should have basic family resemblance.

Perhaps a word initially represents only a single object when it first comes into being. When a person uses a sign, such as a syllable, to denote an entity, the sign is no more than a single person's subjective experience of an objective object, to which she or he subjectively gave a name. This process is very arbitrary as the syllable does not necessarily have any relation with the object denoted (an exception is onomatopoeia which are imitations of various sounds). Another person who communicates with the first person might see the object while hearing the syllable and thus would naturally connect the syllable with the object and form a corresponding relation between the two in his/her mind. The sender of the sign might send his/her message to different receivers, who might then send the same message to other receivers, and after much repetition such a corresponding relation between the sign and the object gradually becomes fixed as an established sign or code accepted by members of a certain community. In the minds of the members of this community, the initial arbitrariness would become a habit. A reverse process would be activated when they hear the syllable—now a word derived from the sign and the image of the objective thing, then the referential meaning of the word will have been created. Words formed in such a process are called semantic primitives, and the objects or things they denote are called prototypical entities.

People have the ability to use language signs to denote things inaccessible directly in time and space. This feature is called **displacement** and is the foundation of abstraction. It should be pointed out that the formation of Chinese characters is not so arbitrary as most European languages because they were developed from simple pictures, which later evolved to become linear pictographic characters, finally developing into **ideograms** built upon **trinities** of **sound**, **form** and **meaning**. But the process of the conceptualization of their meanings is more or less similar to that of words in English.

It is maintained that conceptualization can be divided into several steps. The first is **generalization** or **de-specification**. This means finding things of shared family resemblance, that is, things of the same category in features such as *shape* or *use*, but neglecting less important features such as *size*, *material*, *color*, etc. This will serve as the basis for further abstraction, so that things with fundamental similarities are classified into one category and represented by the same word. This is categorization, which is a process of classification in a more extensive sense. Its standards are based on the prototype but lay more stress on the essential nature of the object, and it is thus more abstract. The result of categorization is the forming of concepts. A prototype is an ideal model sample and a standard for reference, a relatively stable cognitive construction. The classification of categories is the process of the formation of concepts. It can be concluded that category is the combination of things having resemblances, taking the prototype as their reference object. In other words, conceptualization is the deepening of categorization. There are large and small, simple and complicated concepts. Meanings are but concepts represented by words, and concepts are the bases of the meanings of words. Category and concept are related, but the former emphasizes the classification of objective things while the latter mainly refers to the scope of meanings of a word, which is the basic unit of thought. Abstraction is fairly broad, including generalization, conceptualization, and categorization. In a word, the whole process is abstraction, a process of continuous stripping of the concrete features of things and drawing their common ones.

Along with the developments of cognition, concepts formed will continuously expand. Because the course of cognitive processing is different for different people and due to various subjective elements, a concept denoted by a word may differ in the mind of different people. As concepts are based on the family resemblance of things, the so-called standard for resemblance is largely subjective. Consequently, the range of and boundaries between categories are not fixed but fuzzy. For example, people saw many similarities between whales and fish, so they mistook the whale for a kind of fish for a long time.

In communication, senders relay information according to their own perception. The concept stimulated in the mind of receivers is generally only vaguely similar to that in the mind of the senders. Because of the concrete language environment, the concept raised in the mind of receivers is often very concrete, belonging to a certain entity within the category. It may be the same as the one in the senders' mind, particularly if the entity denoted is present at the time of communication. It may also be a different entity bearing family resemblance. Thus, the concepts used in communication are relatively abstract and vague. It is not the meanings of words but the concrete environment of communication or similar experience of the information receiver that provides such concepts with concrete ideas to ensure successful communication.

The syllable /bei/ in Chinese or the character 杯 is a common frequently-used word. It is the superordinate of 碗,碟,杯,盘,罐,盆,etc. 杯 stands for a relatively abstract category. The receiver will think of many different objects represented by it. There are 杯 for holding different drinks and for different uses, like 茶杯 (teacup), 酒杯 (wine cup/glass), 啤酒杯 (mug), 牛奶杯 (milk glass/cup), 咖啡杯 (coffee cup), 水果杯 (fruit cup), 漱口杯 (tooth glass/mug), 洗眼杯 (eyecup), even 烧杯 (beaker), 量杯 (measuring glass), 奖杯 (trophy), etc. 杯 can be of different shapes, including 平底大玻璃杯 (tumbler), 高脚杯 (coupe or goblet), and even 盖杯 (碗) (teacup with a lid). Perhaps one might think of special 杯 like 夜光杯 (luminous wine glass) or 保温 (暖) 杯 (thermal mug or vacuum flask), etc. The various 杯 are all based on direct or indirect cognition of actual, real-life objects, which belong to the same category represented in Chinese by the word 杯, though the conceptual scope of each of these concrete 杯 is narrower than the general concept represented by the word 杯 alone.

People of different nations have different processes of subjective cognition, emphasizing different parts or different features of the same thing. As a result, the concepts thus drawn may belong to different categories in different languages. Different ways of generalization cause different modes of reference and expression, which manifests at the lexical level in the fact that different words are used to represent a given category, or there may be a range of different ways to refer to a given category in different languages, and this causes lexical disparity between English and Chinese.

Category involves many concepts. We think "family resemblance", "centrality", and "membership radiance" raised by Lakoff (one of the Pioneers in Cognitive Linguistics) are the most important in the determination and development of word meaning. Furthermore, categories have different levels, as a large category may contain several subcategories, all of which are somewhat indefinite, as their boundaries tend to be vague and open. Neighboring categories may overlap each other partially. Thus, determining the actual meanings of words often depends on the context of communication.

From the examples of various 杯—the many hyponyms, words with narrower scopes than the concept represented by 杯—we can find that the terms for different 杯 are mostly of the form "modifier + central word". This accords with the most frequently-used method of forming compound words, especially in Chinese. The modifier emphasizes certain specific features and differences apart from the common nature shared among words belonging to the category while the central word, a word symbolic of the category itself, represents shared characteristics and stands for the conformity of the category, which also reflects the fact that Chinese people stress unity. English also uses this method to form compound words, but less frequently. The concept represented by Chinese 杯 is fairly broad and contains some concepts represented by several words in English such as *mug*, *cup*, *glass*, and *tumbler*, which do not belong to the same category and have no superordinate like the Chinese word 杯. One might say that the word *vessel* can serve as their superordinate. But the word *vessel* represents a much larger category and can include *pail* (桶), *kettle* (壶), *bowl* (碗/钵), *jar* (盂, such as in 水盂 water jar; water basin; 痰盂 spittoon; 漱口盂儿 mouth cleansing cup), etc. We can see the shared similarity of members of 杯 shares a broader range than those shared by members of *mug*, *cup* or *glass*.

Of course nothing is absolute: Chinese sometimes also has different names to refer to the same thing. Some items called 杯 are also called 盅 (杯 without a handle), 盏 (small 杯), and in ancient times some 杯 were called 樽, 觞, 觚, 觥, etc. These characters have different radicals and thus may belong to different categories.

The various kinds of 杯 shown above tell us that the meanings of words do have national characters. The concepts of *glass*, *cup*, *mug*, and *tumbler*—English words corresponding to Chinese 杯—have vague boundaries, and factors like shape, size and usage require consideration in its nomenclature. They have many overlaps with their neighboring concepts, like *plate*, *bowl*, and *jar*. To Chinese people all the containers called 杯 have family resemblance and thus can be covered by the same concept represented by the word 杯, perhaps with some modifiers. To English speakers, they are different concepts that obviously belong to different categories, and only some of them have family resemblance. Of course you can say they are all containers, which, however, contain a much larger domain.

But things are never absolute. A book entitled *A History of the World in Six Glasses*, published a few years ago in the United States, divides history into six periods according to six types of drinks: *beer*, *wine*, *liquor*, *coffee*, *tea*, and *Coca-Cola*. If what is emphasized is the drink, the word *cup* might seem more proper for the title than glass. However, "six cups" may mislead people to think of the quantity of drinks rather than different types of drink. We can see that the extended meanings of *cup* and *glass* may differ. Interestingly, the Chinese translation of the title is《六个瓶子里的历史》. Obviously 瓶子 is better than 杯子 here, but not perfect, as *tea* normally is not bottled.

We have mentioned before that the material world is infinite. Besides classification referring to infinite things with limited words, another way is often used: giving new meanings to existing words. This is extension and transfer of word meaning. The new concepts represented by old words must have a logical connection with the original concepts they represent. This is part of the development of abstract thinking.

Now let's see how the meanings of 杯 have developed. Phrases like 喝一杯 (have a glass; enjoy a glass; crush a cup), 碰杯 (clink glasses), 举杯 (lift/raise one's glass), 干杯 (empty one's cup/glass), 贪杯 (be fond of one's glass) are common in daily usage. In these expressions, 杯 no longer stands for the container itself but rather refers to the wine (or occasionally other drinks) contained within it. More meanings may be contained in idioms. For example, in 杯盘狼藉 (wine cups and dishes lying about in disorder after a feast) and 杯觥交错 (the wine cup passes freely; the cups go gaily round). 杯 means "drinking", though on the surface it refers to the container. In 杯水车薪 (trying to put out a blazing cartload of firewood with a cup of water), 杯 stresses "little" amount. These new meanings of 杯 are drawn from different angles in the actual use or deeper subjective cognition from personal experiences. We can see that the corresponding English words *cup* and *glass* share similar usage with 杯; for example, in "He accepted another cup" and "A glass had been poured out", neither cup nor glass refers to the container but to the tea or wine in the container. As for the English translation of 干杯 (drink a toast), the phrase seems to have nothing to do with the container at all, except that it implies that the container glass is used in the process of "drinking a toast".

Finally, let's have a look at a very fashionable term used in China, especially on Internet: 杯具. Well, one would think it means "utensils like the cup and so on", but it is instead an allusion to 悲剧 (tragedy), a homophone of 杯具.

However, there are some uses of the English word *cup* that Chinese 杯 does not have. The Concise Oxford Dictionary has another definition for cup: "a cup-shaped thing". For example, "suction cup", 皮碗/圈/吸盘 in Chinese. The part of a bra that covers a woman's breast is also called a "cup", for which there is no name in Chinese, and the rubber cup (attached to the eyepiece) in the microscope is called 目镜. In American English, holes in the golf field are also called "cups".

The so-called corresponding words in Chinese and English very often have different scopes of meanings, and the differences between the extended meanings of these words are usually very huge. This is a cause of difficulty in translation between the two languages. For example, it is hard to translate a simple sentence like 我今天买了 15 只新杯子, because we don't know whether 杯 here refer to *cups*, *glasses*, or *mugs*.

The character 玉 also has many extended meanings, which are all more abstract. Our ancestors used jade as ornaments and funerary objects as early as 5,000 BC. Jade was believed to signify purity, nobility, and refinement, and as a result the character 玉 has acquired many abstract meanings. People use phrases like 玉体,亭亭玉立, 玉容, 玉颜 and 玉貌 to refer to beautiful women; 玉照 to refer to beautiful photos of females; and 玉洁冰清, 浑金璞玉, and 瑕不掩瑜 metaphorically refer to a fine personality. There is also the use of 玉成, etc., to show respect. The word "jade" in English and many other Western languages can be used often in advertising to call to mind an East Asian flavor. Otherwise, most Americans associate no emotions or personal qualities with the word "jade" at all, which is caused by the two different attitudes towards jade in the two cultures.

The development of the meanings or the process of abstraction of words varies in different languages and cultures, caused by multiple factors such as geography, history, culture, customs, etc., of different nations.

From the examples of 杯 and 玉 in the above section, we have some idea of the development of the meanings of some Chinese characters. The further development of conceptualization is abstraction, in which words gain highly abstract meanings. According to The Concise Oxford Dictionary, "abstract" has more to do with thought than matter, and is about theory rather than practice. The abstract meanings of words denote quality or condition of the intangible rather than concrete objects. And this is the product of the development of people's thinking.

English has pairs of words which distinguish between concrete things and relatively abstract concepts, such as clothes/clothing, leaf/foliage, forest/forestry, machine/machinery, peasant/peasantry, tenant/tenantry, medicine/medication, poem/poetry, etc., but Chinese usually does not distinguish them and thus has only one word corresponding to each of the above pairs: 服装, 叶(子), 森林, 机器, 农民, 佃户, 药(品), 诗(歌). But not every concept has such a distinction in English. Very often a word may have both concrete and abstract meanings. Take the word "life" as an example:

1. Where there is water, there is *life*. 有水就会有生命。(生命, a relatively concrete concept)

2. A *life* without a purpose is a ship without a rudder. 一生无目的,犹如船失去了舵。(一生, somewhat abstract as it refers to a period of time)

3. *Life* is ten percent what you make it and ninety percent how you take it. 生活有百分之十在于你如何塑造它,有百分之九十在于你如何对待它。(生活, way of living; more abstract)

4. *Life* or death, I will do whatever I can for the benefits of the country. 苟利社稷,死生以之。(生 as opposite to 死, a phenomenon or concept)

5. Only a *life* lived for others is a *life* worthwhile. (Albert Einstein) 只有为别人而活的人生才是有价值的人生。(人生, an abstract concept)

6. As a diplomat, he has seen much of *life*. (阅历, experience gained in one's life; an abstract concept)

7. Is there any *life* on Venus? (生物, general term for a big class of concrete things; somewhat concrete)

8. The young girl is full of *life*. (生气/朝气, atmosphere; a highly abstract concept)

We can see from the above examples different degrees of abstraction and fuzziness of the meanings of the word *life*. We can cite many examples of the abstraction of ordinary nouns in English, such as brain: 脑子→智力; chair: 椅子→主持; head: 头→领导; muscle: 肌肉→力量; memory: 记忆→储存器;内存 etc. Similar changes can also be seen in the phenomenon of antonomasia, using the name of a person known for a particular quality to denote anyone with that same quality. For example, in Chinese 伯乐 refers to a person good at recognizing talented people, and 诸葛亮 has become a synonym of wise man. Similarly, in English a "Judas" is a traitor and a "Don Juan" is a womanizer.

This change in word meanings is a manifestation of the development of people's thinking: from thinking in images to abstract thinking. Abstraction is the inevitable result of the development of thinking, which is reflected in science and art as well as in language.

It is generally recognized that logic is a very abstract science of great importance in scientific thinking. Mathematics is another highly abstract science, developed from simply counting objects in the world, or from people's descriptions and explanations of the world. In a sense, music is also very abstract, mainly expressing feelings and emotions through notes of different tones and melodies. Dancing can be regarded as a special language comprised of the movements of the body, especially the arms and legs. It originated in imitations of motions and gestures in people's lives, which can be easily understood. But as it has developed into modern dance that uses motion to represent abstractions, probably only the professional can understand its inner meaning. As for fine arts, traditional fine arts mostly depict realistic and concrete things, people and scenes. But abstract fine arts and the ways artists express ideas in such works are difficult to comprehend. The artistic languages used by modern dancers and artists are too abstract to form commonly agreed-upon expressions that can be understood by laymen.

Many abstract ideas and concepts are gradually formed, and abstract words have appeared to represent them. We have such words in both Chinese and English, such as 艺术(art), 现象 (phenomenon), 文化(culture), 假设(hypothesis), 逻辑(logic), etc., mainly nouns representing areas of knowledge.

Many abstract nouns in Chinese represent the unique ideas and concepts in the traditional Chinese culture, such as 孝, 悌, 忠, 信, 礼, 义, 廉, and 耻, all of which are representative of traditional virtues, embody some basic concepts of Chinese ethics and are loaded with rich cultural contents of Confucianism. It is difficult to find their absolute equivalents in English, if there is any at all. This tells us that concepts are often nation-specific. Actually, the character 仁 contains the implications of 诚, 敬, 忠, 恕, 孝, 慈, 爱, and 恭 within its overall meaning, which makes it very difficult to be translated into just one English version. James Legge held that 仁 contained "kindness", "love", "charity", "generosity", "altruism", "character", and "benevolence". Arthur Waley translated 仁 as the very general term "goodness". Gu Hongming translated it as "humanity, moral sense, and Lin Yutang, however, simply translated it as "true manhood". But none of the above-mentioned versions can truly and wholly represent the cultural connotations of the word 仁.

While many Chinese characters contain profound cultural connotations, English words reflect another type of abstraction, mainly through the formation of words, or **lexicalization**. Chinese compound words are represented often in the form of "modifiers+central elements", with emphasis on the category of meaning. This is because Chinese is an analytic language. As more of a comprehensive language, English stresses more the markers (that is, morphological features) of parts of speech, which makes it easy for English abstraction at the lexical level. The easiest way is **affixation**, especially **nominalization**: turning adjectives and verbs into nouns to express characteristics, action or motion. Some scholars have named such words like "noun-verb" (gerund) (名动词 better rendered as "verbal noun") and "noun-adjective" (名形词, "adjectival noun"). Such nouns have higher degrees of abstraction than their cognate adjectives and verbs, because they "contain the meanings of original adjectives and verbs but can be used in the sentence like ordinary nouns".

Chinese adjectives and verbs can be used as nouns without any morphological change, but now many category words (范畴词, which are sometimes referred to as "suffixes" like 度, 性, 化, 态度, 问题, 局势, 现象, 方法, 问题, 作用, 事件, 态度, 精神) are added as a way of **nominalization**. This is one of the manifestations of the important influence of European languages, especially that of English, on the Chinese language. For example:

necessity 必要性	arrogance 傲慢态度
intensity 强度	operability 可操作性
muddiness 混沌状态	transparency 透明度
infiltration 渗透作用	complexity 复杂局面
loftiness 崇高气质	neutralization 中和作用
jealousy 嫉妒心理	irregularity 越轨行为
dedication 献身精神	togetherness 不分彼此的集体感
assimilation 同化	acculturation 文化适应;文化移入;文化互渗

Abstraction and Sentence Structure

Chinese does not have many abstract nouns referring to actions, motions, or characteristics. Therefore, Chinese usually uses nouns standing for concrete entities or objects to play the various roles of the noun in a sentence, as vague abstract concepts cannot "lead the array"—form the focus of the sentence. English tends to use more nouns as it usually prefers to be stative rather than dynamic. One of the causes of this is the requirements of grammatical structure in the sentence. Nouns can perform many roles in the basic sentence structure of "Subject + Predicate + Object". Cai Jigang lists **eight rhetoric functions of abstract nouns**: simplicity, vividness, variety, balance, emphasis, coherence, rhythm, and euphemism. Speaking from another angle, the abstract noun often forms the focus of the sentence. Please read the following sentences carefully:

1. They were now sitting in the shade, having drinks on the first of the evening **cool**.

这时他们坐在树荫下,趁着夜晚的第一丝凉意喝酒。

Cool in this sentence is a noun. It is translated into Chinese as 凉,somewhat concretized as 凉意(the feel of coldness), something that can be felt.

2. But now the sadness of her dimple shivered away into **pride**.

这时,她的酒窝显示的不再是伤心,而是自豪。

3. There is that precarious moment when the body is tense, the breath is short and all that matters is the next handhold, the right positioning of feet and **clarity** of thought.

有一阵子他感到惶惑,全身绷紧,呼吸短促,关键是下面一个手握的动作,双脚站位要正确,头脑要保持清醒。

4. He fled into the cold sharp **clarity** of the night. 他逃了出去,在夜晚的寒冷中让自己头脑清醒一下。

5. She then ate in the lonely **splendor** in her office.

然后她在自己豪华的办公室里一个人孤零零地吃晚饭。

6. He curled into the downy softness of the bed and drifted into sweet **oblivion**.

他蜷缩在软乎乎的鸭绒被中,进入了甜蜜的梦乡,把所有的烦恼忘得一干二净。

7. She wore a straight tan skirt and a sweater, with a slender belt round her, carefully calculated to emphasize the **smallness** of her waist.

她上身穿着一件毛衣,下身穿着一条褐色的直筒裙,很讲究地束着一根很细的腰带,恰如其分地突显出纤细的腰身。

8. It suddenly revealed the glistening **newness** underneath.

下面突然露出了闪闪发光的崭新的钱币。

9. We agreed that the high points have a way of becoming blurred with the passage of time. But we shared one experience that never will lose its **immediacy**.

我们同意,随着时间的推移,那些高出来的地方会慢慢地被磨平而显露不出来。但是我们有一个共同的感受,在我们心里永远是亲近的。

Concretization of Abstract Nouns

Please look at the following sentences:

1. I knew that sleep was an **impossibility**. 我明白睡觉是不可能的了。

2. They deemed going shopping a total **irrelevance**. 他们认为,去购物完全是件不相干的事。

3. The attacks were also partly an **outpouring** of anger that had been bottled up over the past six months. 之所以攻击别人,是因为过去半年积在心中的怒气终于爆发了。

4. He said it was simply a matter of playing on the **probabilities**. 他说,那只不过是一种概率游戏而已。

5. The town is becoming a growing cultural **complexity**. 这个镇正在成为文化复合体。

6. The machines are a real **delight**. 这些机器真让人感到一种由衷的高兴。

7. The woman was both perfectly pleasant and an agreeable physical **presence**. 这个女人绝对讨人喜欢,非常好相处。

8. The players regarded this as a tedious fate that befell them as part of their duty as public **eminences**. 运动员们把这看成是无法摆脱的命运带给他们的烦恼,是出了名之后必须承担的责任的一部分。

9. As an amusement park employee, he is often asked for **directions** to specific attractions. 作为游乐场的工作人员,常有人向他打听怎么去具体的景点。

10. The storm caused many communication **breakdowns**. 暴风雨造成多处通信中断。

11. But the percentages are estimates, not **certainties**. 但是,这些百分比只是估计出来的,并非确切数字。

The abstract nouns in the above sentences have been concretized, or reified. Although the meanings of words gradually undergo the process of generalization, conceptualization, and abstraction, this is not the only direction or the end of the process because of the interaction between concepts and the objective world, and because most communications involve concrete things as well as abstract concepts, including those formed through perception and cognition. Sometimes abstract nouns would revert to having concrete meanings—that is, referring to concrete things or phenomena. Take the word "glass" that we have discussed before as an example, it is a concrete noun, usually uncountable and somewhat abstract, because it refers to a kind of material. Glass can be made into various objects but most commonly into the container that people use to drink. As a result, the word "glass" has been de-generalized to refer to that object, called 杯 or 玻璃杯 in Chinese. Similar cases abound: a cloth 抹布, a copper 铜板, an iron 熨斗, paper 文件/论文, etc. We could find this de-generalization in some other concrete nouns, too. We all know that usually the concepts represented by words like "fish" and "fruit" are relatively abstract because they denote many different kinds of fish and fruit; so we say "three fish" or "four fruit" without adding the plural suffix -(e)s.

But when we want to emphasize that the fish or fruit are of different types, some people will use the plural suffix to say "three fishes" and "four fruits" because we have more concrete images of them this time.

Abstract nouns have higher degrees of abstraction, but they too can be reified. For example, the word "experience" is uncountable when it means "knowledge or skill derived from one's practice (经验)" because it is a fairly abstract concept. But in the following two sentences it becomes countable.

1. That's quite an experience. 这可真算是一次(有意思的/难忘的)经历。

2. The book is a detailed record of his life experiences. 这本书详细记录了他的生平(经历)。

The word "experience" in the above two sentences has been concretized to refer to "actual observation of or practical acquaintance with facts or events (经历)".

C-E Translation Strategies and Skills 3—Linear vs. Inverse Translation/Interpreting 顺译与逆译

Linear translation or interpreting is, as its name suggests, translation or interpreting of source language into target language in original word order. Inverse translation or interpreting is translation or interpreting in an inverse word order. Please study the following cases.

A. Linear Translation or Interpreting Cases

1. 流水不腐,户枢不蠹。Flowing water does not rot, nor a door-hinge rust.

2. 近水楼台先得月。A waterfront pavilion gets the moonlight first.

3. 我们诚恳地希望,你们在表示祝贺之后,能做出相应的共同努力,以便寻求一个公正可行的办法,来解决这个多年来一直困扰着联合国的问题。We sincerely hope that your congratulations will be matched by your collective endeavour to seek a just and practical solution to the problem which has bedeviled the United Nations for so many years.

4. 他们通常没意识到在很多国家,形形色色的贿赂行为正日益增多。在某些国家,这已成为人们几百年来的生活方式。They often do not realize that bribery in various forms is on the increase in many countries and, in some, has been a way of life for centuries.

5. 她一宿无眠,早早起身,披上毯子,迎着拂面的凉风,凭窗眺望黎明。She had spent a sleepless night, and rising early, had stood, wrapped up, at her window, with the cool air blowing on her face, to watch the dawn.

6. 我们可以断定,当分子之间的距离很小时,就会产生排斥力,并随着分子间距离的减小而迅速增加。We must therefore conclude that when the distance between the molecules is very small, there are forces of repulsion and that these forces increase rapidly as the distance between the molecules decreases.

7. 我们的人民政府是真正代表人民利益的政府,是为人民服务的政府。Our People's Government is one that genuinely represents the people's interests. It is a government that serves the people.

8. 到了20世纪60年代造出了"两弹一星",中国的发展速度是真正的奇迹。By the 1960s, China had detonated two nuclear devices and sent a satellite to space. The speed of the development was nothing short of a miracle.

9. 因此,每个气缸都用一个水套围着,水套形成循环回路的一部分。水泵驱使水在回路中不停地流动,并由外面鼓进空气来使水冷却。鼓风用的大型旋转风扇是由辅助电机带动的。Each cylinder therefore is encased in a water jacket, which forms part of a circuit through which water is pumped continuously, and cooled by means of air drawn in from the outside atmosphere by large rotary

fans, worked by auxiliary motors.

10. 鱼处水而生,人处水而死。Fish can only survive in waters while men will die in waters.

11. 君子之交淡若水,小人之交甘若醴;君子淡以亲,小人甘以绝。A gentleman's friendship is as plain as water, a vulgar man's friendship is as sweet as good wine; gentlemen approach each other for plainness, vulgar men approach each other for gain.

B. Inverse Translation or Interpreting Cases

1. 古老之河不断流。Water never dries up in **an old river**.

2. 远水不解近渴。Water **afar off** does not quench fire.

3. 如果把管子装成能让最热的水上升,而最冷的水流下回到锅炉,那么锅炉中的热水系统不用水泵就能运转,其道理就在于此。This is why the hot water system in a furnace will operate without the use of a water pump, **if** the pipes are arranged so that the hottest water rises while the coldest water runs down again to the furnace.

4. 这犹如无源之水,无本之木。This is like water **without a source**, or a tree **without roots.**

5. 文化越来越成为民族凝聚力和创造力的重要源泉,是综合国力的重要竞争因素。Culture has increasingly become **an important source of national cohesion and creativity**, and **an important competitive factor in overall national strength**.

6. 江苏省历史悠久,文化底蕴深厚。在历史演进过程中,形成了风格多样、特色鲜明的地域文化和水域文化。Jiangsu Province has a long history and profound cultural heritage. In the course of historical evolution, **regional and water cultures with diverse styles and distinctive features have been formed**.

7. 海洋文化是人们基于海水、在海洋活动中创造的物质和精神财富。Marine culture is **the material and spiritual wealth created by people based on sea water and activities on the ocean**.

8. 针对现实困境中的水资源紧缺问题,在全社会提高水文化意识,建设节水型社会是有效的解决方式。Aiming at tackling the problem of water shortage **in the real dilemma**, raising the awareness of water culture **in the whole society** and building a water-saving society are effective solutions.

C. Combination of Linear and Inverse Translation or Interpreting

Actually, absolute linear or inverse translation or interpreting is rather scarce. The two strategies or approaches are often intermixed. Please study the following cases:

1. 人莫鉴于流水,而鉴于止水。唯止能止众止。Men do not use running water as a mirror; they only use the still water. Only things that are still in themselves can still other things.

2. 水能载舟,也能覆舟。The water that bears the boat is the same that swallows it up.

3. 水是风景区的点睛之处。Water is the focal point of a landscape.

4. 欲擒龙王,就得下海。He who would catch fish must not mind getting wet.

5. 水文化建设是推进水利建设的强大动力,要大力发展水文化建设,以先进的文化推动先进的生产力。Water culture construction is a powerful driving force to promote water conservancy construction. We must vigorously develop water culture construction and promote advanced productivity with advanced culture.

6. 高度重视水文化建设,切实加强组织领导,是建设水文化的关键。Attaching great importance to the construction of water culture and effectively strengthening the organization and leadership is the key to the construction of water culture.

7. 水文化事业是指水利行业和与水有关的科学技术、各类教育、文学艺术、新闻出版、体育卫生等事业,这些都要大力发展。Water culture undertakings refer to the water conservancy industry and water-related science and technology, various types of education, literature and art, press and publishing, sports and sanitation and other undertakings, all of which must be vigorously developed.

8. 天下莫柔弱于水,而攻坚强者莫之能胜,以其无以易之。弱之胜强,柔之胜刚,天下莫不知,莫能行。是以圣人云:受国之垢,是为社稷主;受国不祥,是为天下王。正言若反。(《道德经》78 章)Nothing in the world is softer or weaker than water, but nothing is better to win over the hard and the strong, for it cannot be replaced. The weak may surpass the strong and the soft may surpass the

hard. It is well-known to the world, but none can put it into practice. That is the reason why the sage says, "Who can bear the humiliation of a state may become its master; who can endure the disaster of a state may become its ruler." It seems wrong, but it is right.

C-E Guided Translation Practice 3

山水画简介:在魏晋南北朝之前,山水画并不是独立的画种;隋唐时期经济繁荣推动了文化的发展,拓宽了绘画题材的选择范围,山水画发展初具规模;五代时期,山水画出现皴染法,有了不同的山水派系,这一阶段名家辈出;宋代,各个画种全面发展,盛极一时,观念和手法也各有不同,山水画至此达到高峰;元代,随着文人画发展,书法与绘画相互融合,在注重描绘自然景色的同时,更强调主观情感的抒发,山水画趋于写意;明清时期的山水画派系众多,风格多变,画坛百花齐放,东西方艺术开始交流,山水画风貌一新。时至今日,山水画也一直没有停止发展的脚步。(节选自黎越常《立象以尽意:山水画中的写意精神》一文)

第四单元　水文化遗产与水利瑰宝

Unit 4　Water Culture Heritage and Water Conservancy Treasures

第一节　水文化遗产
Section A　Water Culture Heritage

"问渠那得清如许，为有源头活水来。"水是生命之源，是人类生产和生活中必不可缺的自然物质。水与建筑结合，产生了奇妙的化学反应，在中华优秀传统水文化遗产中，工程类水文化遗产建筑成果颇丰，出现了京杭大运河、新疆坎儿井、四川都江堰等家喻户晓的水利建筑。此外，一大批结合水景观的建筑设计也相继问世。

A Chinese poem reads as follows: "The river is always being kept clean, since there is in-flowing water from its source." Water, as the natural source of life, is a necessity in people's daily production and living. Through the utilization of water, many wonderful architectural fruits have been born during different periods, especially those engineering buildings among those magnificent Chinese traditional water-related cultural heritages. For instance, the Beijing-Hangzhou Grand Canal, Xinjiang Karez (an irrigation system of wells connected by underground channels), Sichuan Dujiang Dam and so on. In addition, a large number of architectural designs combined with water landscapes have also come out one after another.

有水便有桥，有桥便有路，也便有了"小桥，流水，人家"的中国情怀。水赋予建筑无与伦比的诗意，人穿行其中，感受着自然韵律的同时，心灵也得到了慰藉。我国与水相关的建筑主要有滨水景观建筑、水乡居民建筑、园林建筑、山水名胜建筑等，无论哪种滨水建筑，无不彰显了水与建筑的融合之美。

Where there is water, there is a bridge; and where there is a bridge, there is a road. All of images have pictured a scene of "a household on a creek flowing under a stone-bridge nearby", which endows the Chinese people with a particular sentiment. Usually, much unparalleled poetic flavor is hidden in water-related architectures where people can physically and mentally console themselves as soon as feeling the natural rhythm through water. Such water-related architectures in China mainly include waterfront landscape architectures, riverside towns, ancient gardens, tourist attractions, etc. No matter what kind of waterfront architecture, they all embody a kind of beauty through the integration of water and architecture.

1. 滨水景观建筑

1. Waterfront landscape architectures

我国自古以来就有在江河湖海等滨水区营造建筑的传统。

Traditionally, most Chinese architectures are located along the banks of rivers, lakes and seas.

得益于天地的钟灵毓秀，观景类建筑多依山傍水，与此同时，滨水风景也因建筑而备受青睐。如依水而建的陕西省汉中市天汉文化公园，风景秀丽，生态良好，文化深厚，不仅是汉中市一道靓丽的滨江风景线，还成为汉中市的一张新名片。

Being abundant in natural resources like mountains and rivers stands out among waterfront architectures in good stead. On the one hand, a collection of buildings can be designed through making good use of such scenery. On the other hand, the splendidly beautiful scenery is getting more appreciation owing to magnificent structures. For example, the Tianhan Cultural Park of Shaanxi Province in northwest China, built along the Han River, owns its wonderful view, pleasant ecological environment and profound culture. Being in possession of a beautiful riverside scenery, the Park has become a new business card of Hanzhong City.

纪念性建筑是为了纪念有功绩的或显赫的人或重大事件而营造的建筑或建筑艺术品。滨水纪念性建筑多是为了纪念与治水或抗洪有关的历史人物及历史事件，如绍兴市治水纪念馆便介绍了治水先贤马臻筑三百里镜湖时的艰难历程。

As the name suggests, the architectural works function as markings of distinguished and influential figures who have made merits and signified important events. Therefore, waterfront architectures are mostly in memory of historical figures and events related to water control and flood fighting. For example, the Shaoxing Water Control Memorial Hall has recorded the difficult and thorny journey of the sage Ma Zhen for his construction of the three-hundred-li Jinghu Lake.

我国古代的建筑常常都是依据风水而建，直至今天风水在建筑工程中仍是一个重要考量因素。如安徽省的西递、宏村于 1999 年被列为世界文化遗产，村内两条溪流均向西流，这与“一江春水向东流”刚好相反，为逆水，“东水西递”是居住风水中著名的聚财局，所以，西递、宏村是“逆水为财”的风水，而此地官商两旺的鼎盛时期维持了长达 200 年之久。

Which is called "fengshui" in Chinese philosophy. When a project is under construction, most Chinese people would like to take the "fengshui" philosophy into serious consideration from the perspective of location, direction, the natural environment and many other factors. Therefore, the style of Chinese architectures is oriented on the "fengshui" philosophy in every age. For example, the Xidi Village and Hong Village in Anhui Province was listed as a World Cultural Heritage in 1999. Both streams in the village flow westward. Considering the philosophy of "the spring river flows east", that phenomenon is the other way around. In China, the flow of water from east to west represents that life will be roses all the way; and in the traditional Chinese residence customs, it propitiously heralds a gathering of wealth. As a result, the Xidi Village and Hong Village is "against the water" but gathering the wealth, which made the prosperity of the officials and merchants here maintained as long as 200 years.

2. 水乡居民建筑

2. Riverside towns

中国人所说的"水乡",一般是指"江南水乡"。中国的"江南",大体上是指长江以南地区,主要城市包括上海、南京、杭州、绍兴、苏州、扬州、无锡等地。江南地区环境温暖,降水充沛,江河湖泊星罗棋布,是中国最富足的鱼米之乡,其独特的"江南水乡"风韵,体现在生活、文化、建筑、物产等各个方面。

Water towns generally refer to "towns in the south of the Yangtze River". "Jiangnan" in China generally refers to the south part of the Yangtze River. The main cities include Shanghai, Nanjing, Hangzhou, Shaoxing, Suzhou, Yangzhou, Wuxi and other places. In possession of the warm environment, abundant precipitation, and rich water resources such as scattered rivers and lakes, the region has become the richest land flowing with milk and honey in China. The unique charm of water towns in the south of the Yangtze River is merged into various aspects like lives, cultures, architectures, and products.

江南水乡的建筑一般都比较密集,湖泊、河流、小巷交叉穿梭存在,水、路、桥和谐地融为一体。房屋傍着河流建造,密集的传统建筑簇拥在水巷两岸,构成了独具特色的水乡建筑特色。如浙江省乌镇以河成街,街桥相连,依河筑屋,水镇一体,组织起水阁、桥梁、石板巷等独具江南韵味的建筑因素,呈现了江南水乡古镇的空间魅力,在中国的文化发展史和建筑发展史上都占据了一席之地。

With ever-expanding network of scattered lakes, rivers and alleys, water towns in the south of the Yangtze River obviously feature a dense architectural style. Water, roads and bridges are harmoniously integrated into one piece. Houses closely stand along the river and traditional buildings densely cluster on two sides of the water lane as well, both of which form the unique architectural characteristics of water towns. Taking Wuzhen Ancient Town in Zhejiang Province as an example, water is largely utilized as an architectural element. These streets are composed of rivers and connected with bridges, as well as houses built along rivers, creating a lot of architectural designs such as water pavilions, bridges, stone alleyways and other elements with unique flavors. For its representation of the spatial charm of ancient water towns, this kind of architecture occupies a significant position in the development history of Chinese culture and architecture.

3. 水与园林建筑

3. Ancient gardens

园林是大自然中山水景色的缩影,这是中国园林的主要特色,体现了自然之美与人工之美的高度结合。在中国园林建筑中,水是人们必须充分考虑的元素之一。

Chinese gardens can be characteristically viewed as the epitome of natural landscape, reflecting the high combination of natural beauty and artificial beauty. When building a Chinese garden, water is one of the essential elements that must be fully considered.

中国园林中的建筑主要是木质建筑,木质材料最怕虫蛀、火烧,园林中的水起到了蓄水、防火等维护园林建筑的基本作用。而用水造景,可以从视觉上丰富空间层次。一方面,水将各个相对独立的建筑空间串联起来,提升了空间整体的氛围感;另一方面,水又将一整个的空间分隔开来,使得园林景观错落有致。作为生命之源的水,是民族文化的象征,这也是水能够成为园林中要素的原因之一。无形无色的水反映出形形色色的景物。在园林景观中,水倒映四周的山石、草木、建筑,不仅延伸了人们的视野,还在无形中扩大了视觉空间,将园林建筑设计的美与妙展现得淋漓尽致。

Chinese gardens are mainly made of wood materials, which can be easily damaged by insect decay and fire, so that water plays a basic role in maintaining garden buildings, such as water storage and fire prevention. Water can visually enrich the level of architectural space. On the one hand, water connects each relatively independent architectural space and improves the overall atmosphere of the space. On the other hand, water separates the whole space, making the landscape well arranged. As the source of life, water is a symbol of national culture, which is also one of the reasons why water has become an important element in garden. Invisible and colorless water reflects all kinds of scenery. In a garden landscape, water reflects its surrounding rocks, plants, and buildings. It not only extends people's vision, but also invisibly expand the space, showing the beauty and wonderful landscape architectural design incisively and vividly.

4. 山水名胜建筑

4. Tourist attractions

中国山水名胜比比皆是,山岳型、湖泊型、河川型、瀑布型、海岛海滨型等名胜景区数不胜数,无数的文人墨客慕名前去观赏。山水文化作为中国传统文化中重要的一部分,是人与自然环境交互作用的结果,是天人合一的产物。

There are many scenic spots in China, such as mountains, lakes, rivers, waterfalls, islands and beaches. As an important part of Chinese traditional culture, landscape culture is not only the result of the interaction between man and the natural environment, but the product of the harmony of nature and man.

名胜添雅意,山水皆有情。风景名胜以自然山水和点缀其间的人文胜迹为审美对象,是自然山水和历史人文的有机融合。一方面,山水的结合以秀丽见长,构成了平山远水的景观特色;另一方面,也彰显了浓郁的人文气息和深厚的历史与地域文化。

Scenic spots add elegance, mountains and rivers are sentient. Scenic spots take natural landscape and interspersed cultural sites as aesthetic objects, which is the organic integration of natural landscape and historical humanity. On the one hand, the combination of mountains and rivers is famous for its beauty, which constitutes the landscape characteristics of near mountains and distant waters. On the other hand, it also demonstrates the rich cultural atmosphere and profound historic and regional culture.

New Words, Phrases and Expressions

heritage [ˈherɪtɪdʒ] *n.* 遗产;传统;世袭财产

as follows 如下

in-flowing [ˈɪnˌfləʊɪŋ] *a.* 流入某地的

necessity [nəˈsesəti] *n.* 必需品;必要,需要;必然性;不可避免的情况

architectural [ˌɑːkɪˈtektʃərəl] *a.* 建筑学的,建筑方面的;与建筑物相似的

magnificent [mæɡˈnɪfɪs(ə)nt] *a.* 宏伟的,壮丽的;令人印象深刻的,出色的;高尚的,高贵的

household [ˈhaʊshəʊld] *n.* 家庭,一家人;(the Household)家务;王室　*a.* 家用的,家务的;全家人的;家喻户晓的;(Household) 皇家的

unparalleled [ʌnˈpærəleld] *a.* 无与伦比的,无双的;前所未有的,从未经历过的;独特的

flavor [ˈfleɪvə(r)] *n.* 情味,风味;香料;滋味　*vt.* 加味于

console [kənˈsəʊl] *v.* 安慰,慰藉

rhythm [ˈrɪðəm] *n.* (声音或运动的)节奏,韵律,节拍;节奏感;规则变化,节律;(艺术作品的)匀称,和谐;(韵文或散文)抑扬节奏

waterfront [ˈwɔːtəfrʌnt] *n.* 滩,海滨;水边　*a.* 滨水区的

commemorate [kəˈmeməreɪt] *vt.* 纪念,用以纪念;庆祝;深切怀念

abundant [əˈbʌndənt] *a.* 大量的,丰富的,充足的

in good stead 有利

possession [pəˈzeʃ(ə)n] *n.* (正式)拥有,持有;个人财产,所有物;持有违禁物,私藏毒品(或武器);(对球的)控制,球权;进攻;领地,殖民地;鬼魂附体,着魔;(观点或情感的)支配,控制

in possession of 拥有

distinguished [dɪˈstɪŋɡwɪʃt] *a.* 卓越的,杰出的;高贵的,尊贵的

signify [ˈsɪɡnɪfaɪ] *v.* 意味着,象征;(正式) 表达,显示(感情、意愿等);(正式) 要紧,有重要性

in memory of 纪念;为了纪念

thorny [ˈθɔːni] *a.* 多刺的,带刺的;棘手的,麻烦的

sage [seɪdʒ] *n.* (正式)智者,圣贤;鼠尾草(叶子用于烹饪);浅灰绿色　*a.* 睿智的,贤明的

orient [ˈɔːrient] *v.* 朝向,面对,使适合;定向放置(某物);确定方位,认识方向 (orient oneself);引导;使熟悉,帮助适应 *n.* 东方,东亚诸国(the Orient);(优质珍珠的)光泽;优质珍珠 *a.*〈文〉东方的,东方国家的;(尤指宝石)光彩夺目的;(太阳等)冉冉上升的,(白昼的光亮等)渐渐变强的

World Cultural Heritage 世界文化遗产

propitiously [prəˈpiʃəsli] *adv.* 吉祥地;顺利地

herald [ˈherəld] *v.* 预示……的来临;宣布,宣传;热烈欢迎;公开称赞 *n.* 预兆;使者,先驱

the richest land flowing with milk and honey 鱼米之乡

merge into 融入

ever-expanding [ɪkˈspændɪŋ] *a.* 不断发展壮大的;不断扩张的

scattered [ˈskætəd] *a.* 分散的,零散的

alley [ˈæli] *n.* 小巷,胡同;(两旁有树木、灌木或石头的)小径;(九柱戏和保龄球等游戏的)球道;(美)双打网球场两边的狭长地带

feature [ˈfiːtʃə(r)] *n.* 特点,特征;五官,面貌(特征);地貌;特写,专题节目;正片; 特点,特征 *v.* 以……为特色,以……为主要组成;起重要作用,占重要地位;放映,上演;担任主演

harmoniously [hɑːˈməʊniəsli] *adv.* 和谐地;调和地

densely [ˈdensli] *adv.* 密集地,稠密地;难懂地,费解地;(非正式)愚笨地,迟钝地

spatial [ˈspeɪʃ(ə)l] *a.* (space 表示"空间"时的形容词)空间的,与空间有关的;空间理解能力的

epitome [ɪˈpɪtəmi] *n.* 典型,缩影;摘要,概要

artificial [ˌɑːtɪˈfɪʃ(ə)l] *a.* 人造的,人工的;人为的;不真挚的,矫揉造作的

decay [dɪˈkeɪ] *v.* (建筑、地方等)破败,衰落;(观念、影响力等)衰败;(使)腐朽,腐烂 *n.* 腐烂;(观念、机构、制度等)衰退

visually [ˈvɪʒuəli] *adv.* 形象化地;外表上

incisively [ɪnˈsaɪsɪvli] *adv.* 敏锐地;激烈地

relics [ˈrelɪks] *n.* 遗迹;遗骸;纪念物 (relic 的复数)

organic [ɔːˈgænɪk] *a.* 有机的,绿色的;有机物的,生物的;构成有机整体的,不可分割的;自然的,演进的;器官的,器质性的;仿自然形态的 *n.* 有机物质;有机食品

sentient [ˈsentiənt] *a.* 有感情的;有感觉力的;意识到的 *n.* 有知觉的人

第二节 水利瑰宝
Section B Water Conservancy Treasures

中国水利起源、发展与中华文明的发展历程同步，水利一直都是国家发展的重要内容之一。兴水利、除水患，历来是中华民族治国安邦的大事。

The origin and development of water conservancy in China are synchronized with the evolution of Chinese civilization. Water conservancy is one of the most important national development goals. Water conservancy development and flood disasters elimination, throughout the ages, have been a vital affair for administering state affairs and ensuring national security.

学者谭徐明认为，水文化遗产是社会历史发展过程中人们对水的认识、利用所保存下来的重要文化遗存，以水利工程、水利文物、水利技术以及与水相关的活动等形态存在。其中，水利是对自然影响最大的人类活动，它源于人类对自然的理解，也源于社会的物质需求。水利是在广大的范围和程度上对自然的改造，改变后的自然环境又反馈给人类社会。

The scholar Tan Xuming believes that water-related culture is an important cultural heritage preserved through people's knowledge and utilization of water in the process of social and historical development. These heritages exist in the form of water conservancy projects, water conservancy cultural relics, water conservancy technologies, and water-related activities. Actually, water conservancy is a human activity which has the greatest impact on nature. It comes from humans' understanding of nature as well as the material needs of society. Water conservancy is the transformation of nature in a wide range and degree. In return, the reshaped natural environment feeds back to human society.

中国水利起源要晚于尼罗河、两河流域，后来黄河流域却较西方更早地完成了向封建社会的过渡，统一了中国，并且在黄河下游建成了规模宏大的堤防工程，开凿了灵渠、邗沟等运河工程和郑国渠、都江堰等灌溉工程，中国因此在水利上达到了世界领先地位。中国水利资源除河湖、湿地等自然景观和文物遗产、特色文化等人文景观之外，还有一批各式各样的水利工程景观。

The origin of China water conservancy is late compared with that of the Nile or the Mesopotamia Basin. However, the Yellow River Basin was earlier in the completed transition to the feudal society than the West. After the unification of the country, our country began to build large-scale embankment engineering and dig ditches such as the canal engineering (e. g. Linqu Canal and Hangou Canal) and other irrigation projects (e. g. Zhengguo Canal and Dujiang Dam) in the lower reaches of the Yellow River. China then reached the world's leading position in water conservancy. In addition to natural landscapes such as rivers, lakes and wetlands, as well as cultural landscapes such as cultural relics and characteristic cultures, there are also other various landscapes of water conservancy projects in China.

从古至今,我国建造的水利工程主要有运河、水利枢纽、堤坝圩堰、水关闸涵、码头渡口、陂塘水利、水文化遗址、水文化建筑、镇水神兽、水利碑刻、水文站、井泉和古桥,等等。它们经过历史的发展和沉淀,逐渐成为优秀的中华文化瑰宝。如江苏省淮安市的码头三闸(惠济闸、通济闸和福兴闸)遗址作为重要的水工遗产点,是世界文化遗产中国大运河淮安段两个遗产区之一的清口枢纽的核心区。诸如此类具有几千年历史的水利工程不仅在抵御洪涝灾害上发挥了重要作用,而且也孕育了丰富的水文化。

The water conservancy projects built in China mainly include canals, water conservancy hubs, dykes, water gate culverts, wharves, pond irrigation works, heritage sites, water-related cultural buildings, water-related holy beasts, irrigation inscription, hydrological stations, wells, springs and ancient bridges, etc. All of these constructions have become exquisite Chinese cultural treasures with historical development. For example, as an important hydraulic heritage site, the Three Quay Sluice (which consists of Huiji Sluice, Tongji Sluice and Fuxing Sluice) in Huai'an, Jiangsu Province, is the core area of Qingkou Junction Station. Such water conservancy projects with thousands of years history play an important role in resisting flood and waterlogging and breed a rich water-related culture.

与此同时,以水利工程为依托,以保护水资源、提升水工程、优化水环境、建设水生态、传播水文化为宗旨的水利风景区也日渐兴起。水利风景区的建设和发展是水利工程的功能拓展和水域景观的场所再造,改变了人们对水利发展和水资源利用的传统观念,满足了人们对良好生态产品的追求,是水利行业改革深化、发展民生水利的重要内容,也是经济社会发展的必然结果。

At the same time, relying on water conservancy projects, water conservancy scenic spots with the purpose of protecting water resources, improving water engineering, optimizing the water environment, constructing water ecology and spreading water culture are also on the rise day by day. Construction and development of water conservancy scenic spots is the very place where the function of the water conservancy project development and water landscape change the traditional concept of water conservancy development and water resource utilization, and meet the people in the pursuit of good ecological products. Water conservancy industry is an important content of deepening reform, development and water conservancy of the people's livelihood, and the inevitable result of economic and social development as well.

New Words, Phrases and Expressions

synchronize [ˈsɪŋkrənaɪz] *v.* (使)同步;对准(钟、表);相符;(电脑)同步化

evolution [ˌiːvəˈluːʃ(ə)n] *n.* 进化(论);演变,发展;(气体的)释放,(热量的)散发;队形变换,位置变换

elimination [ɪˌlɪmɪˈneɪʃn] *n.* 消除,排除;淘汰;消灭,铲除;排泄

throughout the ages 古往今来;这么多年来

administer [ədˈmɪnɪstə(r)] *vt.* 管理,治理;执行,实施;给予(药物或治疗);给予帮助,关心照顾(某人);主持(仪式等);执行遗产管理人的职责

ensure [ɪnˈʃʊə(r)] *vt.* 确保,保证;保护,使安全

utilization [ˌjuːtəlaɪˈzeɪʃn] *n.* 利用,使用 (=utilisation);利用,使用

transformation [ˌtrænsfəˈmeɪʃ(ə)n] *n.* (彻底或重大的)改观,变化,转变;舞台场景的突变;(动物生命周期中的)变态;(物理)嬗变,核的转换;(数学或逻辑)变换;(语言学)转换;遗传转化;细胞转化

reshape [ˌriːˈʃeɪp] *vt.* 改造;重新塑造

the Nile 尼罗河

Mesopotamia [ˌmesəpəˈteɪmiə] *n.* 美索不达米亚(亚洲西南部)

basin [ˈbeɪs(ə)n] *n.* 盆;洗涤槽;流域;盆地,海盆;内港,内湾

the Yellow River Basin 黄河流域

transition [trænˈzɪʃ(ə)n] *n.* 过渡,转变;(分子生物)转换;(乐)临时转调;(物理)跃迁,转变　*v.* 转变,过渡

feudal [ˈfjuːd(ə)l] *a.* 封建(制度)的

embankment [ɪmˈbæŋkmənt] *n.* 路堤;堤防

the lower reaches of the Yellow River 黄河流域下游

irrigation [ˌɪrɪ'geɪʃ(ə)n] *n.* 灌溉;冲洗(尤指伤口)
culvert ['kʌlvət] *n.* 涵洞;阴沟;电缆管道
wharf [wɔːf] *n.* 码头,停泊处 *v.* 靠码头;把货卸在码头上;为……建码头
holy beast 神兽
inscription [ɪn'skrɪpʃ(ə)n] *n.* 题词;铭文;刻印
hydrological [ˌhaɪdrə'lɒdʒɪkəl] *a.* 水文学的
exquisite [ɪk'skwɪzɪt] *a.* 精致的,精美的;剧烈的;细致的,有鉴赏力的
hydraulic [haɪ'drɒlɪk] *a.* (通过水管等)液压的,水力的;(机器)液压驱动的;与水利(或液压)系统有关的;(水泥)水下凝固的;(与)水力学(有关)的
quay [kiː] *n.* 码头
sluice [sluːs] *n.* 水闸;蓄水;洗矿槽 *vt.* 冲洗;开闸放水 *vi.* 奔流
junction ['dʒʌŋkʃ(ə)n] *n.* (公路或铁路的)交叉口,岔道口;汇合处,交叉点;(电子)接口;连接,结合;(高速公路的)出入口;(铁路的)枢纽站,联轨站
waterlogging ['wɔːtəˌlɔgiŋ] *n.* (水文)涝;水浸
breed [briːd] *v.* 交配繁殖;饲养,培育;养育,培养;引起,酿成 *n.* 品种;(人的)类型,种类
ecology [i'kɒlədʒi] *n.* 生态学;生态;生态系统;生态保护运动
inevitable [ɪn'evɪtəb(ə)l] *a.* 必然发生的,不可避免的;总会发生的,惯常的 *n.* 必然发生的事,不可避免的事

C-E Language Disparity 4—Parataxis vs. Syntaxis 意合与形合

Parataxis refers to the connection between words or clauses without linguistic formal means, and the grammatical meaning and logical relationship in sentences are expressed through the meaning of idioms or clauses. (所谓意合,指的是词语或分句之间不用语言形式手段连接,句中的语法意义和逻辑关系通过习语或分句的含义表达。) The American Heritage Dictionary (给"意合"定义为): "The arranging of clauses one after the other without connectives showing the relation between them. For example: *The rain fell*; *the river flooded*; *the house washed away*." 汉语造句主要采用意合法. The so-called **hypotaxis** refers to the phenomenon that the words or clauses in a sentence are connected by linguistic formal means (such as connective words) to express grammatical meaning and logical relations.) (所谓形合,指的是句子中的词语或分句之间通过诸如连接

词语等语言形式手段连接来表达语法意义和逻辑意义）The American Heritage Dictionary（给"形合"定义为）："The dependent or subordinate construction or relationship of clauses with connectives, for example, *I shall despair if you don't come*." 英语造句主要采用形合法。

Chinese Parataxis

In Chinese sentences, formal connective means are rarely used or even not used, and emphasis is placed on covert coherence, logical order, function and meaning, as well as divine form. Chinese has much less hypotaxis than English: there are no relative pronouns, relative adverbs, conjunctive pronouns and conjunctive adverbs, which are commonly used in English. There are only about 30 prepositions, and most of them are "borrowed" from the verbs. In Chinese, there is no morphological change in words, no substitute words such as "it" and "there", and pronouns are seldom used. In short, "all unnecessary formal devices should be avoided as much as possible", and parataxis is emphasized. The relationship between words is often implicit, and grammatical meaning and logical connection are often hidden between the lines.

1. Word Order 语序

a.（因为）她不老实，我不能信任她。Because she is not honest, I can't trust her.

b. 我不能信任她，因为她不老实。I can't trust her, because she is not honest.

c. 人（若）不犯我，我（则）不犯人。We will not attack unless we are attacked.

d. 说是说了，没有结果。（=我虽然说了，但是没结果。）I made proposals, but they proved futile.

e. 打肿脸充胖子，吃亏的是自己。If you get beyond your depth, you will suffer.

f. 人到事中迷，就怕没人提。When a man is lost in a labyrinth, what he needs badly is a hint.

g. 抓住了主要矛盾，一切问题就可以迎刃而解。Once the principal contradiction is grasped, all problems can be readily solved.

2. Repetition/Restatement 反复、Metaphor 隐喻或 Simile 明喻、Contrast 对照、Antithesis 对偶等，这些句式词语整齐、匀称，往往不用关联词

a. 他不来，我不去。If he doesn't come here, I'll not go there.

b. 种瓜得瓜，种豆得豆。As you sow, so will you reap.

c. 聪明一世，糊涂一时。Smart as a rule, but this time a fool.

d. 东边闪电出日头，西边闪电必有雨，南边闪电天气热，北边闪电有雷雨。If it lightens in the east, it will be sunny; if it lightens in the west, it will be rainy; if it lightens in the south, it will be sultry; if it lightens in the north, it will be stormy.

3. Compressed Sentence 紧缩句

a. 有水大家喝。Let everybody share the water if there is any.

b. 不到黄河心不死。Until all is over, ambition never dies.

c. 问遍千家成行家。Learn from numerous advisers, and you'll become a master.

d. 上梁不正下梁歪。If the upper beam is not straight, the lower ones will go aslant. /When those above behave unworthily, those below will do the same.

4. (Two) Four-Character Structure (两)四字格

a. 逆水行舟，不进则退。Learning is like rowing upstream, not to advance is to drop back.

b. 酒令智昏 When one is in, wit is out. = Wine dulls the mind.

c. 水到渠成 Where water flows, a channel is formed. = A canal is formed when water comes. = When conditions are ripe, success is inevitably achieved. = When conditions are ripe, success will come.

d. 滴水穿石 Despite weak power, unremitting efforts will lead to success.

e. 水火无情 Floods and fires occur with violent force and show no mercy.

f. 水落石出 When the water subsides the rocks emerge.

g. 水涨船高 When the river rises, the boat floats high. = When water rises, the boat rises with it. = A ship rises with the tide — a person's social rise benefits those related to him. = Particular things improve with the improvement of the general situation.

Chinese language attaches importance to parataxis, function and meaning, often without connection means, so it is relatively concise. English attaches importance to hypotaxis, structure and form, often with the help of various means of connection, so it is relatively precise. In order to determine the function and meaning of a sentence, we must first analyze its structure and form. In Chinese-English translation, the function and meaning of the sentence should be analyzed before the structure and form of the sentence can be determined. Please appreciate the following examples:

a. 牡丹江水,汹涌澎湃,如万马奔腾,一泻千里。Waves upon waves, the Peony River rushed violently down its long course like a horse galloping.

b. 我躺在床上,睡不着,听着雨点儿落在路面上,啪啪作响。我思绪万千,恍恍惚惚进入了一条幽暗的通道,回想起许多痛苦的往事,心里一阵冰凉,不禁感到毛骨悚然。As I lie awake in bed, listening to the sound of those razor-sharp drops pounding on the pavement, my mind goes reeling down dark corridors teeming with agonizing flashbacks, and a chill from within fills me with dread.

c. 江南水乡的建筑一般都比较密集,湖泊、河流、小巷交叉穿梭存在,水、路、桥和谐地融为一体。With ever-expanding network of scattered lakes, rivers and alleys, water towns in the south of the Yangtze River obviously feature a dense architectural style.

d. 另外,在新的哲学思潮(如玄学)的冲击下,汉朝以来"罢黜百家,独尊儒术"的思想控制日趋软弱松弛,于是出现"越名教而任自然"(嵇康)、"法自然而为化"(阮籍)之类的主张。"自然"指宇宙自然规律,岿然不动的山和变动不居的水,则最充分、最完美地体现了这种规律,也就成了师法的对象,成了精神力量不竭的源泉。In addition, under the impact of new philosophical trends such as metaphysics, the ideological control of "deposing hundreds of schools of thought and respecting Confucius alone" became increasingly weak and lax since the Han Dynasty, hence such propositions as "going beyond all the constraints of all kinds of name and fame, and morals and ethics and letting human nature develop freely" (Ji Kang) and "following the Taoism of Nature and ruling without doing anything" (Ruan Ji) emerged. "Nature" refers to the natural law of the universe, and the immovable mountains and the ever-changing water embody this law most fully and perfectly, and have become the object of teaching and the source of inexhaustible spiritual strength.

English Hypotaxis

A variety of forms are commonly used in English sentence formation to connect words, phrases, clauses, where overt cohesion, sentence form, structural integrity, and form manifestation are emphasized.

1. Relatives and Conjunctions

Relative words include relative pronouns, relative adverbs, conjunctive pronouns, and conjunctive adverbs, such as *who*, *whom*, *whose*, *that*, *which*, *what*, *when*, *where*, *why*, *how*, etc., which are used to connect the main clause with the attributive clause, subject clause, object clause or predicate clause. Conjunctions include juxtative and subordinate conjunctions, such as *and*, *or*, *but*, *yet*, *so*, *however*, *as well as*, *(n)either... (n)or...*, *when*, *while*, *as*, *since*, *until*, *so... what*, *unless*, *lest*, etc. Please study the following examples:

a. 那是个天气晴朗、金色的秋天，美好的秋色为那些青年们送别。待到战后和平时期，黄叶纷飞的秋天再度来临，当日的青年已经失去青春，有的丧失了生命。

It had been a fine, golden autumn, a lovely farewell to those who would lose their youth, and some of them their lives, ***before*** the leaves turned again in a peacetime fall.

b. 但不论水光或山色，必定都是未曾经过诗人知性介入或情绪干扰的山水，也就是山水必须保持耳目所及之本来面目。

But whether it is water or scenery, it must be a landscape that has not been interfered with by the poet's intellect or emotions, ***that is***, the landscape must remain ***as*** it is within the reach of the eyes and ears.

c. 当然，诗中的山水并不局限于荒山野外，其他经过人工点缀的著名风景区，以及城市近郊、宫苑或庄园的山水亦可入诗。

Of course, the landscapes in the poetry are not limited to the barren mountains and wilderness, but also include other artificially decorated famous scenic spots, ***as well as*** the suburbs of cities, palaces ***or*** estates.

d. 山水诗的出现，不仅使山水成为独立的审美对象，为中国诗歌增加了一种题材，而且开启了南朝一代新的诗歌风貌。

The emergence of landscape poetry **not only** made landscape an independent aesthetic object, added a theme to Chinese poetry, ***but also*** initiated a new poetry style of the Southern Dynasty generation.

2. Prepositions

Prepositions include simple prepositions such as *with*, *no*, *in*, *of*, *about*, *between*, *through*, synthetic prepositions such as *inside*, *onto/upon*, *within*, *without*, *throughout*, and idiomatic prepositions such as *according to*, *along with*, *apart from*, *because of*, *in front of*, *on behalf of*, *with regard to*. Please appreciate the following examples:

a. 彩虹有多种颜色,外圈红,内圈紫。

The many colors ***of*** a rainbow range ***from*** red ***on*** the outside ***to*** violet ***on*** the inside.

b. 这是一次精心组织的会议。市政厅里济济一堂、热情洋溢,主持会议的是斯特朗先生。

This was an intelligently organized and fervent meeting ***in*** a packed Town Hall, ***with*** Mr. Strong ***in*** the chair.

c. 第十七回对大观园里的水进行了细致描写,“一带清流,从花木深处曲折泻于石隙之中”,“清溪泻雪,石磴穿云,白石为栏,环抱曲沼,石桥三港,兽面衔吐”,贾宝玉因此有“绕堤柳借三篙翠,隔岸花分一脉香”的联语。

Chapter 17 gives a detailed description of the water in the Grand View Garden, “A clear stream welling up where the trees were thickest wound its way ***through*** clefts in the rocks”, “a crystal stream cascading as white as snow and stone steps going down ***through*** the mist ***to*** a pool; this was enclosed ***by*** marble balustrades and spanned ***by*** a stone bridge ornamented ***with*** the heads ***of*** beasts ***with*** gaping jaws”, Jia Baoyu therefore has this tablet: “Willows ***on*** the dyke lend their verdancy ***to*** three punts;/Flowers ***on*** the further shore spare a breath ***of*** fragrance”.

d. 联语“寒塘渡鹤影,冷月葬花魂”,使整个氛围、情境全都跃然纸上,称得上是《红楼梦》水文化震撼人心的绝唱。白鹤被惊扰而无奈地飞出寒塘,林黛玉和史湘云也会像它一样逃离现实的寒塘啊。月,沉在寒塘里才称得上冷月,两具诗魂葬在里面,真是适得其所。“水”中的意蕴,值得细细咀嚼。

With the couplet“A stork's shadow flit across the chilly pool;/The flowers' spirit is buried in cold moonlight.”, the whole atmosphere and the whole situation all leap ***out of*** the paper, which can be called the shocking swan song ***of*** the water culture of *A Dream **of** Red Mansions*. The stork was disturbed and helplessly flew

out of the cold pond. Just ***like*** the stork, Lin Daiyu and Shi Xiangyun would escape ***from*** the cold pond ***of*** reality. The moon, sunk ***in*** the cold pond, is called the cold moon. The two poetic souls were buried ***in*** the moonlight, which is really suitable ***for*** its place. The implication ***of*** "water" is worth deliberating ***on***.

3. Other means of connection, such as morphological change, including affix change, verb, noun, pronoun, adjective and adverb morphological change (such as gender, number, time, aspect, voice, mood, comparative, person, etc.) are used to maintain consistent relationships. The pronoun is widely used to maintain the relationship of response, and "it" and "there" as substitutes are used to connect. Please study the following examples:

a. 他吹嘘说,任何奴隶一踏上英国的土地就获得自由,而他却出卖穷人家六岁的孩子到工厂干活,每天十六个小时,受尽鞭打责骂。

He boasts that a slave is free ***the moment*** he sets foot ***on*** British soil and he sells the children ***of*** the poor ***at*** six years ***of*** age to work ***under*** the lash ***in*** the factories ***for*** sixteen hours a day.

b. 他们恐怕免不了在有生之年要蒙受不洁之名,人们会说他们贸然采取行动,使最高会议遭到搁浅,而且,可以设想,还可能挑起了一场核战争。

They would have had to live the rest ***of*** their lives ***under*** the stigma ***that*** they had recklessly precipitated an action ***which*** wrecked the Summit Conference and conceivably could have launched a nuclear war.

c. 山川之美,古来共谈。高峰入云,清流见底。两岸石壁,五色交辉。青林翠竹,四时俱备。晓雾将歇,猿鸟乱鸣。夕日欲颓,沉鳞竞跃。实是欲界之仙都。

The beauty ***of*** mountain***s*** and river***s*** has been discuss***ed*** in ancient time***s***. The peak enter***s*** the cloud***s***, and the clear stream bottom***s*** out. The stone wall***s*** ***on*** both side***s*** ***of*** the bank are intertwined ***with*** five color***s***. Green forest***s*** and bamboo are ready ***at*** all time***s***. The mist will vanish, and the ape***s*** will sing. The sun is fall***ing***, and the bottom fish are jump***ing***. It is actually the heavenly capital ***of*** desire and lust.

d. 有关"住",风水学是一门独到的学问,水在其中有着重要的影响。数千年来,我国人民的居住讲究依山傍水、临水而居,据说可以趋福避祸。

As far as dwelling is concerned, "fengshui" is a unique branch of knowledge, in which water has an important impact. This is the very reason ***why*** over thousands of years we Chinese people attach great importance ***to*** living nearby mountain***s*** with water***s*** or living nearby water***s*** with mountain***s***, ***which*** is said to have the potential to avoid misfortune***s*** and advance towards blessing***s***.

C-E Translation Strategies and Skills 4—Amplification vs. Omission 增译与省译

Amplification

Amplification is the addition in the target text of words that did not appear in the source text but without affecting the original meaning.

1. Amplification for Grammatical Purpose 语法增译

a. 他得寸进尺。Give him an inch ***and*** he will take a mile.（增加连词 and）

b. 小不忍则乱大谋。If ***one*** is not patient in petty things, ***one*** will never be able to command great ventures.（增加两个 one）意译：Patience is a virtue./Anger and haste hinder good counsel.

c. 广告是很挣钱的生意，大部分电台和电视台都是靠广告收入生存的。

Commercial business is very profitable, ***and*** most radio and TV stations depend on the income.（增加连词 and）

d. 天长地久有时尽，此恨绵绵无绝期。（白居易）

The eternal universe sometimes comes to an end, ***but*** my unceasing complaint knows no limit.（增加连词 but，明确转折关系）

e. 大多数物质热胀冷缩。

Most substances expand ***in*** heating and contract ***in*** cooling.（增加汉语中没有的两个介词 in）

f. 不同种类的钢，临界温度各不相同。

The critical temperature is different ***for*** different kinds of steel.（增加汉语中没有的介词 for）

g. 她把手插到口袋里。

She put ***her*** hands into pockets.（增加 her 这一形容词性物主代词）

h. 最新数字表明通货膨胀率有所下降。

The latest figures indicate ***a*** fall in the inflation rate.（增加汉语中没有的冠词和不定冠词）

i. 生活没有目标就像航行没有指南针。

Living without ***an*** aim is like sailing without ***a*** compass.（增加汉语中没有的不定冠词 an 和 a）

j. 借助火箭可以把卫星送上太空。

Satellites can be sent into space with ***the*** help of rockets.（增加汉语中没有的冠词）

k. 在电压相同的情况下，导线的电阻越大，流过的电流就越小。

The greater ***the*** resistance of a wire, ***the*** less electric current will pass through it under ***the*** same pressure.（增加汉语中没有的 4 个冠词）

l. 在开始使用本仪器前，请首先仔细阅读说明书。

Before ***you*** begin to work the instrument, first read the instruction carefully.（增加主语 you）

m. 在使用这些仪器前，必须弄清楚它的各种性能。

You must know the **properties** of the device before you use it.（增加主语 you）

n. 要干哪一行爱哪一行。

You have got to like what you do.（增加主语 you）

o. 车未停稳，请勿上下车。

Do not enter or exit ***while*** the vehicle is moving.（增加连词 while 表示连接）

p. 有工作经验的人将优先录用。

The applicants who had worked at a job would be preferred in getting the position ***over those who had not***.（增加介词短语 over those who had not）

q. 大街小巷早就传开了各种流言蜚语。

Rumors had already spread ***along*** the streets and lanes.（增加介词 along）

2. Amplification for Semantic Purpose 意义增译

a. 济公劫富济贫。

Jigong, ***Robin Hood in China***, robbed the rich and helped the poor.（增补背景知识）

b. 三个臭皮匠，顶（抵）个诸葛亮。

Three cobblers ***with their wits combined*** equal Zhuge Liang ***the master***

mind.（增补 with their wits combined 和 the master mind 背景知识）

c. 姜太公钓鱼，愿者上钩。

Jiang Taigong, ***Jiang Shang*** of the 11th century BC was said to fish by the Weishui River (present Shensi) one day, holding a fishing line with the hook three feet above the water, saying at the same time that "Whoever is ordained, come and take the bait."（加注相关文化背景信息，补充典故意义）

d. 诸葛亮 Zhuge Liang, ***the master mind***（音译加注）

老子 Lao Tze, ***an ancient Chinese philosopher***（音译加注）

e. 下海 xiahai (starting a shop or going out doing business at the risk of losing one's permanent job)（音译加注）

f. 油条 youtiao (a Chinese snack, fried sticks made of dough)（音译加注）

g. 雪茄烟 cigar（音译加意译）

波尔卡舞 polka（音译加意译）

3. Amplification for Rhetorical Purpose 修辞增译

a. 本章简单回顾一下计算机的应用理论。

This chapter **provides** a brief review of applicable theory for computer.（增加动词 provides）

b. 重力垂直向下作用，使物体具有"重量"。

The force of gravity acts vertically downwards and gives an object "**weight** or **heaviness**".（增加 weight 的同义词 heaviness）

c. 正如我们所知，电子围绕着原子核旋转。

As we know, electrons revolve about the **nucleus**, or **center**, of an atom.（增加 nucleus 的近义词 center）

d. 黄河流域是中国古代文明的诞生地，也是中国早期历史上最繁荣的地区。

The Yellow River basin is the **cradle** of China's ancient civilization and was once the most prosperous region in the early history of China.

e. 长江流经多种不同的生态系统，是诸多濒危物种的栖息地，灌溉了中国近五分之一的土地。

The Yangtze River, which flows through varied ecosystems along its passage, offers habitats to many endangered species and provides irrigation to about 1/5 of China's land.

Omission

Omission is the reduction in the target text of words that appeared in the source text but without affecting the original meaning. It may be for grammatical purpose, for semantic purpose and for rhetorical purpose.

1. Omission for Grammatical Purpose 语法减译

1）省译动词

a. 目前，欧洲、美国以及亚洲一些发达地区已经开始研究**推行**电子货币的**可能性**。

At the moment, developed areas in Europe, the United States and Asia have already started studying the **possibility** of electronic currency.（省译动词"推行"）

b. 读书使人充实，讨论**使人**智慧，写作**使人**准确。

Reading makes a full man; conference a ready man; and writing an exact man.（省译两个动词"使人"）

c. 我们不会后悔，我们从来没有**后悔**过，我们将来也不会**后悔**。

We don't regret, we never have and never will.（省译"后悔"）

2）省译名词

a. 无知是恐惧的根源，也是敬佩的**根源**。

Ignorance is the **mother** of fear as well as of admiration.（省译第二个"根源"）

b. 不跟人打招呼或是不回应别人的招呼，**便是**失礼、不友好的**表现**。

Failure to greet a person you recognize or to answer a greeting given to you is an unkindness to the other person, and very bad manners.（省译"便是……的表现"）

c. 他**满脸**皱纹，**皮肤**黝黑，头发灰白稀疏。

He was wrinkled and black, with scant gray hair.（省译"满脸"和"皮肤"）

d. 一种新型的飞机正越来越引起人们的注意——这种飞机**体积**不大，**价格**便宜，是无人驾驶飞机。

A new kind of aircraft—small, cheap, pilotless—is attracting increasing attention.（省译"体积"和"价格"）

e. 他读过**书**写过**字**。

He can read and write.（省译作宾语的名词）

3）省译副词

a. 你我**当年**暗中相见，

我**今日**悲痛难言。

In secret we met,

I silence I grieve.（省译“当年”和“今日”，通过 met 这一过去时和 grieve 这一现在时表现出来）

b. 群山**渐渐**没入天际。

Hills melt into the sky.（省译副词“渐渐”）

4）省译语气助词

a. 别**再**提它了。让过去的事过去**吧**。

Don't mention it. Let bygones be bygones.（省译“再”和语气助词“吧”）

b. 勤劳是财富的右手，节俭是她的左手。

Industry is fortune's right hand, and frugality her left.（省译“is”和“hand”）

5）省译连词

他**虽**有很多成就，**但**还是谦虚谨慎。

With all his achievements he remains modest and prudent.（省译“虽”和“但”）

2. Omission for Semantic Purpose 意义减译

a. 剑桥**大学**创建于 13 世纪。

Cambridge was founded in the 13th century.（省译“大学”）

b. 莫高窟壁画的内容**包罗万象，无所不及**，反映了人类生活的各个方面。

The contents of the murals in Mogao Grottoes mainly indicate various sides of ancient Chinese lives.（省译“包罗万象，无所不及”）

c. 本品限于外用，**禁止口服**；切勿喷入口、眼、鼻。

This Aerosol is used externally only. Never spray into mouth, eyes, nostrils.（省译“禁止口服”）

d. 中国**过去不曾**、**现在没有**、**将来也不会**对世界的能源安全构成威胁。

China **did not**, **does not** and **will not** pose any threat to the world's energy security.（省译表示时态的时间概念词“过去不曾、现在没有、将来也不会”，通过英语时态变化即可）

3. Omission for Rhetorical Purpose 修辞减译

a. 友谊可以滋生美德,**也可以催生**邪恶。

Companionship ministers to virtue or vice.

b. 不尝**黄连**苦,怎知**蜂蜜**甜。

Who had not tasted bitter knows not what is sweet. (省译"黄连"和"蜂蜜")

c. 和平与发展仍然是时代的主题,**求**和平、**谋**发展、**促**合作已经成为不可阻挡的时代潮流。

Peace and development remain the main themes of the present era, and **pursuit of peace, development and cooperation** has become an irresistible trend of the times. (省译动词"谋、促",三个动词"求、谋、促"译为"pursuit")

d. **立刻**推出了马车——**瞬间**就套好了马——车夫们**迅速地**跳上车——乘客们**急忙**各就各位。

e. **Out** came the chaise— **in** went the horse— **on** sprang the boys— **in** got the travelers. (通过 out, in, on 以及 in 四个副词倒装,省译表示速度的四个副词"立刻、瞬间、迅速地、急忙")

Please appreciate the following passage:

河流之歌

沿着整条河都可听见歌声。它洪亮而有力度,那是船夫,他们划着木船顺流而下,船尾翘得很高,船边系着桅杆。这也许是比较急促的号子。那些纤夫拉着纤逆流而上,如果拉的是小木船,也许只要五六人,如果拉的是要过急滩、扬着横帆的大船,就要二百多人。一个汉子站在船中央不停地击鼓助威,让他们加劲。于是,他们用尽全身的力量,像着了魔似的,腰弯成两折,有时力量要全部用完了就全身趴在地上匍匐前进,就像田里的牲口。他们用力,拼命用力,对抗着水流无情的磅礴之力。领头的在纤绳前后不停地奔跑,见到有人没有用尽全力,就用竹板打他的光背。每个人都必须竭尽全力,否则就要前功尽弃。就这样他们还是唱着激昂热烈的号子,那汹涌澎湃的河水号子。我不知道用怎样的词语才能描写出这样的拼搏,它体现了除了紧绷的心弦,几乎要断裂的筋肉,同时也体现了人类以不屈不挠的精神克服着无情的自然力。虽然绳子可以扯断,大船可以倒退,但险滩最终能通过,在结束筋疲力竭的一天之后,可以痛快地吃上一顿饱饭……

生活如此艰难、如此残酷,这喊声正是最后的绝望的抗议。这就是河流之歌。

The Song of the River

You hear it all along the river. You hear it, loud and strong, from the rowers as they urge the junk with its high stem, the mast lashed alongside, down the swift running stream. You hear it from the trackers, a more breathless chant, as they pull desperately against the current, half a dozen of them perhaps if they are taking up a sampan, a couple of hundred if they are hauling a splendid junk, its square sail set, over a rapid. On the junk a man stands amid ships beating a drum incessantly to guide their efforts, and they pull with all their strength, like men possessed, bent double; and sometimes in the extremity of their travail they crawl on the ground, on all fours, like the beasts of the field. They strain, strain fiercely, against the pitiless might of the stream. The leader goes up and down the line and when he sees one who is not putting all his will into the task he brings down his split bamboo on the naked back. Each one must do his utmost or the labour of all is vain. All still they sing a vehement, eager chant, the chant of the turbulent waters. I do not know how words can describe what there is in it of effort. It serves to express the straining heart, the breaking muscles, and at the same time the indomitable spirit of man which overcomes the pitiless force of nature. Though the rope may part and the great junk swing back, in the end the rapid will be passed; and at the close of the weary day there is the heavy meal ...

Life is too hard, too cruel, and this is final despairing protest. That is the song the river.

(Written by William Somerset Maugham)

C-E Guided Translation Practice 4

1. 我国水文化底蕴深厚,水文化遗产作为水文化的重要历史沉淀尤为重要。面对水文化遗产严峻的生存形势,应探索解决办法,针对重要的水文化遗产应积极联合文物和文化部门申报国家、省、市级文物保护单位和国家级、省级非物质文化遗产,开展分级保护,在重要的水文化遗产前竖立文物保护碑,介绍该遗产的有关情况及其重要性。针对特定遗产聚集区的不同水文化遗产,应统筹进行有针对性的研究和探讨、制定相应方案,开展跨流域、跨省区的大区域范围内点、线、面相结合的水文化遗产保护。

2. 水文化遗产是人类水事活动中的遗存物，是人类治水历史和社会发展的见证，因此历史性是其显著特性，不同的历史时代、不同地域、不同民族呈现出不同的历史文化特征。水文化遗产具有重要的历史文化价值，表现在三方面。一是记录历史文化。非物质文化遗产当中许多记录人类的水事活动，表述了人类与水的关系。广泛流传于民间的神话、传说、史诗、歌谣、文学、故事中含有大量的水事历史题材，是水文化遗产的重要内容。二是表征社会发展水平，水文化的历史性、时代性，表征出古代的总体社会经济发展水平。一方面，水事活动可以体现古代社会经济状况、农业生产水平；另一方面，通过人与水的协调关系可以透视社会政治、文化艺术和哲学思想。三是传承优秀文化成果和精神思想。水文化是中华民族文化的母体文化，融合和集聚了中华儿女优秀的劳动创造和文化成果，是民族文化的精髓。“治国者必先治水”，治水理念经提炼后可以形成为治国理念，甚至可以上升为哲学思想，并对宗教信仰、道德文化、人生哲理产生深刻影响。

3. 大运河(The Grand Canal)是世界上最长的人工河，北起北京，南至杭州。它是中国历史上最宏伟的工程之一。修建之初是为了运输粮食，后来也用于运输其他商品。大运河沿线区域逐渐发展成为中国的工商业中心。长久以来，大运河对中国的经济发展发挥了重要作用，有力地促进了南北地区之间的人员往来和文化交流。

4. 都江堰(Dujiangyan)坐落在成都平原西部的岷江上，距成都市约 50 公里，始建于公元前 3 世纪。它的独特之处在于无须用堤坝调控水流。两千多年来，都江堰一直有效地发挥着防洪与灌溉作用，使成都平原成为旱涝保收的沃土和中国最重要的粮食产地之一。都江堰工程体现了我国人民与自然和谐共存的智慧，是全世界年代最久、仍在使用、无坝控水的水利工程。

5. 坎儿井(Karez)是新疆干旱地区的一种水利系统，由地下渠道将水井连接而成。该系统将春夏季节渗入(seep into)地下的大量雨水及积雪融水收集起来，通过山体的自然坡度引到地面，用于灌溉农田和满足人们的日常用水需求。坎儿井减少了水在地面的蒸发(evaporation)，对地表破坏很小，因而有效地保护了自然资源与生态环境。坎儿井体现了我国人民与自然和谐共存的智慧，是对人类文明的一大贡献。

6. 生态文明建设是“五位一体”总体布局和“四个全面”战略布局的重要内容。各地区各部门要切实贯彻新发展理念，树立“绿水青山就是金山银山”的强烈意识，努力走向社会主义生态文明新时代。

要深化生态文明体制改革，尽快把生态文明制度的“四梁八柱”建立起来，把生态文明建设纳入制度化、法治化轨道。要结合推进供给侧结构性改革，加快推动绿色、循环、低碳发展，形成节约资源、保护环境的生产生活方式。要加大环境督查工作力度，严肃查处违纪违法行为，着力解决生态环境方面突出问题，让人民群众不断感受到生态环境的改善。各级党委、政府及各有关方面要把生态文明建设作为一项重要任务，扎实工作、合力攻坚，坚持不懈、务求实效，切实把党中央关于生态文明建设的决策部署落到实处，为建设美丽中国、维护全球生态安全作出更大贡献。（2016 年 11 月 28 日，习近平《树立“绿水青山就是金山银山”的强烈意识》）

第五单元　水与科学和工程技术

Unit 5　Water, Science and Engineering Technology

水是人类生存和发展不可缺少的一种宝贵资源，也是所有生物不可缺少的物质基础。人类自诞生起就一直与水打交道，不断积累对水的认识和用水经验。可以说，关于水知识的积累并形成相关学科的历史非常悠久，无法准确说出其起源时间。截至目前，关于水的学科、行业、理论方法及生产实践可以说是“五花八门”，这也符合人类不同阶段、不同层次、不同行业、不同观念、不同信仰对水的认识的多元化。水科学与工程技术作为广义水文化的一部分，在人们生活、社会、经济及贸易发展过程中发挥着非常重要的作用。

Water is not only an indispensable precious resource for human survival and development, but also an indispensable material basis for all organisms. Mankind has been dealing with water since its birth/inception, and has continuously accumulated knowledge and experience in water use. The history of the accumulation of water knowledge and the formation of related disciplines is very long, and it is impossible to ascertain when it started. Up to now, the disciplines, industries, theoretical methods and production practices of water are "of all kinds". This is also in line with the diversification of human understanding of water at different stages and levels, in terms of different industries, concepts, and beliefs. As part of the broad water culture, water science and engineering technology play a very important role in the development of people's lives, society, economy and trade.

第一节　水与科学
Section A　Water and Science

1. 什么是水科学
1. What is water science?

水科学的定义在学界中颇有争议，人们对水科学的理解多种多样，涉及的研究范畴也很难界定清楚。有时候可笼统地用“水科学”这一词汇，但作为一门学科，还需进一步界定其概念、内涵和研究范围。

The definition of water science is quite controversial in academic circles. People have various understandings of water science, and the research scope involved is also difficult to define clearly. Sometimes the term "water science" can be used as a broad term. But as a discipline, its concept, connotation and research scope need to be further defined.

从研究内容来看,可以把水科学描述为对“水”的开发、利用、规划、管理、保护、研究,涉及多个行业、多个区域、多个部门、多个学科、多个观念、多个理论、多个方法、多个政策、多个法规,是一个庞大的系统科学。我们不妨把研究与水有关的学科统称为水科学。具体来说,水科学是一门研究水的物理、化学、生物等特征,分布、运动、循环等规律,开发、利用、规划、管理与保护等方法的知识体系。

From the perspective of research content, water science can be described as the development, utilization, planning, management, protection, and research of "water" involving multiple industries, regions, departments, disciplines, concepts, theories, methods, policies, laws and regulations. It is a huge systematic science. We might as well refer to the study of water-related disciplines collectively as water science. Specifically, water science is a knowledge system that studies the development, utilization, planning, management, and protection of water's physical, chemical, and biological characteristics, distribution, movement, and circulation.

2. 水科学研究什么

2. What does water science study?

因为水科学的涉及范围十分广泛,很多方面仍处于探索阶段,人们对水科学学科体系、研究框架的认识还不是很成熟。大致上,我们可以把水科学的研究分成相互交叉的 10 个方面,即水文学、水资源、水环境、水安全、水工程、水经济、水法律、水文化、水信息、水教育。

Owing to the fact that the scope of water science is very broad and still in the exploratory stage, the understanding of the discipline system and research framework of water science is not yet mature. In general, we can divide the research of water science into 10 intersecting aspects, namely hydrology, the science of water resources, water environment, water safety, water engineering, water economy, water law, water culture, water information, and water education.

水文学是地球科学的一个重要分支,它是一门研究地球上水的起源、存在、分布、循环和运动等变化规律,并运用这些规律为人类服务的知识体系。水文学主要讨论的内容和学科分支有很多,几乎所有涉及地球上自然水体的知识研究都与水文学有密不可分的关系。

Hydrology is an important branch of earth science. It is a knowledge system that studies the origin, existence, distribution, circulation, and movement of water on earth, and uses related laws to serve mankind. There are many main topics and branches of hydrology. Almost all knowledge studies involving natural water bodies on earth are closely related to hydrology.

水资源学是在认识水资源特性、研究和解决日益突出的水资源问题的基础上逐步形成的一门研究水资源形成、转化、运动规律及水资源合理开发利用基础理论并指导水资源开发、利用、保护、规划、管理的知识体系。

Water resources science is a knowledge system that is gradually formed in order to understand the characteristics of water resources, research and solve increasingly prominent water resources problems. It can guide the development, utilization, protection, planning, and management of water resources.

水环境内容较广,涵盖所有与水有关的环境学问题,但不包括环境治理工程的设计、施工等内容。

The content of water environment science is very broad, covering all water-related environmental issues, but excluding the design and construction of environmental treatment projects.

水安全包括洪水、干旱、污染给人们生命和财产带来的安全威胁,讨论危害机理及安全调控。水安全不仅包括常指的洪水、干旱带来的安全问题,还包括由于污染问题带来的水环境变化对人们身体健康产生的影响。

The science of water safety studies the security threats to life and property caused by floods, droughts, and pollution, and discusses the mechanism of hazards and safety regulations. It includes not only the safety problems caused by floods and droughts, but also the impact of water environment changes on people's health caused by pollution.

水经济领域所涉及的研究依旧聚焦于水及其运用管理本身,只是偏向于运用经济学理论来帮助研究水系统中的经济问题。

Research in the field of water economics focuses on water and its use and management itself, especially revolving around applying economic theories to the practical economic issues in the water system.

水法律、水文化、水信息、水教育均属于对水的管理及其与人类社会联系的研究领域,聚焦多个维度,研究水在各个领域内不同的发展,以及水对于各个领域的作用和意义。

The disciplines of water law, water culture, water information, and water education all belong to the research field of water management and its connection with human society, focusing on multiple dimensions, the developments of water in various fields, and the role and significance of water in various fields.

New Words, Phrases and Expressions

organism [ˈɔːɡənɪzəm] *n.* 生物,有机体,(尤指)微生物;有机组织或体系
inception [ɪnˈsepʃ(ə)n] *n.* (机构、组织等的)开端;创始
accumulate [əˈkjuːmjəleɪt] *v.* 积累,积攒
accumulation [əˌkjuːmjəˈleɪʃn] *n.* 积累,堆积;堆积物;堆积量
ascertain [ˌæsəˈteɪn] *vt.* 查明,确定
in line with 与……一致;符合
diversification [daɪˌvɜːsɪfɪˈkeɪʃ(ə)n] *n.* 新产品的开发;多样化经营
controversial [ˌkɒntrəˈvɜːʃ(ə)l] *a.* 有争议的,引发争论的
academic [ˌækəˈdemɪk] *a.* 学业的,学术的;学校的,学院的;学业(成绩)优秀的,善于学习的;不切实际的,空谈的 *n.* 大学教师,学者;(学校或学院的)课程;大学生
connotation [ˌkɒnəˈteɪʃ(ə)n] *n.* 内涵意义,隐含意义,联想意义
might as well 不妨,何妨;还是……的好
distribution [ˌdɪstrɪˈbjuːʃn] *n.* 分发;分销,配送;(电影在各院线的)发行,上映;分配;分布
circulation [ˌsɜːkjəˈleɪʃ(ə)n] *n.* 发行量,销售量;血液循环;流传,流通;参加社交活动,交际;环流,循环;(图书的)借出
exploratory [ɪkˈsplɒrət(ə)rl] *a.* 勘探的;探究的;考察的
mature [məˈtʃʊə(r)] *a.* 成熟的,理智的;成年的,发育完全的;中老年的;技艺精湛的,技巧娴熟的;审慎考虑的,深思熟虑的;(经济、行业或市场等)成熟的 *v.* (使)成熟或长成;变理智,(举止)变成熟
intersect [ˌɪntəˈsekt] *v.* 相交,交叉;横穿,横断;(与……)相交叉,(与……)相关联
hydrology [haɪˈdrɒlədʒɪ] *n.* 水文学,水文地理学
prominent [ˈprɒmɪnənt] *a.* 重要的,著名的;显眼的,突出的;突起的,高耸的
hazard [ˈhæzəd] *n.* 危险,危害;(不可避免的)风险;(高尔夫球道)障碍物(如池塘或沙地);〈文〉机会,机遇 *v.* 冒失地提出,冒险猜测;使遭危险,使处于危险之中

第二节　水与工程技术
Section B　Water and Engineering Technology

1. 水利工程的定义
1. The definition of water conservancy engineering

人类社会为了生存和可持续发展，采取各种措施，适应、保护、调配和改变自然界的水和水域，以求在与自然和谐共处、维护生态环境的前提下，合理开发利用水资源，防治洪涝、干旱、污染等各种灾害。研究这类活动及其对象的技术和理论知识体系称为水利科学，为达到这些目的而修建的工程则称为水利工程。所有与水相关的工程技术中，与我们人类息息相关的正是水利工程。水利工程学以工程设施为手段，控制和改造河流，达到为人类社会谋取经济利益的目的。

For survival and sustainable development, human society has adopted various measures to adapt to, protect, deploy and change natural waters and watersheds, so as to rationally develop and utilize water resources and prevent floods, drought, pollution and other disasters under the premise of coexisting in harmony with nature and protecting the ecological environment. The technical and theoretical knowledge system that studies such activities and their objects is called water conservancy science, and the projects built to achieve these goals are called water conservancy engineering. Among all water-related engineering technologies, the most closely related to human beings is water conservancy engineering, in which engineering facilities serve as a means of controlling and transforming rivers to achieve the goal of seeking economic benefits for human society.

水利工程与水科学息息相关，但又不能等同。水利工程学科中研究水的特征、规律、开发利用等"软"的部分，同样是水科学的一部分；而水利工程中关于工程设计、实验、施工部分内容却不包括在水科学中。这些内容不仅仅适用于水利工程，也适用于其他行业。

Water conservancy projects are closely related to water science, but they are not the same thing at all. The "soft" part of the water conservancy engineering discipline that studies the characteristics, laws, development and utilization of water is also a part of water science. However, the part of water conservancy projects related to engineering design, experimentation, and construction is not included in water science. These contents are applicable not only to water conservancy projects but also to other industries.

2. 水利工程的分类

2. The categories of water conservancy engineering

水利工程按目的或服务对象可分为以下几个方面:

1）防止洪水灾害的防洪工程;

2）防止旱、涝、渍灾,为农业生产服务的农田水利工程(又称灌溉和排水工程);

3）将水能转化为电能的水力发电工程;

4）改善和创建航运条件的航道和港口工程;

5）为工业和生活用水服务,并处理和排除污水和雨水的城镇供水和排水工程;

6）防止水土流失和水质污染,维护生态平衡的水土保持工程和环境水利工程;

7）保护和增加渔业生产的渔业水利工程;

8）围海造田,满足工农业生产或交通运输需要的海涂围垦工程等。

另外,我们称同时为防洪、灌溉、发电、航运等多种目标服务的水利工程为综合利用水利工程。

Water conservancy projects can be divided into:

1) Flood control projects to prevent flood disasters;

2) Farmland water conservancy projects (also known as irrigation and drainage projects) to prevent drought, waterlogging and flooding and to serve agricultural production;

3) Hydropower projects that convert water energy into electrical energy;

4) Channel and port projects to improve and create shipping conditions;

5) Urban water supply and drainage projects that serve industrial and domestic water, and treat and remove sewage and rainwater;

6) Water and soil conservation projects and environmental water conservancy projects to prevent soil erosion and water pollution and maintain ecological balance;

7) Fishery engineering in water conservancy projects to protect and enhance fishery production;

8) Land reclamation and tidal flat reclamation projects that meet the needs of industrial and agricultural production or transportation.

In addition, we refer to water conservancy projects that serve multiple goals such as flood control, irrigation, power generation, and shipping at the same time as comprehensive water utilization projects.

3. 水利工程的特征及发展趋势

3. Characteristics and development trends of water conservancy projects

水利工程需要修建坝、水闸、进水口、堤、渡槽、溢洪道、筏道、渠道、鱼道等不同类型的水工建筑物,以实现其目标。因此,水利工程与其他工程相比有以下特点。

Water conservancy projects concern building different types of hydraulic structures such as dams, sluices, water inlets, embankments, water crossings, spillways, rafts, channels, and fish channels to achieve their goals. Therefore, compared with other projects, water conservancy projects have the following characteristics.

第一,水利工程工作条件复杂。水利工程活动中,各种水工建筑物的施工和运行通常都是在不确定的地质、水文、气象等自然条件下进行的,这就导致其工作环境较其他建筑物更为复杂,对施工的技术要求较高。

First, the working conditions of water conservancy projects are complicated. The construction and operation of various hydraulic structures in hydraulic engineering activities are usually carried out under uncertain geological, hydrological, meteorological and other natural conditions. The technical requirements are relatively strict.

第二,水利工程一般规模较大,工期较长,投资较多,技术较复杂。

Second, water conservancy projects are generally larger in scale and with longer construction periods, and involve more investment and apply more sophisticated technology.

第三,水利工程具有很强的综合性和系统性。单项水利工程是所在地区、流域内水利工程的有机组成部分,这些水利工程相互联系,相辅相成,相互制约。

Third, water conservancy projects are highly comprehensive and systematic. A single water conservancy project is an integral part of the comprehensive water conservancy project in the area or basin where it is located. They are interrelated, complementary and restrict one another.

第四,水利工程的效益具有随机性,其效益随着每年水文状况的变化而变化,其中,农田水利工程的效益直接受年降水量的影响。

Fourth, the benefits of water conservancy projects are random, and their benefits vary with the changes in hydrological conditions each year. Among them, the benefits of farmland water conservancy projects are directly affected by the annual precipitation.

第五,水利工程对环境影响很大。水利工程活动不但对所在地区的经济、政治、社会有影响,而且对湖泊、河流以及相关地区的生态环境、古物遗迹、自然景观,甚至对区域气候,都将产生一定程度的影响。

Fifth, water conservancy projects have a great impact on the environment. Water conservancy project activities not only affect the economy, politics, and society of the region, but also have a certain degree of impact on lakes, rivers and the ecological environment, ancient relics, natural landscapes in related areas, and even on regional climate.

当今世界多数发展中国家都面临人口增长过快、城镇供水紧张、可利用水资源不足、生态环境恶化、能源短缺等重大问题,都与水紧密相关。防治洪水、开发利用水资源关系到很多国家的社会经济发展。水利工程的未来发展趋势主要有以下六个方面。

The population of most developing countries in the world today is growing too fast, and the urban water is in short supply. The available water resources are stretched thin and the ecological environment is deteriorating. Besides, we are also faced with other problems such as energy shortage and so on. All these problems are closely related to water. Prevention and control of flood, development and utilization of water resources are related to the socioeconomic development of many contemporary countries. The future development trends of water conservancy projects are mainly as follows:

第一,将逐步加强对水利工程、水资源的统一调度、统一管理。

First, measures will be taken to further integrate the dispatching and management of water conservancy projects and water resources.

第二,将防治洪水的工程措施与非工程措施进一步结合,非工程措施地位越来越重要。

Second, engineering measures and non-engineering measures should be further combined to prevent and control flood, and non-engineering measures are becoming more and more important.

第三,随着新分析计算、监测试验手段、新勘探技术以及新工艺、新材料的发展,对高水头水工建筑物和复杂地基的施工、建设能力随之得到发展。同时,水利工程施工地的材料将得到更广泛的应用,这就会使水工建筑物的造价大幅降低。

Third, with the development of new analytical calculations, monitoring and testing methods, new exploration technologies, new techniques and new materials, the construction capabilities of high-head hydraulic structures and complex foundations will also be developed. At the same time, materials for construction sites of water conservancy projects will be more widely used, which will greatly reduce the cost of hydraulic structures.

第四,大范围、大区域的水资源调配工程,如跨流域引水工程,将会进一步发展。

Fourth, large-scale water resources allocation projects over large areas, such as inter-basin water diversion projects, will be further developed.

第五,水利工程的开发利用会向功能综合性、目标多样性发展。

Fifth, the development and utilization of water conservancy projects will develop towards comprehensive functions and diversified goals.

第六,水利工程的作用,在满足工农业生产发展、人民日益增长的生活的需要的同时,将其对生态环境的维护、促进生态环境可持续发展的功能提升到新的日程。

Sixth, according to the new agenda, water conservancy projects will be applied not only to meet the needs of the development of industrial and agricultural production and the growing needs of the people, but also to promote the protection of the ecological environment and the sustainable development of the ecological environment.

New Words, Phrases and Expressions

deploy [dɪˈplɔɪ] *vt.* 部署,调度;利用

rationally [ˈræʃnəli] *adv.* 理性地;讲道理地

premise [ˈpremɪs] *n.* 前提,假设;(企业或机构使用的)房屋及土地(premises);上述各项 *v.* 以……为基础或前提;预先提出;事先提到

facilities [fəˈsɪlətiz] *n.* (facility 的复数)设施;工具,设备

means [miːnz] *n.* 方法,手段;财富;金钱

applicable [əˈplɪkəb(ə)l] *a.* 适用的,适当的

drainage [ˈdreɪnɪdʒ] *n.* 排水系统;排水,排泄;排出的(污)水

hydropower [ˈhaɪdrəʊˌpaʊə(r)] *n.* 水力发出的电力;水力发电

convert [kənˈvɜːt] *vt.* (使)转变,(使)转换;(使)改变信仰,(使)皈依

erosion [ɪˈrəʊʒ(ə)n] *n.* 侵蚀,腐蚀;削弱,降低;糜烂,溃疡

fishery [ˈfɪʃəri] *n.* 渔业;渔场;水产业

reclamation [ˌrekləˈmeɪʃ(ə)n] *n.* 开垦;收回;再利用;矫正

comprehensive [ˌkɒmprɪˈhensɪv] *a.* 综合性的,全面的;有理解力的　*n.* 综合中学;专业综合测验

inlet [ˈɪnlet] *n.* 小湖湾,小河湾;(空气、气体或液体进入机器等的)进口;入口

duration [djuˈreɪʃn] *n.* 持续,持续时间

investment [ɪnˈvestmənt] *n.* 投资;值得买的东西;(时间、精力的)投入

sophisticated [səˈfɪstɪkeɪtɪd] *a.* 见多识广的,老练世故的;复杂巧妙的;先进的,精密的;水平高的;在行的;时尚的;精致的

systematic [ˌsɪstəˈmætɪk] *a.* 有系统的;有条理的;仔细周到的;一贯的,惯常的;分类的

complementary [ˌkɒmplɪˈment(ə)ri] *a.* 相互补充的,相辅相成的;互补色的;(与)补充医学(有关)的;(互为)余角的

restrict [rɪˈstrɪkt] *vt.* 限制,控制(大小、数量、范围);限制(活动或行为),妨碍;约束,管束;(以法规)限制;封锁(消息)

random [ˈrændəm] *a.* 任意的,随机的,胡乱的　*n.* 随意,随机

annual [ˈænjuəl] *a.* 一年一度的;年度的;(植物)一年生的　*n.* 一年生植物;年刊,年鉴

deteriorating [dɪˈtɪərɪəˌreɪtɪŋ] *a.* 退化的;恶化的

contemporary [kənˈtemp(ə)rəri] *a.* 当代的;现代的;同时期的,同时代的　*n.* 同时代的人;同龄人,同辈

trend [trend] *n.* 趋势,动态;时尚,风尚;热门话题

dispatch [dɪˈspætʃ] *v./n.* 派遣;发送;迅速处理,迅速办妥;杀死,处决

analytical [ˌænəˈlɪtɪk(ə)l] *a.* 具备分析能力的,善于分析的;分析(性)的

calculation [ˌkælkjuˈleɪʃ(ə)n] *n.* 计算,运算;估算,预测;算计,盘算

diversion [daɪˈvɜːʃ(ə)n] *n.* 转向,转移;绕行路,支路;转移注意力的事物,分心的事物;消遣,娱乐

diversified [daɪˈvɜːsɪfaɪd] *a.* 多样化的;各种的

agenda [ə'dʒendə] *n.* 待议事项,议事日程;(政治)议题;秘密计划或目标
maintenance ['meɪntənəns] *n.* 维护,保养;保持,维持;(依法应负担的)生活费,抚养费
sustainable [sə'steɪnəb(ə)l] *a.* (计划、方法、体制、自然资源等)可持续的,持续性的;站得住脚的

C-E Language Disparity 5—Dynamicity vs. Stativeness 动态与静态

Chinese is a language which is more dynamic than English. This is a very important phenomenon. Chinese dynamicity is reflected in the use of verbs, adverbs, verbal phrases, reduplication of verbs, linkage and parallelism, while English stativenss is manifested in the frequent use of nouns, prepositions, adjectives and compound sentences.

We live in a dynamic world, where motion and change are absolute, while stillness is relative. Every language has a large number of lexical items to express motions and actions, among which the verb is the most important and the most common. In this respect, Chinese and English are no exception. English has a large number of verbs, including verb phrases. It also merits attention that many grammatical meanings in English are expressed through various forms, such as morphological changes in verbs, indicating the tense, the voice, and the mood.

Theoretically, verbs are used to indicate actions, motions, states, and occurrences, usually reflecting dynamicity in the sentence. However, detailed studies find that different English verbs reflect different degrees of dynamicity, and verbs expressing strong dynamicity do not account for the majority in English. Compared with Chinese verbs, English verbs have a much lower degree of dynamicity, showing a strong tendency of stativeness, which is manifested in their function, classification, morphological changes, and pragmatic meanings.

Functions of Verbs

In English the part of speech of a word corresponds to its function in the sentence. Compared with Chinese verbs, English verbs play a lesser role in the sentence (or clause) and usually form the predicate. When used for other parts of the sentence, such as the attributive, they can only appear in the form of verbals. Generally, a sentence can have only one predicate verb (or two or more joined by conjunctions). But Chinese verbs play a much more active part in the sentence. There is no rule to restrict the use of verbs in the sentence: verbs (subject-predicate phrases or verb-object phrases, both of which contain verbs) can act as almost any part of the sentence, that is, as the subject, the object, an attributive, an adverbial, etc. In addition to the predicate, English is theoretically verb-centered, but in fact, it is the noun that occupies a dominant position; but in Chinese it is actually the verb that has much more dominance. It is also pointed out that many English verbs are often used to express such concepts with the notion of action, motion, behavior, change, state, characteristic, emotion, etc. As a matter of fact, the dynamicity of the English sentence is far weaker than that of the Chinese sentence. In this sense, the English sentence tends to be stative, while the Chinese sentence tends to be dynamic.

"Serial verb construction"(连动式)and "pivotal construction"(兼语式) are unique sentence patterns in Chinese. For example, in 她教跳舞,both 跳舞 and 教 appear in their original form without any morphological change, and no sign or marker can be seen to judge the degree of dynamicity. However, the idea must be expressed in English as "she teaches dancing", in which "dancing" has been conceptualized. The English version of 她教我跳舞 is "she taught me (how) to dance". Here the infinitive "to dance" still has a higher degree of conceptualization or abstraction, reflecting very weak dynamicity.

In Chinese, some verbs are found redundant in meaning. The bold words in the following sentences, for example, are puppet verbs.

1. 对经营不善、连年亏损的企业**进行**整顿,是非常必要的。
2. 应该对这样的做法**给予**鼓励。
3. 我们不允许任何人**从事**贩卖妇女儿童的活动。

In a sense, this also shows that Chinese is very dynamic.

Classification of Verbs

English verbs, though usually classified as "transitive" and "intransitive" like Chinese ones, are divided into "action verbs" and "state verbs" according to their degree of dynamicity, with the former reflecting a much stronger degree of dynamicity while the latter being called "stative verbs", for it reflects much weaker dynamicity. English linking verbs (which outnumber their counterparts in Chinese) also belong to a kind of state verbs with even lower degrees of dynamicity. English action verbs can be further divided into "instant verbs", "duration verbs", and "result verbs", duration verbs being less dynamic than instant verbs and result verbs being less dynamic still.

Chinese Dynamicity

The Chinese language has the habit of using verbs more oftentimes. Some Chinese sentences use verbs alone. Chinese verbs can be classified into the following types:

Behaviour verbs 行为动词:吃,喝,玩,踢

Existence or change verbs 存在和变化动词:有,在,出现,消失

Motion causing verbs 使动动词:惊天地,泣鬼神

Trend verbs 趋向动词:起来,来到,去到

Notion verbs 意念动词: 想

Linking verbs 关系动词:是

In Chinese, the past, present and future dynamicity are demonstrated by Chinese characters, such as"着、了、过".

Look at the following cases:

1) 说着话、跳着舞。(表示动作开始后、终结前的进行时)

2) 电视机开着。(表示动作完成后的存在形态)

3) 他正穿着新衣服呢!(动作进行)

4) 她穿着一身晚礼服。(动作完成后遗留状态的持续)

5) 年纪大了。(表示具备了年纪大的性状)

6) 来了五个人。(表示动作实现了、完成了)

7) 她现在到了南京。(现在实现)

8) 到了南京就来信。(将来实现)

9) 昨天我离开时她已经到了南京。(过去实现)

10) 我们去过黄山。(表示曾经发生"去"的动作)

11) 我打过毛衣。(表示曾经有打毛衣的经验)

12) 年前冷过一阵子。(表示曾经具有"冷"的状态)

13) 她年轻时也曾漂亮过。(表示过去有过"漂亮"的状态)

Chinese verbs are more dynamic than their English counterparts.

There are many ways of forming compound verbs in Chinese:

1. Repetition of the same verb or two synonymous verbs

Repetition of the same verb(s), such as 看看,玩玩,试试看, 挥挥手,蹦蹦跳跳,说说笑笑,走走看看,商量商量,合计合计,考虑考虑. Two verbs used together would surely add to the dynamicity. English hardly has any such usages, which makes its dynamicity much weaker than Chinese.

2. Use of two synonymous verbs

测量 (measure),思考 (think),比较 (compare),庆祝 (celebrate),欢呼 (cheer),批判 (criticize).

3. A verb plus its object 宾语

吃饭 (have/eat dinner),上学 (go to school),开会 (hold a meeting),走路 (walk on one's way),睡觉 (sleep),洗澡 (bathe),鞠躬 (bow),打架 (fight).

4. A verb plus its complement 补语

打碎 (break), 揭穿 (expose), 弄脏 (dirty), 搞臭 (defame), 打败 (defeat),粉碎 (smash).

When Chinese is being translated into English, Chinese dynamicity is often transformed into English stativeness, vice versa.

Please appreciate the following cases:

a. 这是一个秋天的下午。细雨淅沥,秋风瑟瑟。他们撑着雨伞,攀沿一个弯曲的山间小道去拜望一位隐居在深山的朋友。

They **walked** with umbrellas **up** a **winding** mountain path on a **drizzling** and windy autumn afternoon for a visit to a friend **living** in seclusion.

b. 我躺在床上,睡不着,听着雨点儿打在路面上,啪啪作响。我思绪万千, 恍恍惚惚进入了一条幽暗的通道,回想起许多痛苦的往事, 心里一阵冰凉,不禁感到毛骨悚然。

As I **lie awake in bed**, **listening to** the sound of those razor-sharp drops **pounding** on the pavement, my mind **goes** reeling down dark corridors **teeming with agonizing** flashbacks, and a chill from within fills me with dread.

c. 他信步至一山环水旋、茂林修竹之处,隐隐有座庙宇,门巷倾颓。

He **came to** luxuriant woods and bamboo groves **set** among hills and **interlaced** by streams, with a temple half hidden among the foliage, whose entrance **was** in ruins.

d. 医生迅速到达，并非常仔细地检查了病人，因此病人很快就康复了。

The doctor's extremely quick **arrival** and uncommonly careful **examination** of the patient brought about his very speedy **recovery**.

e. 她说这话时，挑衅地瞟了一眼，还把牙一龇。

She said this with a **provocative glance** and a gleam of teeth.

5. The use of verbs in the sentences

Chinese sentences have a particular preference for dynamic verbs while English sentences prefer stative verbs.

The Chinese action verb is replaced by a linking verb in English. This is by no means a rare case. The following are more examples:

a. 现在他们都准备好了。They ***are*** now all ***at the ready***.

b. 岸上密密麻麻长满了草。Now the bank ***was thick with*** grass.

c. 他们很快发现他们真的很走运。They soon ***found*** they ***were really lucky***.

d. 他父亲很明显因为他不懂规矩而不高兴地皱着眉。His father ***was*** clearly ***frowning*** because he didn't know the rules.

In Chinese, there is a frequent use of verb repetition, while in English, single actions are frequently expressed with the "verb + object" structure. For example, *have a look (at)*, *take a walk*, *do some washing*, *take care (of)*, *pay attention (to)*, *get rid (of)*, etc. Verbs in such structures like *have*, *take*, *do*, *pay*, etc., have been "weakened" and have lost their original meanings. (As action verbs, *take*, *do*, *pay*, etc., have stronger dynamicity than *have*.) In other words, their meanings have been made abstract, thereby retaining little dynamicity. Nouns serving as objects in this structure, though derived from verbs, hardly reflect any dynamicity, as they express a kind of conception. Comparatively speaking, Chinese often uses single verbs to express the same action or motion, reflecting strong dynamicity. English nouns in such structures may have adjectival modifiers (attributives), which, however, are often turned into adverbials modifying verbs when translated into Chinese.

English Stativeness

English uses fewer predicate verbs or other means to express the natural tendency of the meaning of the action. Generally speaking, each English sentence has only one single finite verb, except compound verbs.

Classification of English verbs:

Please classify the following verbs: *love*, *ask*, *think*, *talk*, *enlarge*, *remain*, *bathe*, *resemble*, *smell*, *kick*, *persuade*, *feel*, *materialize*, *hate*, *like*.

Action/Behaviour verbs: *ask*, *think*, *talk*, *bathe*, *kick*, *smell*

State verbs: *love*, *remain*, *resemble*, *smell*, *feel*, *hate*, *like*

Result verbs: *enlarge*, *persuade*, *materialize*

Morphological changes of English verbs:

English verbs have various morphological changes to express various grammatical meanings. However, verbs in different forms reflect different degrees of dynamicity. Study the following sentences:

a. She *goes* to school at 7 o'clock in the morning on weekdays. (with weaker dynamicity)

b. She *is going* to school with her younger brother. (with stronger dynamicity)

c. She *went* to school late yesterday because of staying up at night. (dynamicity is not so strong)

d. She *was going* to school with her classmate at this time. (with stronger dynamicity)

e. She *has studied* 4 years in that primary school. (dynamicity is not so strong)

f. She *can hardly remember* what had happened to her. (with weak dynamicity)

In a sense, English linking verbs can also be understood as a kind of state verb, especially the verb *to be*, whose dynamicity is even weaker than that of linking verbs like *become*, *turn* (*into*), which express changes.

Action or motion may be implied in other parts of speech: 1) Nouns; 2) Adjectives; 3) Prepositions.

English is a noun-dominated language, and many nouns imply the concept of action or motion, especially abstract nouns derived from verbs.

1. Nouns

a. 过去我自己也常有点儿胡思乱想。I used to be a bit of a *fancier* myself.

b. 可得小心点。大家都知道他可是动不动就要怪罪别人的。Be careful!

He is known as a ***blame shifter.***

c. 我们的免疫系统还不足以对抗这种新的疾病。Our immune systems are no *match* for this new disease.

2. Adjectives

a. 她说该提议具有建设性。She said the proposal was ***constructive***.

b. 成本太高,令人望而却步。High cost proved to be ***prohibitive***.

c. 许多投资者仍然对当地政策多变怀有戒心。Many investors are still ***fearful*** of the ever-changing local policies.

The comparative degree of English adjectives and adverbs also contain some implied action or motion as they often suggest the change of state or situation.

a. 我们都盼望情况会好转。We all expect a *better* situation.

b. 不断增强的综合国力使我们对外援的依赖性减少了。Increasing comprehensive national strength made us less dependent on foreign aid.

3. Prepositions

a. 她出了一身冷汗。She was ***in*** a cold sweat.

b. 说完这些话,她站起来走开了。***With*** these words she stood up and went away.

c. 我们主张有/讲原则的团结。We are ***for*** principled unity.

Please look at the following Chinese posters and their English equivalents:

a. 免费入场! 免票入场! Admittance Free!

b. 游客禁止入内! Off-limits for tourists!

c. 非公莫入! 员工专用! Staff only!

d. 前方危险! Danger ahead!

e. 仅限授权车辆! Authorized cars only!

C-E Translation Strategies and Skills 5—Conversion of Parts of Speech 词性转换

A. 汉语动词转为英语名词

1. 她教英语。She is a teacher of English.
2. 他能吃又能睡。He is a ***good eater*** and a ***good sleeper.***

3. 现在极需新的补救方法。Now, there is a ***crying need*** for a remedy.

4. 他希望还能再次访问中国。He ***expressed the hope*** that he would come over to visit China again.

5. 我过去常常有点喜欢胡思乱想。I used to be a bit of a ***fancier*** myself.

6. 你一定很不善于学习,要不然就是教你的人很不会教。You must be a very bad ***learner***; or else you must be going to a very bad ***teacher.***

7. 使用电子计算机可以大大提高劳动生产率。The ***application*** of electronic computers makes for a tremendous rise in labor productivity.

8. 他通晓多种不常使用的语言,这使我们大家感到惊讶。His ***familiarity with*** many rarely used languages ***surprised*** us all.

9. 了解一点世界史对研究时事很有帮助。An ***acquaintance with*** the world history is ***helpful to*** the ***study of*** the current affairs.

10. 激光是近年来最轰动的科学成就之一,因为它可以应用于许多科学领域,并且适合各种实际用途。Laser is one of the most sensational developments in recent years, because of its ***applicability*** to many fields of science and its ***adaptability*** to practical uses.

11. 通过润滑减少运动部件间的摩擦,大大地延长了机器的寿命。The ***reduction*** of friction between moving parts ***by lubrication*** has greatly ***prolonged*** the life of machines.

12. 由于粗心,他今年高考落榜了。***Carelessness caused*** his ***failure*** in this year's college entrance examination.

B. 汉语动词转为英语形容词

1. 有人认为,未来的计算机将具有智能。

Some people think tomorrow's computers will be **intelligent**.

2. 科学家们深信一切物质是不灭的。

Scientists are **confident** that all matter is indestructible.

3. 她正在眺望大海,显然没有看见他。

She was gazing across the sea, apparently **ignorant** of him.

C. 汉语动词转为英语介词

1. 发展的道路是漫长的,但是我们已经坚定地走上这条道路。

The road to development is long but we are firmly ***on*** it.

2. 他们反对这项提议。They are ***against*** the proposal.

3. 任何机器的输入功都等于输出功加上克服摩擦所做的功。

In any machine input work equals output work ***plus*** work done ***against*** friction.

D. 汉语动词转为英语副词

打开阀门,让空气进入。

Open the valve to let air **in**.

E. 汉语名词转为英语动词

1. 设计的目的在于可自动操作,调节方便,维护简易,生产率高。

The design **aims at** automatic operation, easy regulation, simple maintenance and high productivity.

2. 该仪器的特点是结构紧凑、携带方便。

The instrument is **characterized** by its compactness and portability.

F. 汉语名词转为英语形容词

1. 操作系统的质量决定着计算机的应用效能。

The quality of the operating system determines **how useful** the computer is.

2. 刀具必须有足够的强度、韧性、硬度,而且耐磨。

The cutting tools must be **strong**, **tough**, **hard** and **wear-resistant**.

G. 汉语名词词组转为英语副词

1. 但是,他们的思想工作没有他们的组织工作做得好。

They have not done so well ***ideologically***, however, as organizationally.

2. 他身体很弱。He is ***physically*** weak.

H. 汉语副词转为英语形容词

1. 图表可以直观地显示要说明的关系。

A graph gives a ***visual*** representation of the relationship.

2. 不断提高密封容器内气体的温度,会使气体的内压力不断增大。

A ***continuous*** increase in the temperature of a gas confined in a container will lead to a continuous increase in the internal pressure within the gas.

3. 她说这话时,挑衅地瞟了一眼,还把牙一龇。

She said this with a ***provocative*** **glance** and a gleam of teeth.（还包括动词"瞟"转译为名词 glance）

I. 汉语形容词转为英语名词

电子计算机和微处理器对我们来说十分重要。

Electronic computers and microprocessors are of great **importance** to us.

J. 汉语形容词转为英语动词

1. 他们说,这知识对他们要发明的一种有效的地震早期预警系统是必要的。

They said that such knowledge is **needed** before they can develop a successful early warning system for earthquakes.

2. 光束运载的信息比无线电信号运载的信息多。

Light beams can **carry** more information than radio signals.

K. 汉语形容词转为英语副词

1. 这台水压机的主要特点是操作简单、维修容易。

This hydraulic press is ***chiefly*** characterized by its simplicity of operation and the ease with which it can be maintained.

2. 袖珍式瓦斯检测器的主要特点是体积小、重量轻、功能齐全、连续工作时间长。

The miniature gas detector is ***chiefly*** featured by small size, light weight, complete functions and long continuous working time.

3. 牡丹江水,汹涌澎湃,如万马奔腾,一泻千里。

Waves upon waves, the Peony River rushed ***violently*** down its long course like a horse galloping.

4. 季节的每一更迭,气候的每一转变,乃至一天中的每一小时,都给这些山峦的奇幻色彩和形态带来变化,远近的主妇都把这些看作是精确的晴雨表。

Every change of season, every change of weather, indeed, every hour of the day, produces some change in the magical hues and shape of these mountains, and they are regarded by all good wives, ***far and near***, as perfect barometers.

Please appreciate the following and pay special attention to the

translation of Chinese verbs:

1. 世上最美的莫过于从泪水中挣脱出来的一丝微笑。

There's nothing more beautiful than a smile that **struggles through** tears.

2. 雪花大如棉桃,小如柳絮,纷纷扬扬,铺天盖地。

Snowflakes, as big as cotton bolls, as small as willow catkins, were **falling down heavily**, **covering** the world **with a cloak of snow**.

3. 婚姻好比鸟笼,外面的鸟儿想进进不去,里面的鸟儿想出出不来。

Marriage may be **compared** to a cage: the birds outside **despair** to **get in** and those within **despair** to **get out**.

4. 青年兴则国家兴,中国发展要靠广大青年挺膺担当。年轻充满朝气,青春孕育希望。广大青年要厚植家国情怀、涵养进取品格,以奋斗姿态激扬青春,不负时代,不负华年。(2023 年 1 月 1 日,国家主席习近平发表 2023 年新年贺词)

A nation will **prosper** only when its young people **thrive**. For China to **develop** further, our young people must **step forward** and **take on** their responsibilities. Youth is full of vigor and is a source of hope. Youngsters should keep their country in mind, **cultivate** keen enterprise, and live youth to the fullest with great drive, to **prove worthy of** the times and the splendor of youth.

5. 只要有愚公移山的志气、滴水穿石的毅力,脚踏实地,埋头苦干,积跬步以至千里,就一定能够把宏伟目标变为美好现实。(2023 年 1 月 1 日,国家主席习近平发表 2023 年新年贺词)

As long as we **have** the resolve to **move** mountains and the perseverance to **plod** on, as long as we **keep** our feet on the ground and **forge ahead** with our journey by **making steady progress**, we will **turn** our grand goals **into** reality.

6. 新中国诞生伊始,毛泽东就把治理长江等大江大河纳入议事日程。他曾多次实地考察长江水情,并亲自参与三峡工程的规划、设计与论证。

At the beginning of the birth of new China, Mao Zedong **put** the management of the Yangtze River and other major rivers ***on the agenda***. He **conducted field investigations** of the water situation of the Yangtze River many times and personally **participated in** the planning, design and demonstration of the Three Gorges Project.

7. 白求恩同志毫不利己专门利人的精神,表现在他对工作的极端的负责任,对同志对人民的极端的热忱。(毛泽东《纪念白求恩》,1939 年 12 月

21 日）

Comrade Bethune's spirit of dedicating himself exclusively to the interests of others without regard for himself was **demonstrated** in his utmost sense of responsibility in **performing** his work and his greatest enthusiasm in **helping** comrades and other people.

8.《道德经》讲："上善若水。"古往今来，江河给中华民族带来巨大福祉，但也造成了无穷无尽的灾难。毛泽东深谙治水与兴国安邦的关系，早在1934 年 1 月，他就在《我们的经济政策》一文中明确提出了"水利是农业的命脉"的著名论断。

Lao Tzu said: "The supreme goodness is like water." Throughout the ages, rivers have **brought** great benefits to the Chinese nation, but they have also **caused** endless disasters. Mao Zedong was **well aware of** the relationship between water management and the rejuvenation of the nation and security, and as early as January 1934, he clearly **stated** in his article "Our Economic Policy" that "water conservancy is the lifeblood of agriculture".

9. 中国在推进建设网络强国战略部署的同时，将秉持以合作共赢为核心的新型国际关系理念，致力于与国际社会携起手来，加强沟通交流，深化互利合作，构建合作新伙伴，同心打造人类命运共同体，为建设一个安全、稳定、繁荣的网络空间作出更大贡献。（2017 年 3 月 1 日《网络空间国际合作战略》）

While moving forward with the national strategy for cyber development, China will, **guided** by the vision for a new type of international relations **featuring** win-win cooperation, **work** with the international community to **strengthen** communication, **deepen** mutually beneficial cooperation, **forge** partnership and **build** a community of **shared** future for mankind, thus **making** greater **contributions to** a secure, stable and prosperous cyberspace.

10. 共同推动全球信息基础设施建设，铺就信息畅通之路。推动与周边及其他国家信息基础设施互联互通和"一带一路"建设，让更多国家和人民共享互联网带来的发展机遇。（2017 年 3 月 1 日《网络空间国际合作战略》）

China will work with other countries to strengthen global information infrastructure to **facilitate** smooth flow of information. It will **promote** information infrastructure connectivity and the Belt and Road Initiative with neighboring countries and beyond, so that more countries and their people can **share** the development opportunities **brought by** the Internet.

11. 经济全球化遭遇波折，多边主义受到冲击，国际金融市场震荡，特别是中美经贸摩擦给一些企业生产经营、市场预期带来不利影响。（《2019 年政府工作报告》）

Setbacks in economic globalization, **challenges** to multilateralism, **shocks** in the international financial market, and especially the China-US **economic and trade frictions**, **had an adverse effect** on the production and business operations of some companies and on market expectations.

12. 营造良好的科研生态，就一定能够迎来各类英才竞现、创新成果泉涌的生动局面。（《2019 年政府工作报告》）

If we **foster** a healthy research environment, we'll be sure to **see** brilliant and capable people **emerge** in all fields and **create** a boundless stream of innovations.

13. 面对新情况新变化，我们坚持不搞"大水漫灌"式强刺激，保持宏观政策连续性稳定性，在区间调控基础上加强定向、相机调控，主动预调、微调。（《2019 年政府工作报告》）

Facing new circumstances and developments, we **were firm** in **choosing** not to **adopt** a deluge of strong stimulus policies, and we **maintained** the continuity and consistency of macro policies. As we **conducted** regulation to **keep** main economic indicators within an appropriate range, we also **improved** targeted and well-timed regulation, and **carried out** anticipatory adjustments and fine-tuning.

14. 严格落实中央八项规定及其实施细则精神，坚定不移纠正"四风"。严肃查处各类违法违规行为，惩处腐败分子。（《2019 年政府工作报告》）

We **acted** in strict accordance with the central Party leadership's eight-point decision on conduct and the rules for its implementation. We **took stern action against** formalities **performed** for formalities' sake, bureaucratism, hedonism, and extravagance.

15. 中国将努力构建总体稳定、均衡发展的大国关系框架，积极同美国发展新型大国关系，同俄罗斯发展全面战略协作伙伴关系，同欧洲发展和平、增长、改革、文明伙伴关系，同金砖国家发展团结合作的伙伴关系。中国将继续坚持正确义利观，深化同发展中国家务实合作，实现同呼吸、共命运、齐发展。中国将按照亲诚惠容理念同周边国家深化互利合作，秉持真实亲诚对非政策理念同非洲国家共谋发展，推动中拉全面合作伙伴关系实现新发展。（国家主席习近平 2017 年 1 月 18 日在联合国日内瓦总部发表了题为《共同构建人类命运共同体》的演讲）

China will **endeavor to put in place** a framework of relations with major powers **featuring** general stability and balanced growth. We will **strive to build** a new model of major country relations with the United States, a comprehensive strategic partnership of coordination with Russia, partnership for peace, growth, reform and among different civilizations with Europe, and a partnership of unity and cooperation with BRICS countries. China will **continue to uphold** justice and friendship and **pursue** shared interests, and **boost** pragmatic cooperation with other developing countries to **achieve** common development. We will further **enhance** mutually beneficial cooperation with our neighbors under the principle of amity, sincerity, mutual benefit and inclusiveness. We will **pursue** common development with African countries **in a spirit of** sincerity, being result oriented, affinity and good faith. And we will **elevate** our comprehensive cooperative partnership with Latin America **to a higher level**.

16. “海纳百川，有容乃大。”开放包容，筑就了日内瓦多边外交大舞台。我们要推进国际关系民主化，不能搞“一国独霸”或“几方共治”。世界命运应该由各国共同掌握，国际规则应该由各国共同书写，全球事务应该由各国共同治理，发展成果应该由各国共同分享。（国家主席习近平2017年1月18日在联合国日内瓦总部发表了题为《共同构建人类命运共同体》的演讲）

“The ocean is vast because it admits all rivers.” Openness and inclusiveness have made Geneva **a center of multilateral diplomacy**. We should **advance** democracy in international relations and **reject dominance** by just one or several countries. All countries should jointly shape the future of the world, **write** international rules, **manage** global affairs and **ensure** that development outcomes are shared by all.

17. 坚持绿色发展。绿水青山就是金山银山。保护生态环境就是保护生产力，改善生态环境就是发展生产力，这是朴素的真理。我们要摒弃损害甚至破坏生态环境的发展模式，摒弃以牺牲环境换取一时发展的短视做法。要顺应当代科技革命和产业变革大方向，抓住绿色转型带来的巨大发展机遇，以创新为驱动，大力推进经济、能源、产业结构转型升级，让良好生态环境成为全球经济社会可持续发展的支撑。（《共同构建人与自然生命共同体》，习近平2021年4月22日在“领导人气候峰会”上的讲话）

We must **be committed** to green development. Green mountains are gold mountains. To **protect** the environment is to **protect** productivity, and to **improve** the environment is to **boost** productivity — the truth is as simple as that. We must **abandon** development models that **harm** or **undermine** the environment, and must **say no to** shortsighted approaches of **going after** near-term development gains at the expense of the environment. Much to the contrary, we **need to ride the trend of** technological revolution and industrial transformation, **seize** the enormous opportunity in green transition, and **let** the power of innovation **drive** us to **upgrade** our economic, energy and industrial structures, and **make sure** that a sound environment is there to **buttress** sustainable economic and social development worldwide.

C-E Guided Translation Practice 5

1. 瑞士作家、诺贝尔文学奖获得者黑塞说:"不应为战争和毁灭效劳,而应为和平与谅解服务。"国家之间要构建对话不对抗、结伴不结盟的伙伴关系。大国要尊重彼此核心利益和重大关切,管控矛盾分歧,努力构建不冲突不对抗、相互尊重、合作共赢的新型关系。只要坚持沟通、真诚相处,"修昔底德陷阱"就可以避免。大国对小国要平等相待,不搞唯我独尊、强买强卖的霸道。任何国家都不能随意发动战争,不能破坏国际法治,不能打开潘多拉的盒子。核武器是悬在人类头上的"达摩克利斯之剑",应该全面禁止并最终彻底销毁,实现无核世界。要秉持和平、主权、普惠、共治原则,把深海、极地、外空、互联网等领域打造成各方合作的新疆域,而不是相互博弈的竞技场。(国家主席习近平 2017 年 1 月 18 日在联合国日内瓦总部发表了题为《共同构建人类命运共同体》的演讲)

2. 三峡水电站,即长江三峡水利枢纽工程,又称三峡工程。中国湖北省宜昌市境内的长江西陵峡段与下游的葛洲坝水电站构成梯级电站。三峡水电站是目前世界上规模最大的水电站和清洁能源生产基地,也是目前中国有史以来建设最大型的工程项目之一。三峡水电站的功能有十多种,航运、发电、种植等。三峡水电站 1992 年获得中国全国人民代表大会批准建设,1994 年正式动工兴建,2003 年 6 月 1 日下午开始蓄水发电,于 2009 年全部完工。机组设备主要由德国伏伊特(VOITH)公司、美国通用电气(GE)公司、德国西门子(SIEMENS)公司组成的 VGS 联营体和法国阿尔斯通(ALSTOM)公司、瑞士 ABB 公司组成的 ALSTOM 联营体提供。

三峡水电站大坝高程 185 米，蓄水高程 175 米，水库长 2335 米，总投资 954.6 亿元人民币，安装 32 台单机容量为 70 万千瓦的水电机组。三峡电站最后一台水电机组于 2012 年 7 月 4 日投产，这意味着装机容量达到 2240 万千瓦的三峡水电站在 2012 年 7 月 4 日已成为全世界最大的水力发电站和清洁能源生产基地。

第六单元　水与体育运动和卫生健康

Unit 6　Water, Sports and Games, and Health and Hygiene

随着社会发展不断多元化，体育产业发展的规模和水平已成为衡量一个国家、社会发展进步的重要指标。水上体育运动作为现代体育运动项目的重要组成部分，丰富了人民的休闲娱乐活动，在国家经济建设中发挥了一定的作用，有着巨大的发展空间与潜力。

With the diversification of social development, the scale and progress of sports industry have become important indicators of the development of a country and society. As an important part of modern sports, water sports have enriched people's leisure and entertainment activities. With huge development, this industry has emerged as a main driving force for national economic growth.

水乃生命之源，人类的生存离不开水，离不开卫生、健康的水。随着知识水平提高，安全意识提升，人们越发重视饮用水安全、灾后水卫生等问题。“水碧无尘埃”也成了全体中国人民乃至世界人民共同的美好追求。

As the source of all life, water, especially clean and safety water, is essential to human survival. With the improvement of knowledge level and safety awareness, people pay more attention to issues such as drinking water safety and post-disaster water hygiene. "Clean and dust-free water" has become the common pursuit of people around the world.

第一节　水与体育运动
Section A　Water and Sports and Games

1. 水上运动的定义
1. Definition of water sports

水上运动是体育运动的一类，指在水域中，依靠肢体动作或借助船艇和其他器物进行体育运动的总称。其运动全部过程或主要运动过程都是在水下、水面或水上进行的。它是为了区别于陆上和空中体育项目，根据所处的运动环境而命名的。

Water sports is a kind of sports. The term refers to the general term for sports in waters that rely on body movements, boats and other implements. The whole process or the main process of water sports competitions and activities should be carried out underwater, on the surface of water or above the water. The term is named according to sports environments so as to distinguish it from land and aerial sports.

2. 水上运动的分类

2. Classification of water sports

水上运动可分为水上竞技项目、船类竞技项目、滑水运动、潜水运动。

Water sports can be divided into: aquatic sports, boat sports, water skiing, and scuba diving.

1）水上竞技项目主要包括游泳、跳水、水球和花样游泳四项。

1) Aquatic sports mainly include swimming, diving, water polo and synchronized swimming.

2）船类竞技项目主要包括划船运动、赛艇运动、皮划艇运动、帆板运动、摩托艇运动。

2) Boat sports mainly include boating, rowing, kayaking, windsurfing, and motor boating.

3）滑水运动是指人借助动力的牵引在水面上“行走”的水上运动。滑水运动包括水橇、滑水板和冲浪。

3) Water skiing is a surface water sport in which people"walk" on the water with the help of other instruments. It includes water skiing, wakeboarding, surfing, etc.

4)潜水运动是指运动员借助于轻便的潜水装具,在水下进行的竞赛和体育活动。包括竞速潜泳、水下橄榄球等。

4) Scuba diving sports refer to competitions and activities carried out underwater with light diving equipment. It includes racing snorkeling, underwater rugby, etc.

3. 水上运动产业发展现状

3. Current status of water sports industry

水上运动产业是以海洋、江河、湖泊为载体,以竞技、休闲、娱乐、探险、旅游为主要形式,向大众提供相关产品和服务的一系列经济活动,主要涵盖帆船、赛艇、皮划艇、龙舟、摩托艇、滑水、潜水等项目。

Taking major forms of competition, leisure, entertainment, adventure, and tourism, water sports industry consists of a series of economic activities that provide related products and services to the public with oceans, rivers, and lakes as its carriers. The industry covers different activities, including sailing, rowing, kayaking, dragon boat racing, motorboating, water skiing and scuba diving.

我国水上项目开展较晚，2004 年雅典奥运会上孟关良、杨文军获得男子双人划艇 500 米金牌，才实现了中国水上运动奥运金牌零的突破。自此，水上运动开始获得人民群众的广泛关注。目前，尽管我国水上运动产业仍处于起步阶段，但各类数据表明人们对水上运动的关注度不断增加，参与人群日益广泛，健身需求快速增长。据统计局数据表示，2019 年我国水上娱乐项目门票收入超过 190 亿元。其中，潜水、帆船、游泳、摩托艇等项目成为创收主力。

China's sports industry starts rather late. In 2004, Meng Guanliang and Yang Wenjun won men's Canoe Double (C2) 500m gold medal at the Athens Olympic Games, which was China's first Olympic gold medal in water sports. Since then, water sports began to gain extensive attention in China. At present, China's water sports industry is still in the initial stage. However, statistics show that people's interests in these activities have significantly increased. Therefore, there is a wider group of water sports participants and higher demand for physical health. According to the National Bureau of Statistics, the total revenue of China's water entertainment programs exceeded 19 billion *yuan* in 2019, among which scuba diving, sailing, swimming, motorboating and other projects were the major generators.

同时，根据体育总局等印发的《水上运动产业发展规划》，在确保我国水上运动产业快速发展的同时，必须按照“五位一体”总体布局和“四个全面”战略布局，牢固树立和贯彻落实创新、协调、绿色、开放、共享的五大发展理念，推进水上运动产业实现长久可持续发展。因此，在推动水上运动产业发展过程中，我们还需高度重视水资源浪费污染、多元产业融合、水资源管理体系优化、赛事活动供给等问题。

At the same time, according to the Water Sports Industry Development Plan issued by General Administration of Sport of China, as we push forward the progress of water sports industry, we must stay committed to the Five-sphere Integrated Plan and the Four-pronged Comprehensive Strategy. Moreover, we should work to achieve sustainable development of water sports industry in keeping with the Five Major Development Concepts, that is, innovation, coordination, green, openness and sharing. Thus, we must give high priority to water resources protection, industries integration, water resources system upgrade and supply for sports activities and competitions.

New Words, Phrases and Expressions

hygiene [ˈhaɪdʒiːn] *n.* 卫生;保健;卫生学,保健学

diversification [daɪˌvɜːsɪfɪˈkeɪʃ(ə)n] *n.* 新产品的开发,多样化经营

indicator [ˈɪndɪkeɪtə(r)] *n.* 标志,迹象;方向灯,转向指示灯;指示器/剂,显示器;指示(物)

entertainment [ˌentəˈteɪnmənt] *n.* 娱乐,娱乐表演;招待,款待

emerge [ɪˈmɜːdʒ] *vi.* 浮现,出现;显露,知悉;恢复过来,幸存下来;形成,兴起

survival [səˈvaɪv(ə)l] *n.* 生存,存活,幸存;遗留物,幸存物,残存物　*a.* 幸存的,赖以生存的,救生用的

underwater [ˌʌndəˈwɔːtə(r)] *a.* 水下的

distinguish [dɪˈstɪŋgwɪʃ] *vt.* 使有别于;看清,认出;区别,分清

aerial [ˈeəriəl] *a.* 航空的,从飞机上的;空中的,地表以上的;由飞机实施的;(植物的某部分)气生的;在空中翱翔的;(在)大气(中)的　*n.* 天线;(滑雪等运动的)空中腾越

classification [ˌklæsɪfɪˈkeɪʃ(ə)n] *n.* 分类,分级;类别,级别;(动植物等的)分类学,分类法;(图书馆的书、磁带、杂志等的)分类系统,编目

scuba [ˈskuːbə] *n.* (self-contained underwater breathing apparatus)水下呼吸器,水肺;带水肺潜水　*a.* 使用水肺的,有水下呼吸器的

water polo [ˈwɔːtə pəʊləʊ] *n.* 水球

synchronized [ˈsɪŋkrənaɪzd] *a.* 同步的;同步化的

kayaking [ˈkaɪækɪŋ] *n.* 皮划艇;皮艇运动

windsurfing [ˈwɪndsɜːfɪŋ] *n.* 帆板运动

motorboating [ˈməʊtəbəʊtɪŋ] *n.* 驾汽艇运动;汽船声

water skiing 滑水

snorkeling [ˈsnɔːklɪŋ] *n.* 潜;潜水;浅滩潜水

underwater rugby [ˈrʌgbi] *n.* 水下橄榄球

the Athens Olympic Games 雅典奥运会

extensive [ɪkˈstensɪv] *a.* 广阔的;广泛的;巨大的,大量的;(农业)粗放(经营)的

initial [ɪˈnɪʃ(ə)l] *a.* 开始的,最初的;(字母)位于词首的　*n.* (姓名的)首字母

participant [pɑːˈtɪsɪpənt] *n.* 参加者,参与者　*a.* 参与的

bureau [ˈbjʊərəʊ] *n.* 局,处,科;办事处,办公室;五斗橱,衣柜;书桌

revenue [ˈrevənjuː] *n.* (企业、组织的)收入,收益;(政府的)税收

exceed [ɪkˈsiːd] *vt.* 超过,超出;超越(限制);优于,胜过

billion [ˈbɪljən] *num.* 十亿

generator [ˈdʒenəreɪtə(r)] *n.* 发电机；产生者；电力公司；母点，母线，母面

push forward 推进；抓紧进行

integrated [ˈɪntɪgreɪtɪd] *a.* 各部分密切协调的，综合的；（机构、团体等）废止隔离（尤指种族隔离）的；（温度、面积等的）平均值的，总量的

overall [ˌəʊvərˈɔːl] *a.* 总的，全面的；所有的，包括一切的 *adv.* 全部，总共；总的说来，大体上 *n.* （英）（工作时穿的）罩衣；（英）（上下连身的）工作服，防护服（overalls）；（美）背带工装裤（overalls）；（英）骑马裤，紧身制服裤（overalls）

pronged [prɒŋd] *a.* 尖端分叉的；分为不同方向的

comprehensive [ˌkɒmprɪˈhensɪv] *a.* 综合性的，全面的；有理解力的 *n.* 综合中学；专业综合测验

strategy [ˈstrætədʒi] *n.*（尤指为获得某物制定长期的）策略，行动计划；战略，战略学

priority [praɪˈɒrəti] *n.* 优先事项，最重要的事；优先，优先权，重点；（英）优先通行权 *a.* 优先的

第二节　水与卫生健康
Section B　Water and Health and Hygiene

1. 水的重要性
1. The importance of water

水作为地球上众多生物体的主要组成部分，存在于日常生活中的每个角落。由于地理位置、肥胖指数、年龄和性别各异，每个人体内平均含有55%到60%的水。

As a major component of many organisms on earth, water exists in every corner of daily life. In spite of the geographical locations, obesity indices, ages and genders, generally speaking, as for a human body, 55% ~ 60% is composed of water.

日常生活中，维持体内水平衡对人体生命健康至关重要。人体平均每天会通过汗液、尿液、肠胃运动和呼吸等方式流失2到3升水。过多的水量流失会导致体内水含量过低，引发脱水或过度脱水症状。脱水会导致尿液浓缩，引起黑尿。而过度脱水则会引发眩晕、头痛、血压降低、神经紧张和认知障碍等症状；极端情况下，过度脱水会导致癫痫和死亡。因此，人体需及时补充体液流失，维持体内水平衡，避免脱水或过度脱水的情况发生。

In daily life, maintaining a balanced water level is essential for human life and health. On average, each person loses two to three liters of water a day through sweat, urine, gastrointestinal movements and breathing. Excessive water loss can lead to low levels of water in the body, leading to dehydration or excessive dehydration. Dehydration leads to concentrated, dark urine while excessive dehydration can cause dizziness, headaches, low blood pressure, nervousness and cognitive impairment. In extreme cases, excessive dehydration even results in seizures and death. Therefore, the body needs to compensate for the fluid loss and maintain a balanced water level in order to avoid dehydration or excessive dehydration.

那么,一天究竟该喝多少水呢？一般来说,我们所需的饮水量主要取决于体重和所处环境。男性推荐的每天水摄入量为2.5到3.7升,女性为2到2.7升。这一范围可根据自身身体状况进行适当增减。

So, how much water should we drink every day? The amount of water we need depends largely on our weight and the environment. The recommended daily intake of water varies from between 2.5 to 3.7 liters for men and about 2 to 2.7 liters for women. This range can be pushed up or down according to our health condition.

长期良好的饮水习惯对身体益处良多。研究显示,适当的体内水平衡能降低中风风险、控制肥胖、减少患癌率。总之,合理摄入安全、洁净的饮用水对维持基本身体健康至关重要。

Long-term good drinking habits are beneficial to our body. Studies have shown that proper drinking habits can reduce the risk of stroke, cancer and obesity. In conclusion, proper intake of safe and clean drinking water is crucial for physical health.

2. 水与人类生命安全

2. Water and human security

水,作为人体重要的能量来源,在生命的维系中起着不可或缺的作用。然而,纵观人类历史,水质问题或灾后介水传染病对人类造成健康危害的事件比比皆是。

As an important energy source of the human body, water plays an indispensable role in life. However, throughout human history, water pollution or water-borne communicable diseases caused by disasters have contributed to countless health hazards.

古话有言"大灾之后必有大疫",指的是洪水、海啸、地震等重大自然灾害后易暴发传染性疾病。在台风、暴雨等灾害后产生的大量积水会改变蚊子、苍蝇、老鼠等虫媒生物的生存环境,催生出大量蚊虫,为后续引发疟疾、登革热、痢疾等传染病提供了条件。有研究表明,1992—2021 年这 20 年间,全球共有 19 次灾后疫情暴发,其中最常发生的传染病是因饮食和饮水不洁导致的腹泻以及蚊虫传播的疾病。

There is an old saying that "there must be a severe epidemic after a major disaster", which means major natural disasters such as floods, tsunamis, and earthquakes are more often than not followed by infectious diseases. The large amount of stagnant water produced after disasters like typhoons and heavy rains will change the living environment of mosquitoes, flies, mice and other vector-borne organisms, spawning a large number of mosquitoes and providing conditions for subsequent infectious diseases including malaria, dengue fever and dysentery. Studies have shown that from 1992 to 2021, there had been 19 post-disaster outbreaks around the world. The most common infectious diseases are diarrhea caused by unclean food and drinking water and diseases transmitted by mosquitoes.

大规模的水安全事件,让人们越来越坚信饮用水安全是我们生存的基础。随着科学技术的发展,研究水平的提高和用水安全意识的提升,洪涝灾害后,卫生人员高度重视灾后介水传染病防治,极大避免了传染病暴发,保障了人民生命安全。现如今,"大灾之后必有大疫"在我们国家已经成为历史,我们早已实现了"大灾之后无大疫"的目标,但各类灾后水卫生问题仍需我们时刻警惕,加强关注。

Through large-scale water safety incidents, people reaffirm such a fact that safe drinking water is the basis of our survival. With the development of science and technology and the improvement of research level and water safety awareness, health workers attach great importance to the prevention and control of water-borne communicable diseases. Thus, we can avoid the outbreak of infectious diseases and ensure the safety of people's lives. Nowadays, what is described in the saying that "there will be a severe epidemic after a major disaster" has become a history in China. We have long realized the goal that there will be no severe epidemic after any major disaster. However, we still need to be vigilant and alert to water safety and sanitation problems after disasters.

3. 中国饮用水发展概述

3. A brief review of China's drinking water history

回顾历史，每一个政治、经济、社会的重要发展时期都离不开水卫生的支撑。新中国成立初期，由于历年的战争和灾荒，卫生环境恶劣，疾病流行，同时人民卫生意识薄弱，卫生管理人才缺乏，饮用水安全得不到保障。

An examination of history reveals that every important period of political, economic and social development relies on the support of water sanitation. In the early years of the People's Republic of China, due to years of wars and famine, the sanitation environment was poor and diseases were prevalent. Therefore, the safety of drinking water could not be effectively guaranteed because of the weak public awareness of sanitation and the lack of health management personnel.

饮水标准代表着饮水水平，饮水水平反映了一个国家的卫生安全意识、文明发展程度。改革开放后，中国与世界接轨，各类标准开始更新迭代。国家卫生主管部门决定更新中国生活饮用水卫生标准，让国人喝上更健康的饮用水。然而，中国幅员辽阔，各地水质状况、居民身体状况差距很大，水资源的数据采集和分析是一个很漫长的过程。在经过大量的研究，投入大量的精力后，中国结合国情和世界卫生组织饮水水质准则，彻底改变了中国饮用水标准。1985 年，《生活饮用水卫生标准》(GB 5749-1985) 出台，创新性地提出符合我国国情的水卫生标准。此标准在中国执行了 21 年。2006 年，卫生部同各有关部门完成对 1985 年水卫生标准的修订，持续为国人饮用水健康保驾护航。

Drinking water standards represent the quality of drinking water, while drinking water quality reflects a country's awareness of health and safety, civilization and development. Since reform and opening-up, China has taken measures in line with the rest of the world and updated various standards. The national health authorities decided to improve China's drinking water sanitation standards so that people can drink healthier drinking water. However, vast territory, different water quality and health conditions of residents have made data collection and water resources analysis tough jobs. After a lot of research and hard work, China has made progress in its drinking water standards with a thorough consideration of both national conditions and guidelines of WHO for drinking water quality. In 1985, the upgraded *Drinking Water Sanitation Standard* (GB 5749-1985) was rolled out, which later proved to go well with China's national conditions. This standard has been implemented in China for 21 years. In 2006, the Ministry of Health and other relevant departments revised the original standards and continued to protect the health of Chinese people.

世界卫生组织认为,"享有安全用水是人类的一项根本需求"。安全的饮用水保障了人类的生命安全和健康,推动了人类文明的进步。截至目前,全球仍然有18亿人口使用未经任何处理的饮用水,对与水相关的疾病没有任何防范。

The World Health Organization (WHO) believes that "access to safe water is a fundamental need of man". Safe drinking water guarantees the safety and health of human life and promotes the progress of human civilization. Today, there is a population of 1.8 billion people in the world living with untreated drinking water and lacking prevention of water-related diseases.

今天,中国已经进入绿色发展、高质量发展的新时代,共建共享、全民健康的理念引领着全体中国人民在追求高品质饮用水、健康水的道路上砥砺前行,为全世界饮用水卫生事业添砖加瓦。

At present, China has entered a new era of green and high-quality development. Guided by the concept of health for all, Chinese people will forge ahead to pursue high-quality and healthy drinking water so as to make great contributions to the cause of global drinking water safety.

New Words, Phrases and Expressions

geographical [ˌdʒiːəˈɡræfɪk(ə)l] *a.* 地理的,地理学的

location [ləʊˈkeɪʃn] *n.* 地点,位置;(电影的)外景拍摄地;定位;(计算机内存里的)地址

obesity [əʊˈbiːsəti] *n.* 过度肥胖,肥胖症

index [ˈɪndeks] *n.* 索引;(物价和工资等)指数;指标,量度;幂,根指数;指针 *v.* 为……编索引,将……编入索引;使指数化,将(工资等)与(物价水平等)挂钩;(机器、部件)转位

urine [ˈjʊərɪn] *n.* 尿液,小便

gastrointestinal [ˌɡæstrəʊɪnˈtestɪnl] *a.* 胃肠的

excessive [ɪkˈsesɪv] *a.* 过度的;过多的

dehydration [ˌdiːhaɪˈdreɪʃ(ə)n] *n.* 脱水

concentrated [ˈkɒnsntreɪtɪd] *a.* 集中的;全神贯注的,全力以赴的;浓缩的

dizziness [ˈdɪzinəs] *n.* 头晕;头昏眼花

nervousness [ˈnɜːvəsnəs] *n.* 神经质;(心理)神经过敏;紧张不安

cognitive [ˈkɒgnətɪv] *a.* 认识的,认知的

impairment [ɪmˈpeəmənt] *n.* (身体或智力方面)损伤,缺陷,障碍

seizure [ˈsiːʒə(r)] *n.* 夺取,控制;扣押,没收;(疾病的)突然发作

compensate [ˈkɒmpenseɪt] (for) *v.* 赔偿,偿付;弥补,补偿;抵消;酬报(某人)

recommended [ˌrekəˈmendɪd] *a.* 被推荐的

beneficial [ˌbenɪˈfɪʃ(ə)l] *a.* 有益的,有利的;(法律)(与)权益(有关)的,有财产使用权的

stroke [strəʊk] *n.* 中风;(使用武器的)击,打;击球,一击,一抽;(划船用语)划桨,划法,划桨法;泳式,游泳姿势;(指挥船上其他桨手的)尾桨手;轻抚,抚摸;一笔,一划;(灵感的)突发,(天才的)一举;(突发或突然想到的)好事;斜线(号);(雷电的)闪光;来回动作,上下动作;(一系列重复运动的)节奏,律动;(鸟翼的)一次扑打;准时,准点;(时钟报时的)鸣响,钟声 *v.* 轻抚,抚摸;轻挪,轻触,轻拭;击球

intake [ˈɪnteɪk] *n.* (食物、饮料、空气等的)摄取量,吸入量;摄入,吸入;(一定时期内)纳入的人数;入口,进口

throughout human history 纵观人类历史

water-borne [ˈwɔːtər-bɔːrn] *a.* 水传播的;由水浮起的;水运的;饮水传染的(等于waterborne)

communicable [kəˈmjuːnɪkəbl] *a.* 可传达的;会传染的;爱说话的

epidemic [ˌepɪˈdemɪk]*n.* 流行病,传染病;(迅速的)盛行,蔓延 *a.* 盛行的,泛滥的

outbreak [ˈaʊtbreɪk] *n.* (战争、疾病、暴力等的)爆发(暴发),突然发生

infectious [ɪnˈfekʃəs] *a.* 传染的,传染性的;有感染力的,有影响力的

stagnant [ˈstægnənt] *a.* (经济、社会等)停滞不前的,不景气的;不流动的;污浊的

typhoon [taɪˈfuːn] *n.* (印度洋及西太平洋的)台风

mosquito [məˈskiːtəʊ] *n.* 蚊子

fly [flaɪ] *n.* 苍蝇;裤门襟;腾空球,高飞球;(帐篷的)篷顶;(剧院)吊景区,悬吊布景的空间;(英)单马出租马车

vector-borne [ˈvektə(r)-bɔːn] *a.* 媒介传播的

subsequent [ˈsʌbsɪkwənt] *a.* 随后的;接着的;(河、谷)后成的

malaria [məˈleəriə] *n.* 疟疾

dengue [ˈdeŋgi] fever 登革热

dysentery [ˈdɪsəntri] *n.* 痢疾

diarrhea [ˌdaɪəˈrɪə] *n.* 腹泻(=diarrhoea)

transmit [trænzˈmɪt] *vt.* 播送,传输,发射;传递,传达(思想、情感);传播,传染(病毒、疾病等);传导(声、电等),透(光等)

devastating [ˈdevəsteɪtɪŋ] *a.* 毁灭性的，极具破坏力的；令人极为震惊的；令人印象深刻的，吸引人的；极有效的，强有力的

submerge [səbˈmɜːdʒ] *v.* （使）潜入水中，（使）没入水中，浸没；湮没，掩盖（思想、感情等）；使（自己）集中精力于，使（自己）沉浸于

post-disaster [dɪˈzɑːstə(r)] *a.* 灾后的

reaffirm [ˌriːəˈfɜːm] *vt.* 再肯定，重申；再断言

attach great importance to 认为重要

vigilant [ˈvɪdʒɪlənt] *a.* 警觉的，警惕的

alert [əˈlɜːt] *a.* 警惕的，警觉的；机敏的，敏捷的；意识到，注意到（alert to） *v.* 向……报警，使警觉；提示，提醒（某人） *n.* 警报，警示；警戒，警惕；（电子设备的）提示信号；警戒期

sanitation [ˌsænɪˈteɪʃ(ə)n] *n.* 公共/环境卫生；下水道设施，卫生设备

reveal [rɪˈviːl] *vt.* 揭示，透露；表明，证明；展/显示；（通过神或超自然手段）启示

famine [ˈfæmɪn] *n.* 饥荒，饥馑；匮乏，短缺

prevalent [ˈprevələnt] *a.* 盛行的，普遍的

personnel [ˌpɜːsəˈnel] *n.* （公司、组织或军队中的）全体人员，员工；人事部门 *a.* 人员的，有关人事的

stable [ˈsteɪb(ə)l] *a.* 稳定的，牢固的；稳重的，沉稳的；（化学结构或物理状态）稳定的

exploitation [ˌeksplɔɪˈteɪʃ(ə)n] *n.* 剥削，压榨；开发，开采；（出于私利、不公正的）利用

give rise to 产生

represent [ˌreprɪˈzent] *vt.* 代表；为……代言（辩护）；代表（选区、政党、群体）任国会议员（或其他立法机构议员）；代表（国家、学校、城镇等参加比赛）；作为某人的代表（尤指在正式场合或仪式中）；等于，相当于；（符号或象征）代表，表示；象征，体现；展示，描绘；（尤指不真实地）描述，描写；扮演；（正式）明确讲述，清楚说明；声称；正式提出（意见、抗议等）

update [ˌʌpˈdeɪt] *v.* 为……增加最新信息，更新；使现代化；向……提供最新信息 *n.* 最新报道，最新消息；（计算机软件的）更新；新型，新版

Ministry of Health 卫生部

relevant [ˈreləvənt] *a.* 有关的，切题的；正确的，适宜的；有价值的，有意义的

revise [rɪˈvaɪz] *vt.* 改变，修正；修改，修订（书刊、估算等）；（英）温习，复习

World Health Organization （**WHO**）世界卫生组织

fundamental [ˌfʌndəˈment(ə)l] *a.* 根本的，基本的；必需的，必不可少的；不能再分的 n. 基本原理；基音，基频

guarantee [ˌgærənˈtiː] *vt.* 确保,保证;担保,为……作保;保修,包换　*n.* 保证,担保;保修单,质量保证书;担保金,抵押品
forge [fɔːdʒ] **ahead** 继续进行;取得进展
make great contributions to 为……作出巨大贡献

C-E Language Disparity 6—Covertness vs. Overtness 隐性与显性

Markers

It is universally acknowledged that Chinese is a semantic language while English is a morphological language. That is, Chinese grammar is often implicit while English grammar is comparatively explicit. English overtness is achieved mostly through markers, which are signals of explicitness. Generally, words have two types of meanings: semantic meanings and grammatical meanings. The latter refer to **gender**, number, case, tense, voice, mood, **coherence**, etc. Many English words adopt morphological changes to show some of such meanings, like the plural forms of countable nouns *-s*, the cases of pronouns, the infinitive sign *to*, the present tense of the verb of the third person singular *-s*, the continuous aspect of the verb *-ing*, the perfect aspect of the verb *have* plus past participle *-ed/-en*, the past tense of the verb *-ed*, the passive voice of the verb *be* plus past participle *-ed/-en*, etc. These morphological changes are easily recognized, and thus are called *overt* or *marked*, and the above-mentioned elements are called **markers.**

"Marker" is defined as "an element that indicates grammatical class or function; a derivation of inflectional morphemes". There are far more markers in English than in Chinese, and Chinese also has markers that show some grammatical meanings, such as auxiliaries like 了,过,(正)在(used to mark aspects), and 被 (used sometimes to show the passive voice), etc. But they are not compulsive and can often be left out when the context clearly implies such grammatical meanings. English "markers" include **suffixes denoting the noun**, such as *-ation*, *-ace*, *-ance*, *-cy*, *-dom*, *-ence*, *-er*, *-ess*, *-hood*, *-ism*, *-ist*, *-ity*, *-ment*, *-ness*, *-or*, *-ship*, *-tion*, *-ty*, etc., **adjective markers** such as *-able*,

-eous, *-al*, *-ful*, *-ic*, *-ical*, *-ish*, *-ive*, *-less*, *-like*, *-y*, etc., **verb markers** such as *-ize*, *-en*, *em-*, *en-*, etc., and **adverb markers** such as *-ly*, *-wise*. Broadly speaking, the blank between two words, the indention at the beginning of a paragraph, capitalization, and other special positions of words in the sentence are all markers.

Of course, Chinese and English have similar **markers of negation**. At the syntactic level, English has **negative adverbs** such as *not*, *never*, *nowhere*, **negative pronouns** such as *none*, *nobody*, *neither*, *nothing*, **negative conjunctions** such as *but*, *neither...nor*, *unless*, *lest*, **negative prepositions** such as *without*. At the lexical level, there are many **negative prefixes** such as *a-* / *ab-*, *anti-*, *contra-*, *counter-*, *ob-* (*of-*, op-), *de-*, *dis-*, *il-*, *im-*, *in-*, *ir-*, *ne-*, *non-*, *un-*, *mal-* /*male-*, *mis-*, *re-*, *under-*, etc., and **negative suffixes** such as *-less*, *-free*, etc. Some grammarians also classify *few*, *little*, *hardly*, *scarcely*, *rarely*, *seldom*, *barely*, *too*, *until*, etc. as markers of negation, which are defined as "**semi-negative words**". Chinese markers of negation are mostly adverbs, including 不(不能,不行,不可以,不要,不会,不喜欢,不才等),无(无头绪,无语,无虞,无可奈何等),非(非法,非分,非礼,非命,非人,非笑,非议等),未(未必,未曾,未卜先知,未尝,未竟,未免,未能免俗,未然,未始,未遂,未雨绸缪等),否(否决,否定,否认,否则等),没(没有,没谱,没道理,没事,没来由,没关系等),莫(爱莫能助,一筹莫展,莫可奈何),免(免费,免冠,免考,免提,免检,免试,免刑,免修,免役,免疫,免职,免罪等),休(休想,休息,休假,休克,休眠,休学,休业,休战,休止等),弗(自愧弗如),别(别动,别管,别具匠心,别论,别具一格,别无二致,别无长物,别提等), etc. Such adjectives as 异,禁,止,亡,失,白,乏,鲜 and conjunctions such as 除非,未必,不但,不论,不管, etc. can be regarded as markers of negation.

The Chinese language has no morphological changes and therefore in most cases adopts other means to express grammatical meanings—most often through context, but also by the use of auxiliary words and word order. So the grammatical meanings of Chinese words are usually "covert" or "unmarked".

Parts of Speech

The following table roughly compares the division of parts of speech between Chinese and English.

A Comparison of Chinese and English Parts of Speech

Chinese	English	Chinese	English
实词	Notional Word	拟声词	Onomatopoeia
名词	Noun	虚词	Functional Word
代词	Pronoun	介词	Preposition
形容词	Adjective	连词	Conjunction
动词	Verb	叹词	Interjection
副词	Adverb	助词(语气词)	Auxiliary word
数词	Numeral Word	冠词	Article
量词	Quantifier		

In terms of "markedness" and "unmarkedness", the English article has a special status, which includes the **indefinite** article *a/an* and the **definite** article *the*. Most Chinese students find it confusingly difficult to use these articles.

The article, a kind of determiner 限定词, is "a structural word specifying the noun", a marker of the noun and always comes before a noun or a noun phrase, with no independent meaning except denoting an indefinite or a definite reference. There is no article in Chinese.

The definite article *the* is sometimes translated into 这 or 那, but generally 这 and 那 correspond to the English demonstrative pronouns "this" and "that", which contain certain concepts of time and space while the definite article *the* does not contain any concept of either time or space. The use of the definite article is complicated and it is by no means an easy job for Chinese learners to master it. For example, "she is in hospital" and "she is in the hospital" have different meanings, with the former implying that she is treated as patient and the whole treatment process is associated with the hospital and the latter meaning that she is in a certain hospital.

The English suffix-(*e*)*s* is a marker of the plural form of countable nouns. Some plural forms of English nouns have very different meanings from their singular forms. Please look at the following table carefully:

序号	单数	意义	复数	意义
1	air	大气;空气;空中,天空	*airs*	装腔作势;架子
2	arm	手臂;上肢;扶手	*arms*	武器;军备;怀里
3	ash	灰;灰烬	*ashes*	骨灰;遗骸;废墟;灰烬
4	custom	风俗,习俗;习惯;光顾	*customs*	海关;关税
5	effect	作用,影响	*effects*	动产,财物
6	element	基本部分,要素;元素;有点,少量;一群人	*elements*	(恶劣的)天气;基本原理
7	experience	经验;阅历	*experiences*	经历
8	force	力,力量;暴力,武力	*forces*	军队;势力;武装力量
9	good	善行;合乎道德的行为;好事	*goods*	商品;动产;私人财产;货物
10	green	绿色;青春	*greens*	青菜;绿地;绿色物
11	ground	地,地面;土地	*grounds*	理由;根据;基础;证据
12	letter	信,信函;字母	*letters*	正式文件/法律文书;文学;知识;文化修养
13	look	看;寻找;表情;	*looks*	面貌;容貌
14	minute	分钟;片刻;一会儿;时刻	*minutes*	笔记;会议记录;摘要
15	paper	纸;纸张;论文	*papers*	文件;证件;论文数
16	quarter	四分之一;一刻钟;十五分钟	*quarters*	处所;营房
17	remain	剩余	*remains*	遗体;残骸
18	spirit	精神;心灵;心境;勇气	*spirits*	酒精;烈酒;情绪
19	water	水;雨水	*waters*	矿泉水(the waters);水体,水域;局域;羊水

The Chinese character 们 can be used to express plurality, and some people say it is a marker like the English -(*e*)*s*. But the use of 们 has its own rules.

Some English nouns always appear in the plural form such as *annals*, *trousers*, *remains*, etc.

The plural forms of such nouns are habitually used as *congratulations*, *greetings*, *regards*, *condolences*, *properties*, *gallows*, etc.

Some abstract nouns often appear in the plural to denote specific ideas such as *sufferings*, *hardships*, *blessings*, etc.

Certain terms are in plural form but are treated as singulars: *the United States*, *the United Nations*, *the Philippines*, etc.

The Passive Voice

The passive voice is an important English grammatical construction that is introduced with markers, formed through morphological change of the verb: be + past participle *-ed/-en* ("get" is often used to replace "be", very often the *-ed* participle implies the passive voice enough on its own). As for the logical relation between the verb and its object, Chinese also has passive voice, but it is expressed in covert ways, as many active forms can express or imply a passive voice. But such usage is limited in English, as the language does not have the tendency of putting the object of the action in the usual position of the agent like Chinese. Some people consider the verbs in such patterns linking verbs.

Of course, there are markers for the passive in Chinese, but such markers are by no means as definite as the "*be* +*-ed* participle" structure in English. 被-sentences have a much lower frequency in the Chinese language compared with the passive voice in English, and 被 still does not completely correspond to passive voice, as it does not always indicate passive voice for example, the sentence "一不小心还是被它跑了" means "It escaped because of our carelessness."

Punctuation Marks

Punctuation marks are also a kind of obvious discourse markers. In English, punctuation marks are part of the grammar system and perform important functions. While a comma suggests a pause, a semicolon separates two parallel clauses, and a full stop, a question mark or an exclamation mark marks the end of a complete sentence. A sentence or a line of a poem always begins with a capital letter.

Capitalization of a whole word often shows emphasis. For example, "This is MY business" means it is nobody else's business and implies that no one else is allowed to interfere with this matter. The first letter in the names of addresses, dynasties, persons, places, companies, projects, such as in Jiangsu Province, The Qing Dynasty, Samuel Johnson, The People's Republic of China, Giant Panda Company, The Three Gorges Dam, must be capitalized. Capitalization is also one of the means used in English to distinguish meanings, such as may 可能/May 五月; green 绿色的/Green 格林; smith 铁匠/Smith 史密斯(姓氏); turkey 火鸡/Turkey 土耳其; polish 抛光;修改/ Polish 波兰的;波兰人, etc.

Ancient Chinese had no punctuation marks, so it is difficult to determine where sentences begin and end in some classic works. Chinese punctuation marks were borrowed from European languages but have not become an important part of Chinese grammar, which itself is fairly loose. They suggest breathing pauses rather than grammatical meanings, thus it is very common to use commas all the way through a paragraph until the last sentence, which could very well be the only one marked with a full stop.

Indention 缩排 and **spacing** 字距 can also be considered special punctuation marks. The former marks the beginning of a paragraph and the latter serves to separate two words. As there is no spacing in written Chinese, sometimes ambiguity will arise; therefore, the relationship between characters in a sentence has to be analyzed to prevent such ambiguity:

1. 王林待在实验室里半个月,好像与世隔绝了,所以他回到家,强迫着自己看了十天的报纸。

2. 校门口一边站着一个学生。

3. 北京图书馆收藏着不少章太炎的书。

4. 学校领导对他的批评是有充分思想准备的。

5. 妹妹找不到,爸爸妈妈很着急。

Please appreciate the following translations:

1. 水上运动内容丰富多彩,它寓运动竞赛、科学技术于一体,以独有的惊险和优美等特点,正在得到广大群众,尤其是青少年体育爱好者的青睐。参加水上体育运动,既能锻炼身体、增强体质,又可以磨炼意志、增长才智。在城市的公园和旅游区开展多种多样的水上运动,不仅能为优美环境增添新的生活气息,丰富人们的文化精神生活,而且为城市生活增添了一道美丽的风景线。

Water sports are rich in content, integrating sports competition, science and technology, with unique thrilling and beautiful characteristics, are appealing to the masses, especially young sports enthusiasts. Participating in water sports can not only exercise one's body, invigorate one's physique, but also strengthen one's mind and sharpen one's intelligence. To carry out a variety of water sports in the parks and tourist areas of the city can not only breathe new life into the beautiful environment, enrich people's cultural and spiritual life, but also add a beautiful landscape to city life.

2. 水上运动一般是在优越的天然环境里进行的,可使人们充分体验阳光、空气和水这健身三要素。水上运动已经成为健身运动的新时尚。半个世纪以来,水上运动的发展异常迅猛,新项目不断涌现,传统项目一再更新。参加水上运动的人数越来越多,在一些发达国家已相当普及,仅法国就拥有潜水俱乐部2200多个,有90%的人参加该项活动。赛艇已成为世界上排名第四位的最受欢迎的项目。帆板项目从出现至今仅二十几年的历史,现已成为世界体育运动中发展最快、最热门的项目。航海模型寓体育和科技教育于娱乐之中,是广大青少年钟爱的水上运动项目,在日本几乎每个儿童都有一种或几种模型。

Water sports are generally carried out in a superior natural environment, so that people can fully experience the charm of the three elements of fitness, namely *sunshine*, *air* and *water*. Water sports have become a new fashion for fitness sports. Over the past fifty years, the development of water sports has been extremely rapid, with new projects constantly emerging and traditional projects repeatedly updated. The number of the people participating in water sports is on the increase. Some water sports have become very popular in developed countries. France alone has more than 2,200 diving clubs, and 90% of French people participate in diving. Rowing has become the fourth most popular sport in the world. Windsurfing has only 20 years of history, and has now developed into the fastest growing and most popular sport in the world. Model boat sailing, which combines sports and science and technology education with entertainment, is a popular water sport for the majority of teenagers, and almost every child in Japan has one or several boat models.

3. 我国有着漫长的海岸线,拥有大量的江、河、湖泊,水域资源极为丰富,具有开展水上运动的有利条件。各级体育部门对水上运动项目逐步重视起来。特别是改革开放以来,水上运动越来越受到人们的青睐和欢迎,各项目运动技术水平得到了迅速提高。赛艇、女子皮划艇、帆板、潜水、航海模型等项目,在一些重大国际比赛中曾多次打破世界纪录,获得金牌,为祖国争得了荣誉。随着我国经济的不断发展,水上运动将大有可为。但是,我国的水上运动项目普遍开展时间不长,单纯靠国家有限的财力投入,多数项目局限于少数人的训练,主要是应对各种类型的比赛,广大群众离这些项目较远,缺乏对水上运动和其发展前景的认识,水上运动市场没有打开,我国优越的水域资源没有得到开发,不少项目的场地器材设施还处于落后状态,一些项目同世界先进水平相比还有很大差距。

China has a long coastline, with a large number of rivers, lakes, and extremely rich water resources, which offer favorable conditions to carry out water sports. Sports departments at all levels are gradually paying increasing attention to water sports. Especially since the reform and opening up, water sports have been more and more favored and welcomed by people, and the technical level of each sport has been rapidly improved. In rowing, women's canoeing, windsurfing, diving, sailing model and other events in some major international competitions, world records have been broken for many times, gold medals and honors have been won for the motherland. With the continuous development of our economy, water sports will have great success. However, China's water sports projects, generally carried out for a short time, rely solely on the limited financial investment of the state. Most of the projects are limited to the training of few people, mainly to deal with various types of competitions. The broad masses are far away from these projects, resulting in lack of awareness of water sports and their development prospects. China's superior water resources have not been fully developed, and the site equipment and facilities of many projects are still backward. There are still big gaps in some projects between China and the world's advanced levels.

C-E Translation Strategies and Skills 6—Conversion of Active and Passive Voice 语态转换

Chinese uses fewer passive voice sentences than English. In translating, you should translate covert Chinese sentences into proper overt English versions according to contexts.

1) 强调受事,突出被动状态。

a. 地球上早期的火是大自然而不是人类引燃的。Early fires on the earth were ***caused*** by nature, not by man.

b. 利用发电机可以将机械能再转变成电能。The mechanical energy can

be ***changed*** back into electrical energy ***by means of a generator***.

c. 刀具由零件程序自动调用。The tool can be automatically ***called for use by*** the part program.

d. 地球不时为太阳发出的带电粒子流所袭击。The earth is ***hit*** from time to time by streams of electrically charged particles ***poured out*** by the sun.

2）因各种原因，不出现或无须说明施事者。

a. 这种书是给儿童写的。Such books are ***written*** for children.

b. 有人给你打电话。You are ***wanted*** on the phone.

c. 水污染问题应予以重视。The water pollution should be ***paid attention to***.

d. 墨汁斑渍是洗不掉的。　China-ink stains ***cannot be washed out***.

e. 要不是下大雨，货物早该装运完毕。The goods ***would have been shipped*** but for the heavy rain.

f. 惊涛骇浪，方显英雄本色。The good seaman ***is known*** in bad weather.

3）使句子结构匀称，文气连贯。

a. 他出现在台上，群众报以热烈的掌声。He appeared on the stage and was warmly ***applauded*** by the audience.

b. 电子产生的是 X 射线，能让医生透视病人的身体。Produced by electrons are the X-rays, ***which*** allow the doctor to look inside a patient's body.

c. 应该具有双重素质，即对偶然发生的事情既好奇又敏感，而且拥有自己的一套能揭示这些偶然事件真正重要意义的学术参考体系，也许这就是他所说的"机会只垂青有备之士"的意思吧。This dual quality of being sensitive to, and curious about, small accidental occurrences, and of possessing a frame of reference of revealing their true significance, is probably what he meant when he said"Chance favors only the ***prepared*** mind."

d. 读者为了满足自己的阅读渴望，越读越想读，直到进入如痴如醉的状态。To appease their thirst, its readers drank deeper than before, until they were ***seized with*** a kind of delirium.

4）汉语中的某些习惯用语或泛指人称为主语的主动句。

a. 大家都认为这样做是不妥当的。***It is generally considered*** not advisable to act that way.

b. 大家知道，金属在我们的生活中是很重要的。***It is known that*** metals are very important in our life.

c. 已经证明,能量是不可能消灭的,只能转换为其他形式。***It has been proved that*** energy cannot be destroyed; it can only be changed into other forms.

d. 可见,磁性材料广泛用于现代电子设备中。***It can be seen that*** magnetic materials are used in a wide range of modern electronic equipment.

e. 公认的是,光传播信息的容量极大。***It is generally recognized that*** light has a vast capacity for transmitting information.

f. 应当注意,增加导线的长度会增加其电阻。***It should be noted that*** increasing the length of the wire will increase its resistance.

C-E Guided Translation Practice 6

1. 石油埋藏于地层深处。因此,仅研究地层表面,无法确定有无石油,必须勘测地下的岩石结构。如果确定了某一区域的岩石蕴藏着石油,就此安装钻机。它的主要部分是机架,用以撑起一节一节的钢管,让其下到井孔。一边钻井,一边下钢管,以防周围土层塌陷。一旦出油,就紧固管盖,让油从各个阀门喷出。

2. 她们或许是我们的奶奶,满头银丝,满脸皱纹,世人多用"慈祥"去形容她们,但很少有人能品味皱纹背后那岁月与历史浮过的幽香。她们无须再用铅华刻意雕饰,我却分明看见她和她的老伴共同演出那首动人的歌——《牵手》。

3. 眼泪是上苍对一切感情动物的馈赠,爱为心之声,泪因爱而凝,流泪是女人爱的宣泄,情的倾诉,女人流泪时最美。(节选自《女人什么时候最美》一文,《英语沙龙》,1999 年 08 期)

4. 洞庭湖作为龙舟赛的发源地,在中国文化中享有盛名。据说龙舟赛始于洞庭湖东岸,为的是搜寻楚国爱国诗人屈原的遗体。龙舟赛与洞庭湖及周边的美景,每年都吸引着成千上万来自全国和世界各地的游客。

5. 青海湖位于跨越亚洲的几条候鸟迁徙路线的交叉处。许多鸟类把青海湖作为迁徙过程中的暂息地,湖的西侧是著名的"鸟岛",吸引着来自世界各地的观鸟者。每年夏天,游客们也来这里观看国际自行车比赛。

6. 水是除阳光、空气之外的人类生存三大自然要素之一。水孕育了生命。一般来说,婴幼儿体内的水分占体重的 70%,成年妇女占 52%,成年男性占 61%。一个成年人每天约需两公升的水才能维持正常生存,如果缺水,数日内就会死亡。

7. 地球表面的 3/4 为海洋所覆盖，所以水是人类重要的外环境之一。同样，水也是人类内环境的重要组成部分，因为水是人体新陈代谢的介质。人的机体需要不断地从外界吸取水分和养分，既要通过水把各种营养物质输送到机体各部分去，又要通过水把代谢产物排出体外。水中还含有多种微量元素。若水质不良，或中途被污染，其引起的健康问题可想而知。

8. 天然水是无色、无臭、无味且透明的。例如一条河流，从发源地开始就是如此。但经过漫长的河道，流过大大小小的工厂区和村镇，汇集了四面八方的工业废水和生活污水后，使本来清澈的河水增加了大量的病原体、化学物质和悬浮物，河水已受到严重污染。污染原因有自然的和人为的两方面。污染了的水是绝对不能饮用的。如果未经卫生处理的污染水被人们饮用，根据污染情况，可发生由病毒、细菌、寄生虫、昆虫污染而引起的各种疾病；会因为水中所含的有毒金属而引起急慢性中毒；会因为水中所含致癌物质引发癌症。当然，应用这些污染水也会影响工农业生产的正常进行。

第七单元　中外治水与可持续发展

Unit 7　Water Conservation and Sustainable Development at Home and Abroad

当前,建设可持续发展社会是时代主题。然而,践行这个主题,会面临一些需要回答的问题,即人与水是什么样的关系,人应该以什么样的态度来对待水,以什么样的行为来使用水。古往今来,治水问题在中国,乃至全世界都是极为重要的民生工程。然而,随着全球变暖,暴雨、热浪、台风等极端天气频发,洪旱灾害在区域乃至全球范围愈加频繁地发生,给人们的生产生活造成严重影响,导致生命及财产的重大损失。如今,水危机的实质是治理危机,是其体制长期滞后于需求的累积结果。因此要改变当下局面,根本出路在于治水理念及治水模式的变革和转型。

At present, building a sustainable development society is the theme of the times. However, the practice of this theme will face some questions that need to be answered, that is, what is the relationship between humanity and water? What attitude(s) should people take towards water? What kind of behavior should people take towards using water? Through the ages, issues of water conservation have been an extremely important livelihood project not only in China, but also throughout the world. However, with global warming, extreme cases of weather such as heavy rains, heat waves, and typhoons have occurred frequently. Floods and droughts have occurred in increasing frequency in some regions and even around the world, which have an important impact on people's production and life, resulting in heavy losses of life and property. Today, the essence of the water crisis is the governance crisis, which is the cumulative result of its system lagging behind the demand for a long time. Therefore, in order to change the current situation, the reformation and transformation of the concept and mode of water conversation is the only fundamental way out.

第一节　中国治水与可持续发展
Section A　Water Conservation and Sustainable Development in China

水是生存之本、文明之源,中华民族的发展史就是一部治水史。传说中,大禹治水"三过家门而不入",春秋时期的管子也提出"善为国者必先除水旱之害"。治水是立国之本。我国历史上出现的一些"盛世"局面,无不得益于统治者对水利的重视,得益于水利工程及其成就。所以,除水害、兴水利,历来是兴国安邦的大事。

Water is the foundation of survival and the source of civilization. The history of the development of the Chinese nation is a history of water conservation. According to legend, Dayu tamed the flood "three times without entering the house", and Guan Zi in the Spring and Autumn Period also proposed that "Those who are good at governing the country should first solve the problems of floods and droughts." Water control is the foundation of building up a country. Some of the "golden times" in the Chinese history have all benefited from the rulers' attention to water governance and from water conservancy engineering and its achievements. Therefore, eliminating water hazards and constructing water projects have always been major events for rejuvenating and stabilizing a country or a nation.

1. 创新治水理念

1. Innovating the concept of water conservation

经济的增长和社会的进步必然会产生对水利需求的不断增长和跃升,这要求治水理念不断更新和发展,治水理念如果落后于水利需求,必然会影响和阻碍现代水利的可持续发展。

Economic growth and social progress will inevitably lead to continuous leaps and bounds in demand for water conservancy, which requires the continuous updating and development of water conservation concepts. If the concept of water conservation lags behind the needs of water conservancy, it will inevitably affect and hinder the sustainable development of modern water conservancy.

一要突出"人与自然和谐相处"的治水理念。在治水中,我们首先要坚持按自然规律办事,从向大自然无节制的索取转变为与自然和谐相处;从重点对水资源进行开发、利用、治理转变为更强调对水资源的配置、节约和保护。二是要牢固树立系统治水、科学治水理念。不断优化污水处理措施方案,打造一批能层层过滤、循环净化的生态"海绵体",积极探索低成本、可持续的生态治水之路,实现河畅、水清、岸绿、景美。在水利工程的实施中,要始终致力于弘扬水利人文精神,推广水利文化。不仅要从工程水利向可持续发展水利转变,还要在继续做好防洪抗旱、防灾减灾的同时,把解决水资源短缺和水污染放到重要地位。三要确立城乡统筹的理念。在推进工业化、城镇化过程中,要充分体现"以水定城"理念。充分考虑城市所在地的水资源禀赋,以此来规划城市空间、产业发展,不断强化用水需求和用水过程治理,统筹兼顾、科学规划,构建城乡水利工程新格局。把水环境综合整治与城镇化建设、治污保洁等工作有机结合起来，全方位、多角度开展水污染综合治理，促进城市及周边地区的共同可持续发展。四是要严格贯彻水资源管理制度，坚持依法管水，优化配置，促进水资源的可持续利用。要合理利用好水资源，既要积极发挥市场机制在水资源配置中的基础作用，还要坚持水利社会管理和公共服务的与时俱进。切实转变职能，依法调整水事关系，规范水事行为，从而保障水资源的可持续利用。

First, it is necessary to highlight the water conservation concept of "harmonious coexistence between man and nature". In the process of water conservation, we must first adhere to the law of nature, changing from uncontrolled demands from nature to living in harmony with nature, and from focusing on the development, utilization and governance of water resources to putting more emphasis on the allocation, conservation and protection of water resources. Second, it is necessary to firmly establish the concept of systematic and scientific water conservation. We must continue to optimize sewage treatment measures, create a batch of ecological "sponges" that can filter and purify waste water at different levels, and actively explore low-cost sustainable ecological water treatment methods to realize smooth rivers, clear waters, green shores and beautiful scenery. Then in implementing water conservancy projects, we should always dedicate/devote/commit ourselves to carrying forward the humanistic spirit of water conservancy and promoting its culture. We should not only change from engineering water conservancy to sustainable development of water conservancy, but also put the solutions to the shortage of water resources and water pollution in an important position while continuing to do a good job in flood control, drought prevention and disaster prevention and reduction. Third, we should establish the concept of overall development of urban and rural areas. In the process of promoting industrialization and urbanization, the concept of "governing the city by water" should be fully embodied. We should fully consider the endowment of water resources where the city is located to plan urban space and industrial development. We should constantly strengthen the management of water demand and water use process by taking all factors into consideration and making scientific plans to establish a new pattern of urban and rural water conservancy projects. We will integrate comprehensive governance of the water environment with urbanization, pollution control and cleaning, and carry out comprehensive treatment of water pollution in an all-round and multi-angle manner to promote the common sustainable development of cities and their surrounding areas. Fourth, it is necessary to strictly implement the water resources management system, adhere to governing water resources in accordance with the law, optimize the allocation, and promote the sustainable utilization of water resources. In order to make good use of water resources, we should not only give full play to the basic role of market mechanism in water resources allocation, but also adhere to the advancement of water conservancy social management and public services. It is necessary to change the functions, adjust the water relations in accordance with law, and standardize the water affairs behavior, so as to ensure the sustainable utilization of water resources.

2. 创新治水手段

2. Innovating means of water conservation

治水要标本兼治。在传统治水理念下，我国对水资源的管理主要是借助于行政手段，很少考虑以市场为导向的经济和制度手段。但是单纯依靠行政手段治理水资源，不但交易成本高、效率低，而且调节机制十分僵化，难以根据实际情况的变化灵活调节水资源的供需。表现在治水方面，首先要考虑如何灵活发挥经济和制度手段在优化水资源配置和提高水资源利用效率方面的作用，如何与自然相协调。

It is necessary to address both the symptoms and the root causes of water conservation. Under the guidance of the traditional concept of water conservation, China mainly relies on administrative/executive means for water resources management, and seldom considers market-oriented economic and institutional means. However, relying solely on administrative means to govern water resources not only has high transaction costs and low efficiency, but also has a very rigid adjustment mechanism, making it difficult to flexibly adjust the supply of and demand for water resources according to changes in actual conditions. In terms of water governance, we should first consider how to flexibly play the role of economic and institutional means in optimizing the allocation of water resources and improving the efficiency of water resources utilization, and how to achieve harmony with nature.

一是要兴建绿色水利工程，加大水利生态投入。在原有传统经验基础上，不仅要修复河道堤防，而且要重点抓好上中游水土保持，完善各类水工程的管理系统、防汛报警系统。水利建设可以帮助恢复和提高自然的承受能力，减轻水旱灾害，做到人与自然和谐相处的可持续发展。另外，对于具有较高环境质量的河流，应限制流域开发；对于环境质量较差的河流，应最大限度地减轻损害。二是要建立相应的水权制度，鼓励用水户参与水资源管理，明晰水资源的用水权利。在我国，水权制度建设的核心是水资源使用权的确认和流转。完善这项制度，从根本上说，是为了更好地发挥市场在水资源配置中的作用，提高水资源利用效率与效益。在具体实施方面，相关部门要加快界定初始水权，如从流域层面完成水资源分配。从用户层面，必须通过取水许可管理明确水资源使用权。针对一些地区水资源归属权依旧不明确、配置手段单一的问题，要健全水权配置体系，开展水资源使用权确权登记，形成归属清晰、权责明确、监管有效的水资源资产产权制度。

First, it is necessary to build green water conservancy projects and increase ecological investment in it. On the basis of the original traditional experience, we should not only repair river dikes, but also focus on soil and water conservation in the upper and middle reaches, and improve the management system and flood control alarm system of all kinds of water projects. Water conservancy construction can help restore and improve the bearing capacity of nature, thus reducing the flood and drought disasters and contributing to sustainable development in harmony between man and nature. In addition, for rivers with relatively good environmental quality, we should restrict the development of the basin; but for rivers with poor environmental quality, we should minimize the damage. Second, it is necessary to establish a corresponding water rights system, encourage water users to participate in water resources management and clarify their rights of using water resources. In our country, the core of the construction of the water right system is the confirmation and circulation of the right to use water resources. Fundamentally speaking, the improvement of this system is to better play the role of the market in the allocation of water resources and improve the efficiency and benefit of water resources utilization. In terms of specific implementation, relevant departments are speeding up the definition of initial water rights, such as the completion of water resources allocation at the river basin level. From the user level, the right to use water resources needs to be clarified through the management of water abstraction permits. In response to the unclear ownership of water resources and single allocation method in some areas, it is necessary to improve the water rights allocation system and carry out the confirmation and registration of water use rights, so as to form a water asset and property rights system with clear ownership, clear rights and responsibilities, and effective supervision.

New Words, Phrases and Expressions

theme [θiːm] *n.* 题目,主题;主旋律;主题音乐,主题曲;(学生的)作文;(聚会、房间等的)风格;(句子的)主位;(名词、动词等)词干　*a.* 以奇想主题布置的

livelihood [ˈlaɪvlihʊd] *n.* 生计;营生

project [ˈprɒdʒekt] *n.* 项目,计划;(学校的)课题,研究项目;(美)廉租房区,公共房屋区

global warming 全球变暖

drought [draʊt] *n.* 干旱,旱灾;长期缺水;水严重短缺

property [ˈprɒpəti] *n.* 所有物,财产;地产,房地产;房地产(或投资)(properties);(法律)所有权,处置权;特性,性质

governance [ˈgʌvənəns] *n.* 统治方式,管理方法

cumulative [ˈkjuːmjələtɪv] *a.* 积累的,渐增的;累计的,累积的

lag behind 落后于

current [ˈkʌrənt] *a.* 现行的,当前的;通用的,流行的;最近的　*n.* 水流,气流,电流;思潮,趋势

according to legend [ˈledʒənd] 据传(说)

tame [teɪm] *a.* 驯服的,不怕人的;平淡无奇的,枯燥乏味的;听使唤的,温顺的;(美)(植物)经栽培的;(土地)经开垦的　*v.* 驯化,驯服;制服,控制;开垦,开辟

eliminate [ɪˈlɪmɪneɪt] *v.* 剔除,根除;对……不予考虑,把……排除在外;(比赛中)淘汰;铲除,杀害;(生理)排除,排泄;消去

rejuvenate [rɪˈdʒuːvəneɪt] *vt.* 使年轻;使更新;使恢复精神;使复原　*vi.* 复原;变年轻

stabilize [ˈsteɪbəlaɪz] *v.* (使)稳定,稳固;使不易移动;使稳定,使不易分解

affect [əˈfekt] *v.* 影响;(疾病)侵袭,感染;(在感情上)深深打动,震撼;〈正式〉假装;佯装　*n.* [ˈæfekt](尤指影响行为或行动的)情感,感情

hinder [ˈhɪndə(r)] *v.* 阻碍,妨碍　*a.* (尤指身体部位)后面的

highlight [ˈhaɪlaɪt] *v.* 突出,强调;用亮色突出;挑染　*n.* 最好(或最精彩、最激动人心)的部分;强光部分

harmonious [hɑːˈməʊniəs] *a.* 和睦的,融洽的;悦耳的;和谐的,协调的

coexistence [ˌkəʊɪgˈzɪstəns] *n.* 共存

adhere [ədˈhɪə(r)] **to** 坚持

systematic [ˌsɪstəˈmætɪk] *a.* 有系统的,有条理的,仔细周到的;一贯的,惯常的;分

类的

optimize [ˈɒptɪmaɪz] *v.* 优化;充分利用(形势、机会、资源);使(数据、软件等)优化;持乐观态度

filter [ˈfɪltə(r)] *v.* 过滤;渗入,透过;(消息、信息等)慢慢传开,走漏;缓慢进入,陆续步入;(车辆)看到分流指示灯的信号后转弯;(用程序)筛选

purify [ˈpjʊərɪfaɪ] *v.* 使(某物)洁净,净化;变纯净;洗涤(思想),净化(心灵);提纯,精炼

implementation [ˌɪmplɪmenˈteɪʃ(ə)n] *n.* 实施,执行

humanistic [ˌhjuːməˈnɪstɪk] *a.* 人文主义的;人道主义的

allocation [ˌæləˈkeɪʃ(ə)n] *n.* 配给量,划拨款,份额;分配,分派

in accordance [əˈkɔːd(ə)ns] **with** 按照,依据,与……一致

standardize [ˈstændədaɪz] *v.* 使标准化,使符合标准(或规格);定出标准,立下标准;(对照标准)确定……的性能,确定……的特性

symptom [ˈsɪmptəm] *n.* (医) 症状;(大问题的)迹象,征兆,征候

administrative [ədˈmɪnɪstrətɪv] *a.* 管理的,行政的

executive [ɪɡˈzekjətɪv] *a.* 行政的,有执行权的;高档的,豪华的;供主管人员使用的;(有关)经营管理的,领导的 *n.* 主管,经理;行政部门,执行委员会

rigid [ˈrɪdʒɪd] *a.* (方法、体制等)严格死板的,僵化的;(人)顽固的,不通融的;刚硬的,不易弯曲的;(因强烈的感情而)僵硬的,僵直的;精确的

flexibly [ˈfleksəbli] *adv.* 灵活地;易曲地;柔软地;有弹性地

in terms of 依据;按照;在……方面;以……措辞

dike [daɪk] *n.* (同 dyke) 堤坝,大坝;(英)壕沟

bearing capacity [kəˈpæsəti] *n.* 承载量;结果能力;产仔能力

restrict [rɪˈstrɪkt] *v.* 控制(大小、数量、范围);限制(活动或行为),妨碍;约束,管束;(以法规)限制;封锁(消息)

minimize [ˈmɪnɪmaɪz] *v.* 使减少到最低限度;贬低,使显得不重要;使最小化

clarify [ˈklærəfaɪ] *vt.* 澄清,阐明;(通过加热)使净化,使纯净

confirmation [ˌkɒnfəˈmeɪʃ(ə)n] *n.* 确认/定;证实/明;批准,许可

relevant [ˈreləvənt] *a.* (to) 有关的,切题的;正确的,适宜的;有价值的,有意义的

speed up 加速;使加速

abstraction [æbˈstrækʃn] *n.* 抽象;提取;抽象概念;空想;心不在焉

permit [ˈpɜːmɪt] *n.* 许可证,特许证(尤指限期的)

registration [ˌredʒɪˈstreɪʃ(ə)n] *n.* 登记,注册,挂号;登记证,注册证;(英)(汽车)牌照号码(=registration number);(英)(教师对上课学生的)点名

supervision [ˌsuːpəˈvɪʒ(ə)n] *n.* 监督,管理

第二节 外国治水与可持续发展
Section B Water Conservation and Sustainable Development Abroad

随着经济的飞速发展以及全球环境的日益恶化，国际上对水生态环境的重视程度提高，水生态保护地位愈加突出。从顶层设计到项目施工，各国加快了治水理念和技术的转变。国外的水环境治理与中国不同，基本上走的是一条先污染后治理的道路。如今，国外水环境治理更倾向于统筹考虑流域内所有环境要素，从经济、环境、社会问题的角度转变治水理念，创新措施，对流域生态系统进行综合治理。

With the rapid economic development and the deteriorating global environment, the international community has paid more attention to the water ecological environment, and the status of water ecological protection has become more prominent. From top-level design to project construction, countries have accelerated the transformation of water conservation concepts and technologies. The water environment governance in foreign countries is different from that in China, which basically pollutes water resources first and then conducts governance. Nowadays, foreign water environmental governance is more inclined to consider all environmental elements in the basin as a whole. They have changed the concept of water conservation from the perspective of economic, environmental, and social issues, and innovated measures to comprehensively conduct management of the basin ecosystem.

1. 创新治水理念

1. Innovating the concept of water conservation

早期国外对于水资源的治理多强调防洪和排涝，忽略了河湖的生态功能，继而带来河道淤积、自净能力减弱、生物多样性遭破坏等一系列问题。这些问题的出现促使西方国家不断更新水资源治理理念，逐渐实现水资源可持续利用，进一步改善了生态环境。

In the early days, the governance of water resources in foreign countries put more emphasis on flood prevention and drainage, ignoring the ecological functions of rivers and lakes, which led to a series of problems such as river sedimentation, weakening of self-purification capacity, and destruction of biodiversity. The emergence of these problems has prompted Western countries to continuously update the concept of water resources governance, gradually realize the sustainable use of water resources, and further improve the ecological environment.

二十世纪三十年代，德国提出“近自然河道治理理念”，该理念以保护生物多样性、减少洪涝灾害，以及促进可持续利用自然资源为目的，提倡进一步认识生态系统，对河湖进行生态整治。到二十世纪八十年代，一些发达国家提出“河流再自然化”概念，希望能有效降低人类行为对环境的冲击，减少工程行为对自然生态的破坏，保留和恢复自然系统。与此同时，在该理念的倡导下，国外对于防范洪涝灾害的理念也相继发生了改变。早期，他们也是更多地依靠大规模水利建设工程，如修建大型水坝、大规模排水系统来保证水资源的合理管控；如今，这些国家则更看重运用生态方法改善河道治理，将水资源利用与城市防洪除涝相结合，通过工程、技术、法律、经济等多种手段强化节水和水循环利用，全面、持久地提升水资源利用率以及城市的防洪排涝效能。

In the 1930s, Germany put forward the concept of "near-natural river management". For the purpose of protecting biodiversity, reducing flood disasters and promoting sustainable use of natural resources, the concept advocates further understanding of ecosystems and ecological renovation of rivers and lakes. In the 1980s, some developed countries proposed the concept of "river re-naturalization", hoping to effectively reduce the impact of human behavior on the environment and reduce the damage to the natural ecology caused by engineering behavior. They called for the preservation and restoration of ecosystem. At the same time, under the advocacy of this concept, the concept of preventing flood disasters in foreign countries has also changed one after another. In the early days, they also relied more on large-scale water conservancy construction projects, such as building large dams and large-scale drainage systems to ensure the reasonable management and control of water resources. But today, these countries pay more attention to the use of ecological methods to improve river governance, combining water resource use with urban flood control and waterlogging prevention. Through engineering, technical, legal, economic and other means, they strengthened water saving and water recycling, comprehensively and lastingly improved the utilization rate of water resources and the effectiveness of urban flood control and drainage.

2. 创新治水手段

2. Innovating means of water conservation

水环境治理是一个典型的复杂问题,没有任何一个单一的治理模式能够解决所有维度上的问题。为了提升政策在实施过程中的效率,许多西方国家从多方面对水资源进行治理。

Water environment governance is a typical complex problem, and no single governance model can solve problems in all dimensions. In order to improve the efficiency of policy implementation, many Western countries govern water resources from various aspects.

一是要治污水。对于许多国家,尤其是发展中国家而言,污水处理是一种成本负担,然而,对很多发达国家而言,如德国,污水处理不仅不会增加成本,甚至是一种能够收取回报的产业投资。首先,要依法用水、管水和治水。其次,要实现城乡治水一体化。规定部门统一负责管理及进行不同区域的划分。相应部门制定总体发展规划,提出发展目标和措施,组织实施和检查。最后,要加大投入。保护和管理水资源,控制水污染,需要付出巨大成本。

First, it is necessary to treat sewage. For many countries, especially developing countries, sewage treatment is a burden of cost. However, for many developed countries, such as Germany, sewage treatment, far from increasing the cost, has become yielded a good return on industrial investment. First of all, it is necessary to use, manage and control water in accordance with the law. Next, it is necessary to realize the integration of urban and rural water governance. It is stipulated that all the departments should be responsible for the management and the division of different areas and that the corresponding departments should formulate an overall development plan, put forward development goals and measures, and organize the implementation and inspection of the plan. Finally, we need to increase investment. It is a huge cost to protect and manage water resources and control water pollution.

二是要防洪水。美国防洪减灾的核心就是建立多流域的洪水预警系统,并且利用先进的专业技术和现代信息技术加以辅助。同时,还要发挥储排水工程的重要作用。日本非常重视保留河道和湖泊的原始状态,致力于建设和改善城市下水道系统与排水设施,为城市蓄洪溢洪保留足够空间。

Second, it is necessary to prevent floods. In the United States, the core of flood control and disaster reduction is to establish an early multi-basin flood warning system, which is assisted by advanced professional technology and modern information technology. At the same time, the important role of storage and drainage projects must also be brought into play. Japan attaches great importance to preserving the original state of rivers and lakes, and is committed to building and improving urban sewer systems and drainage facilities to reserve enough space for urban flood storage and spilling.

三是要排涝水。这就要求政府将下水道设施的建设和管理作为重要事务，维护好下水道网络，包括清扫坑道、修理管道。在巴黎地下那条世界闻名的下水道正是践行了这些原则，每年才能吸引众多游客前往观赏。

Third, it is necessary to drain waterlogging. This requires that the government should take the construction and management of sewer facilities as a matter of importance and maintain the sewer network, including cleaning tunnels and repairing pipes. The world-famous sewer beneath Paris practices these principles and attracts many tourists every year.

四是要保供水。在国外，政府不能保障以充足的资金对供水行业的基础设施进行投入已是共性问题，为此近年来各国都进行了许多改革。德国建立了良好的供水和污水处理基础设施，供水和污水处理产业主要是国家所有，政府经营。而其他一些发达国家，如美国、英国、法国等则是鼓励私人企业进入供水行业，开放供水行业市场。

Fourth, it is necessary to ensure water supply. In foreign countries, it is a common problem that the government cannot guarantee sufficient funds to invest in the infrastructure of the water supply industry. For this reason, many countries have carried out many reforms in recent years. Germany has established a sound water supply and sewage treatment infrastructure. The industry is mainly owned by the state and operated by the government. Some other developed countries, such as the United States, Great Britain and France, have encouraged private enterprises to enter the water supply industry and open up the water supply industry market.

五是要抓节水。学校要开展“水资源教育”，不断强调日益严重的水资源紧缺问题，使人们真正提高节水意识。政府也应该设立相关法规，通过提高水费和罚款等经济手段来鼓励节水，调节全社会的水资源进行合理分配，提高水资源利用率。

Fifth, it is necessary to save water. The school should carry out “water resources education" and constantly emphasize the increasingly serious problem of water shortage, so as to make people really improve their awareness of water conservation. The government should also set up laws and regulations to advocate the concept of water-saving through economic measures such as increasing water fees and fines, and then rationally allocate water resources for the entire society and improve the utilization rate of water resources.

New Words, Phrases and Expressions

the international community 国际社会

prominent [ˈprɒmɪnənt] *a.* 重要的,著名的;显眼的;突出的;突起的,高耸的

accelerate [əkˈseləreɪt] *v.* (使)加快,促进;(车辆或驾驶者)加速

inclined [ɪnˈklaɪnd] *a.* 有……意向,倾向于……;对……有兴趣的,有天赋的;倾斜的,有坡度的

innovate [ˈɪnəveɪt] *v.* 革新,创新

comprehensively [ˌkɒmprɪˈhensɪvli] *adv.* 包括地;包括一切地;完全地;彻底地;全面地

siltation [sɪlˈteɪʃən] *n.* 淤积;聚积

prompt [prɒmpt] *a.* 立即的;迅速的;及时的;敏捷的;迅速的;准时的

advocate [ˈædvəkeɪt] *v.* 拥护,提倡　[ˈædvəkət] *n.* 拥护者;支持者;提倡者

renovation [ˌrenəˈveɪʃ(ə)n] *n.* 翻新,整修

naturalization [ˌnætʃrəlaɪˈzeɪʃn] *n.* 归化,移入;移植

preservation [ˌprezəˈveɪʃ(ə)n] *n.* 保护,维护;保留,维持;(食物的)保存,保藏;保存的状况,保养的程度

restoration [ˌrestəˈreɪʃ(ə)n] *n.* 修复;恢复,重新实施;归还,返还;恢复,还原;(牙科)修补;修复物(或图),重建物(或图);原有地位的恢复,复位

advocacy [ˈædvəkəsi] *n.* 拥护,提倡;辩护,辩护术;游说(团体或组织);律师职业(或工作)

stipulate [ˈstɪpjuleɪt] *v.* 规定,明确要求

division [dɪˈvɪʒ(ə)n] *n.* 分开,分配;除法;部门;分歧,不和;分界线;(军队编制中的)师;(足球等体育运动中联赛的)级

corresponding [ˌkɒrəˈspɒndɪŋ] *a.* 相应的,相关的

formulate [ˈfɔːmjuleɪt] *v.* 制定,规划;确切表达,认真阐述;用公式表示

assist [əˈsɪst] *v.* 帮助,协助　*n.* (球赛中的)助攻;资助,帮助

bring into play 发挥;启用

original [əˈrɪdʒən(ə)l] *a.* 起初的,原先的;原作的,真迹的;新创作的;未发表的;独创

的，新颖的；有独到见解或独创性的　*n.*（艺术作品或文件的）原件，原稿；（文学作品中人物或地点的）原型；原版书，原版唱片

be committed/devoted/dedicated to 致力于

spill [spɪl] *v.* 溢出；洒落；（一群人）迅速涌出；（球赛中）掉球；向（某人）说出秘密　*n.* 洒出量；摔下，跌落

waterlogged [ˈwɔːtəlɒgd] *a.* 涝的；浸满水的，吸饱水的

a matter of importance 重要的事

sewer [ˈsuːə(r)；ˈsjuːə(r)] *n.* 下水道，阴沟；缝纫工，缝纫机　*v.* 为……铺设污水管道，用下水道排除……的污水；清洗污水管

infrastructure [ˈɪnfrəstrʌktʃə(r)] *n.* 下面结构；永久性军事设施；基础设施，基础建设

enterprise [ˈentəpraɪz] *n.* 企事业单位；事业心，进取心；事业；创业，企业经营

C-E Language Disparity 7—Rigidity vs. Flexibility 刚性与柔性

Differences in Grammar between Chinese and English

Generally speaking, Chinese language is "under the rule of man" while English language is "under the rule of law", which follows strict grammar rules and changes grammatical forms in terms of gender, tense, number, aspect, etc. Chinese grammar is often hidden and its rules are loose and flexible, which is the very reason why some even say that the Chinese language has no grammar.

The meaning of Chinese sentences often determines their form. Chinese characters have not undergone any such radical morphological change as English words. Chinese grammatical meanings of number, gender, tense (time and aspect), voice, mood, etc., are hidden in sentences.

In addition to lexicology, grammar is chiefly concerned with syntax, i.e. the sentence structure. This part concentrates on the sentence just because it is the basic operational unit in translation.

What is a sentence? To put it simply, the sentence is "a complete expression of a single thought". The sentence is essentially an assumed abstract unit connected with other ideas and put in an actual context to have a certain meaning. Speakers or writers express their ideas through sentences or groups of sentences and listeners or readers receive and respond to them.

Chinese and English sentences are not exactly corresponding language units. Generally, the form of an English sentence usually commands its spirit. It is a tree-like structure following strict formulas, usually with a definite verb as its nucleus and a fixed point of observation of structural changes. The form of an English sentense is self-sufficient and the relationships between its parts are integral while the point of observation of the Chinese sentence is flowing, whose form seems loose but meaning is integral. Please look at the following Chinese sentences:

1. 她工作。
校长叫她工作。
有三个年轻教师和她一起工作。
没有哪个校长会叫她工作到深夜一点钟才休息。

2. 妥妥的。
安排得妥妥的。
把一切安排得妥妥的。
竟然把一切安排得妥妥的。
他竟然把一切安排得妥妥的。
没料到他竟然把一切安排得妥妥的。
的确没料到他竟然把一切安排得妥妥的。
她说她的确没料到他竟然把一切安排得妥妥的。
我听她说她的确没料到他竟然把一切安排得妥妥的。

3. 哪儿去了?
什么哪儿去了?
你说什么哪儿去了?
我哪儿知道你说什么哪儿去了?
你怎么会不知道我说什么哪儿去了?
你怎么会知道我一定知道你说什么哪儿去了?

It can be seen that Chinese sentences are open at the beginning or the end. But an English sentence is open only at the end. Please study the following cases carefully:

1. He teaches.

He teaches English.

He teaches English in a night school.

He teaches English in a night school not far from here.

He teaches English in a night school not far from here with my brother.

This is especially so since one can add many relative clauses:

2. This is the rat.

This is the rat that ate the malt.

This is the rat that ate the malt that lay in the house.

This is the rat that ate the malt that lay in the house Jack built.

The following is an extended English sentence:

The tall girl standing in the corner who became angry because you **knocked over** her glass after you waved to her when you entered is Miranda. (Its main part is "The girl is Miranda.")

What do you think of the following translation (which retains the attributive structure)?

在你进来时挥手打翻了她的杯子、惹她生气的、站在拐角上的那位高个子姑娘是米兰达。

The major difference between the Chinese sentence and the English sentence is that, morphologically speaking, the Chinese sentence is of a loose structure and its process is often dynamic. However, in a static English sentence, there is a morphological focus, taking the predicate verb as the center so that the "Subject+Predicate" structure is always clear, and secondary parts of the sentence all have clear levels, which is why some scholars compare the Chinese sentence to a "lion" and the English sentence to a "peacock".

Generally speaking, English sentences have the following five patterns:

Pattern 1: Subject+Intransitive Verb

We disagreed. /The baby girl was crying.

Pattern 2: Subject+Transitive Verb+Object

She is living a contented life. /We shall do our best.

Pattern 3: Subject+Dative Verb+Indirect Object+Direct Object

My father told us many stories. /Her mother bought her a dictionary.

Pattern 4: Subject+Transitive Verb + Object +Complement to the Object

They elected her monitor. /She felt the office building shaking.

Pattern 5: Subject+Linking Verb+Predicate (also known as "complement to the subject")

Edgar is my classmate. /The elderly woman doesn't look fifty.

There are three varieties of Pattern 5:

Pattern 5-1: Subject + Intransitive Verb + Predicate (also known as "complement to the subject")

They parted good friends.

Pattern 5-2: There be + Subject + Prepositional Phrase (called "existential sentence")

There are two pictures on the wall.

Pattern 5-3: It be that... (the emphatic pattern)

a. It was he that/who told me the news.

是他告诉我这个消息的。/告诉我这个消息的是他。

b. It isn't everybody that can do this job.

不是人人都能干这活的。/这活不是人人都能干的。

Chinese sentences also have patterns similar to the five listed above, except for Pattern 5-2 and Pattern 5-3. Also, Chinese sentences of Pattern 5 often leave out the linking verb. The usual pattern for existential sentences in Chinese is "Place +有+Object": 桌上有 5 本书。Pattern 5 is the most frequently used in English, with a frequency of about one-third.

Structuralists classify sentences into four formulas:

1) Noun/Pronoun + Verb

2) Noun/Pronoun + Verb + Adjective

3) Noun/Pronoun + Verb + Noun/Pronoun

4) Noun/Pronoun + Verb + Noun/Pronoun-1+ Noun/Pronoun-2

Upon the basic elements of these four formulas, determiners, auxiliaries, prepositions and other function words and modifiers may be added.

Chinese and English sentences have similar basic structures, with two major parts: the subject and the predicate. In Chinese sentences, adjectives, adverbs, and nouns can also function as the predicate while in English, the predicate can be performed only by verbs. As Chinese sentences are essentially not "grammatical" but "semantic", more and more people are now analyzing Chinese sentences by dividing them into the topic (theme) and the comment (rheme). Topic and comment emphasize the content, while theme and rheme emphasize their position in the sentence. These are terms referring to information transmission. The "topic" or "theme" usually contains known information, and the "comment" or "rheme" contains new information. English is a "subject-prominent" language and Chinese is a "topic-prominent" language.

Chinese sentences can be used like phrases to serve as the subject, the object and so on in a sentence. The agent, the object or the tool (of the action) can be expressed as the subject, the object, or even as the attributive or the adverbial. Such basic structures can be combined to form various types of sentences.

How many basic sentence patterns are there in Chinese? It is hard to give a definite answer, as grammarians themselves have not reached any consensus yet. Basically, Chinese sentences are of two major types: the "Subject + Predicate" sentence and the "Non-subject + Predicate" sentence. The latter includes the "zero-subject" sentence and the "one-member" sentence. But there are four types of the former according to the formation of the predicate:

A. Verb predicate sentence (动词谓语句)

a. 太阳升起来了。(Subject + Predicate)
b. 我们热爱和平进步。(Subject + Predicate + Object)
c. 北京是中国的首都。(Subject + Predicate + Object)

Usually the verb 是 is regarded as a transitive verb and what follows is the object, though some people analyze it more along the lines of Western grammar by calling 是 a "linking verb" followed by a predicate.

B. Adjective predicate sentence(形容词谓语句)

a. 天亮/黑/晴了。(Subject+Predicate)
b. 他们的干劲儿大得很。(Subject+Predicate+Complement)

C. Noun predicate sentence(名词谓语句)

a. 后天星期六。(Subject+Predicate)
b. 她江苏南京人。(Subject+Predicate)

D. "Subject predicate" predicate sentence（主谓谓语句）

a. 他身高长了 15 厘米。
b. 那人你可小看不得。

Special Chinese sentence patterns

There are also some special Chinese sentence patterns with no counterparts in English. Here are some of them：

A. The 把-sentence（"把"字句）

a. 小赵把那瓶盐水喝了。
b. 她把那本《英汉汉英水科技双解词典》弄脏了。
c. 他把她狠狠地教训了一通。
d. 父亲含辛茹苦地把五个孩子都拉扯成人。

The 把-sentence can put the object in front of the verb and thus express a kind of emphasis.

Usually the object of the preposition 把 is a noun, a pronoun, or a noun phrase. It may also include other structures.

a. 暑假期间，我把水球学会了。
b. 南京人民把开发江北、振兴江北看作头等大事。

However, there are some restraints in the usage of this pattern：1) its verb should have the meaning of "disposing" and do not express actions, such as 是，有，像，存在，etc.，and verbs referring to the senses, such as 感到，看见，etc.，are not used in the pattern；2) the object introduced by 把 should be definite or specific；hence it is incorrect to say 他把任何人都批评了一通；3) there should be some other elements before or after the verb, therefore, a single verb, especially one made up of a single character, cannot be used in this pattern；4) the negation word in most cases comes before 把, except in sayings like 把事不当事，把这件事不当回事，or the sentence should be a double negative.

B. The 被-sentence（"被"字句）

被 is originally a verb meaning "suffer/bear". It is most frequently used as a preposition, often to show passiveness. Some people call sentences with "被" 被

字句. But as several other words serve the same function as 被,some scholars call this type of sentence 被动句(passive sentence). The 被-sentence has the following characteristics: 1) the subject (the patient of the action) in most cases is definite; 2) it is not used in imperative sentences; 3) most of such sentences indicate something already accomplished. The 被-sentence mainly appears in the form of affirmative sentences and is seldom used in negative sentences or questions. It may fall into the following patterns:

a. Patient (subject)+被+Agent+Verb: 他被几个小无赖戏弄了。

Variations: 被(为),所(给): 他被小无赖所戏弄。

b. Patient (subject)+被+Verb: 她家被偷了。

c. Patient (subject)+被+Verb+Noum (direct object)

c1. 那部水文化系列剧已被她译成英语。

c2. 她被(恶霸)害死了妹妹。(妹妹 belongs to 她)

The following verbs can be used instead of 被 to form "quasi-被-sentences": 挨, 遭, 受, 遭受, 由, 用, 归, 该, 可, etc.

It must be pointed out that 被 does not always indicate the passive voice, such as in 被它跑了. We find in recent media a funny phenomenon—被 is used with intransitive verbs, such as 被增长,被就业,被捐款,and even 被自愿. Such extraordinary usage reflects the hopelessness of people who are forced to do things against their own will but are officially said to be willing to do these things.

C. The "Verb + Verb" pattern (连动式,also called 连谓式)

a. 她走过去闻了闻。(continuous action)

b. 快叫出租车上医院看病。(purpose)

c. 我们每天晚上都来这儿自习。(purpose)

d. 她老躲在宿舍里不出门。(apposition)

e. 小张搞创新教学信心不足。(The first verb in a way serves as an adverbial to denote the scope. The sentence means 小张在搞创新教学方面信心不足.)

D. Telescopic form (兼语式, in which the object of the first verb also serves as subject of the second verb)

a. 你能安排我教自由泳吗?

b. 她让你们游过泳、睡过午觉后再来。

E. Double reference pattern (复指句)

a. 那篇《河流之歌》散文,我非常喜欢它。
b. 小张、小陈、小李,还有小龚,他们四个人都去游泳馆了。

F. 的-phrase subject sentence ("的"字式主语句)

是梁山好汉的,站出来!

G. Double predicate pattern(复谓句)

a. 他喝酒喝醉了。
b. 她洗被单、毛衣,一洗就是大半天。
c. 昨天他找你找了四次才找着。

Sentence Elements

1. The subject

The "subject" has the meaning of "topic" and "theme", and thus is often syntactically connected with the theme of the sentence. The role of the English subject is mainly played by a noun, a pronoun, a noun phrase, or a noun clause, typically a "what" clause.

The Chinese subject has the following characteristics: 1) there can be a pause, or words like 啊,呢,么,吧,呀 can be inserted between the subject and the predicate without changing the meaning of the sentence; 2) the subject can be and is often omitted as long as no misunderstanding arises; 3) the subject relates known information about someone or something definite; 4) if what is emphasized is the whole thing, the subject refers to the whole; 5) the subject may be neither the agent nor the patient of the action of the predicate.

Some people hold that there is no subject in the Chinese sentence; it has only the theme or the agent of the action. Generally, the subject of the Chinese sentence is different from that of the English sentence. The term "theme" is semantic rather than grammatical. But some people think the theme of the Chinese sentence can be one of the two types.

A. Subject theme:

a. **地球人**都知道。

b. **那栋大楼**轰的一声倒下了。

B. Topic theme:

a. **那座房子**幸亏去年没有下这么大的雨。

b. **赴宴而不喝酒**,可得有点本事才行。

The Chinese subject may be a noun, a pronoun or equivalent elements and other structures.

a. **水稻**是南方常见的一种农作物。(theme)

b. **他们**买了一大堆菜。(agent of the action)

c. **提水站**建在村南头坡地上。(patient of the action)

d. **前天**又下了一场大雪。(time)

e. **海边**盖了几栋新楼。(place)

f. **一把菜刀**闹革命。(tool)

g. **这个情况**暂时要保密。(relation)

h. **这点儿橡皮泥**还不够捏个小猫呢。(participant of the action)

i. **一千**就是十个百,一百个十,一千个一。(numerical)

j. **再好也比**不上他大哥。(degree)

k. **大声说出来**好。(verb)

l. **你知道我们的难处**就好了。("S + P + O" structure)

m. 三十多年前**所发生的那些乱七八糟的事我现在脑子里**真的一点印象都没有。(multi-level structure)

In a broad sense, there is another kind of theme like those found in the following sentences, but it is better to understand them as adverbials merely placed at the beginning of the sentence.

a. 下午,你有其他安排吗?

b. 对他,我真的没有太高的期望。

c. 厨房里,新买了一套水池。

Such structures are similar to those of reversed sentences in English (called thematic fronting).

a. *A terrible mess* you've made.

b. *Miranda* he gave nothing but *Susan* he gave twenty pounds.

c. *Out* ran the woman and her husband.

d. *Of all his daughters*, Elizabeth is the most beautiful.

In sentences with "S+P" structures serving as the predicate, there might be different semantic relations between the "major subject" (the subject of the whole sentence) and the "minor subject" (the subject in the predicate).

a. 这首河流之歌,我会唱了。

b. 她一口水都没喝。

c. 高警察,她自己有两个儿子参加海军了。

d. 村东边那片地,我已种上水稻。

In some sentences of such structure, the "major subject" and the "minor subject" may both be connected to the whole idea or constitute a double reference.

a. 孙女士,她是个守信用的人。

b. 那瓶红葡萄酒,这家伙一口气就喝去大半瓶。

c. 这种电影,我只看进口大片。

Sometimes the subject does not have any direct semantic relation with the predicate, rather with the whole "S+P" structure serving as the predicate of the sentence.

a. 这场暴风雨,幸亏我们早有准备。

b. 这笔业务,你是怎么操作的?

When a complicated structure (such as "V+O" structure and "S+P" structure) is used as the subject, it usually appears in the first part of the sentence while a logical structure similar to the subject in the English sentence usually appears in the latter part. This shows that Chinese has a higher degree of nominalization than English, while English has a stronger sense of clauses with higher independence.

a. 认识您真荣幸。It's my honor to know you.

b. 一个人竟会堕落到如此地步,真是难以置信。It is hardly believable that a man should fall so low.

Now look at the following sentences:

a. 她喜欢海鱼,我不喜欢。

b. 海鱼她喜欢,我不喜欢。

c. 吃海鱼她最带劲,我不在乎。

d. 她今天海鱼吃得不过瘾。

e. 她今天海鱼吃得不过瘾,我不能不知道。

There are one, two, three, and four themes respectively in the above sentences. The corresponding English for the first sentence might be "She likes seafish, but I don't." The second can be translated into English by using reversed order ("Seafish she likes, but I don't."), though it does not sound very natural. There is no corresponding structure in English for the third sentence, which can only be translated as "She is crazy about seafish, but I don't care." The fourth sentence can be translated as "She didn't have enough seafish today." As for the fifth sentence, the topic part of the Chinese sentence turns into an object (clause) when translated into English: "I surely know that she didn't have enough seafish today." or "She didn't have enough seafish today, which I surely know."

Long themes of the Chinese sentence often express a kind of front weight:

a. 被人缠上是件尴尬事,被人在大街上无缘无故地缠上更是令人尴尬万分。

b. 凡是有岗哨的地方,我们的侦察兵都绕过去了。

In translating Chinese into English, it is necessary to analyze the sentence so as to determine the theme of the Chinese translation and then make corresponding adjustments.

Please compare the following similar paragraphs in Chinese and English:

冰心出生于1900年10月5日,原名谢婉莹,福建长乐人,中国民主促进会(民进)成员。中国诗人,现代作家,翻译家,儿童文学作家,社会活动家,散文家。笔名冰心取自"一片冰心在玉壶"。1919年8月的《晨报》上,冰心发表第一篇散文《二十一日听审的感想》和第一篇小说《两个家庭》。1923年出国留学前后,开始陆续发表总名为《寄小读者》的通讯散文,成为中国儿童文学的奠基之作。1946年在日本被东京大学聘为第一位外籍女教授,讲授"中国新文学"课程,于1951年返回中国。1999年2月28日21时12分,冰心在北京医院逝世,享年99岁,被称为"世纪老人"。

Arthur Clarke was born in Minehead, England. Early interested in science, ***he*** constructed ***his*** first telescope at the age of thirteen. ***He*** served in the Royal Air Force as a radar specialist during World War II. ***He*** originated the proposal for the use of satellites in communication.

Careful comparison will reveal that there are several zero-subject sentences in the Chinese paragraph. The name 冰心 or pronoun 她 is omitted because the reference is clear. The English paragraph, however, has to use three *he* and one *his*.

2. Relation between verbs and their objects

Another manifestation of the paratactic character of the Chinese language is the relationship between verbs and their objects. Semantically, the object can perform any of the following roles with respect to the verb:

a. Real object or target object, that is, the patient of the action: 修空调,撰写可行性报告,卖家用电器

b. Object showing a result: 装修教学大楼,撰写翻译报告,修建地铁

c. Object showing a place or time: 长住酒店,游遍美洲,他们管白天我们管晚上

d. Object showing a means or tool: 过地磅,用手机,上电视

e. Object showing quantity:买了 7 本书,再读 5 遍

f. Object showing existence: 招进几十人,买洗漱用品

g. Object showing a cause: 养身体,避难

h. Object showing a purpose: 跑原材料,保健

i. Object showing a logical subject or an agent: 看医生,剩最后 1 天,刮起一阵大风

j. Object showing content: 了解行情,(天气预报)说有大雪

k. Object showing a manner: 利用时间差,打防守反击

l. Object showing a role: 踢中锋,唱主角

m. Object showing a judgment: 真是个坏蛋

n. Object showing a comparison: 活像个死人

It seems that the Chinese object can refer to anything that has something to do with the action; thus, there may be various relations between the predicate verb and the object.

a. 他考博士研究生。(博士研究生 is the patient or purpose of the action 考)

b. 飞机上午 9 点到桂林。(桂林 is the object of 到)

c. 她星期六就去吃麦当劳。(麦当劳 is considered the object of 吃 even though it refers to the place; the sentence can be changed into 她星期六到麦当劳

吃快餐。)

吃 can be metaphorically used as a transitive verb：吃闭门羹(be denied entry; find the host not at home and the door locked)，吃了豹子胆（become extremely bold)，吃天鹅肉(yearn for something impossible)，吃花生米(be killed by a bullet)，吃醋(be jealous)，吃定心丸（rest reassured)，吃仙丹(to have taken the elixir of life)，吃后悔药(regret)，吃粉笔灰（be a teacher)，吃软不吃硬(be open to persuasion but not to coercion)，吃罪（take the blame)，吃斋（abstain from meat and fish and chant Buddhist scriptures)，吃闲饭(unemployed and without income；be a loafer)，吃现成饭（reap without sowing；feed on the fruits of others' labour)，etc. But 吃请（accept a dinner invitation)，吃亏（suffer losses；come to grief；get the worst of it)，(你以为我是)吃素(的)，(在那里吃饭是)吃情调，etc.，are a different case altogether. They are words rather than a "V+O" structure. 吃 in phrases like 吃紧[a(n) tense/critical/important/essential situation]，吃力（strenuous；painstaking)，吃香(popular；in great demand；much sought after)，吃不住(be unable to bear or stand)，吃得开(workable，practical；popular)，吃得消（be able to endure or stand)，etc.，is intransitive.

Please appreciate the following C-E version：

The following is taken from a short essay through which we may see how complicated the usage of 吃 can be.

"吃"的流行——中国"文化"

谋生叫糊口；工作叫饭碗；受雇叫混饭；靠积蓄过日子是吃老本；混得好叫吃得开；女人漂亮叫秀色可餐；受人欢迎叫吃香；受偏爱、受照顾叫吃小灶；不顾他人叫吃独食；没人理会叫吃闭门羹；有苦难言叫吃哑巴亏；嫉妒叫吃醋；理解不透叫囫囵吞枣；理解深刻叫吃透；广泛流传叫脍炙人口；收入太少叫吃不饱；负担太重叫吃不消；犹豫不决叫吃不准；干不成叫干什么吃的；负不起责任叫吃不了兜着走；打招呼说"吃了吗"。

The Popularity of "Eating"—Chinese Culture

Making a living is called "living from hand to mouth". One's work is called "one's rice bowl". Being employed is called "working for a living". Living on savings is called "living on thrift". Blending/Fitting in well is called "getting well along with others". A beautiful woman is called "food delicate enough to feast one's eyes on". Being popular is called "being much sought-after". Being favored and taken care of is called "enjoying some kind of privilege". Disregarding others is called "eating alone without sharing with others". Not taking notice is called "being left out in the cold". Suffering is called "eating (swallowing) dumb loss". Jealousy is called "drinking vinegar" or "being jealous". Not understanding thoroughly is called "swallowing jujube". Deep understanding is called "having a thorough grasp". Being widely spread is called "being pleasant to eat/hear". Too little income is "not enough to eat"; too heavy a burden is "hard to eat/bear". Hesitancy means "uncertainty". Failure to make it in time is due to not doing it earlier. Inability to bear the responsibility will "land yourself in serious trouble". When greeting each other, Chinese people always start with "Have you eaten?"

C-E Translation Strategies and Skills 7—Reordering of Sentence Structures 句子重组

1. 我曾多次见他画小鸡,毛茸茸,很可爱;也见过他画鱼鹰,水是绿的,钻进水里的,很生动。

On several occasions, I watched him paint fluffy little chicks, and (I also watched him paint) vivid cormorants with their heads in clear green water.

2. 当所发生的事情与你的价值观完全相反或者对你的机构所支持的项目有威胁时,你需要为你的观点而战。(句尾为重)

You need to fight for your point of view when something is counter to your values or threatens a project the organization supports.

3. 我们认为,如果不尊重一个国家大多数人民的正当愿望,任何和平局面都不会是持久的。

We maintain that no peace is permanent without taking into account the legitimate wishes of the majority of the people of a country.

4. 他心中的所谓文化,与人的精神心灵有关,不能用物质的丰富,甚至艺术文明来衡量。他跟东方人交往很久,也同情东方人;在东方人心目中,文化也是如此。

Culture to him, as to the Orientals, with whom he lived so much and sympathized so deeply, was an affair of the spirit and of mind not to be measured by material progress, or, even by the arts.

5. 现代核心家庭渴望享受更平等的婚姻关系所带来的幸福生活。在这样的家庭里，父母间由于理性的爱所带来的友好关系保证了他们能共同抚养孩子和共同在孩子身上投入。

The modern nuclear family was rooted in the desire to live happily in the form of a more equal marriage, where the raising of children and investment of both parents in the children's lives were guaranteed by bonds of friendship between the parents, which were based on rational love.

6. 杭州的春天，淡妆浓抹，无不相宜；夏日荷香阵阵，沁人心脾；秋天，桂枝飘香，菊花斗艳；冬日，琼装玉琢，俏丽媚人。西湖以变化多姿的风韵，令人心旷神怡。

Sunny or rainy, Hangzhou looks its best in spring. In summer the fragrance of lotus flowers gladdens the heart and refreshes the mind. Autumn brings with it the sweet scent of laurel flowers, and chrysanthemums are in full bloom. In winter the snow scenery looks just like jade-carvings, charming and beautiful. The ever-changing aspects of the beauty of West Lake makes one care-free and joyous.

7. "泰坦尼克"号起航后的第四天，正行驶在北大西洋冰冷的海面上。突然，瞭望员发现正前方有一座冰山。警报拉响后，巨轮急转弯，以避免与冰山正面相撞。"泰坦尼克"号这个弯儿拐得及时，紧贴着高出海面 100 英尺的巨大冰墙擦了过去。

Four days after setting out, while the Titanic was sailing across the icy waters of the North Atlantic, a huge iceberg was suddenly spotted by a lookout. After the alarm had been given, the great ship turned sharply to avoid a direct collision. The Titanic turned just in time, narrowly missing the immense wall of ice which rose over 100 feet out of the water.

8. 只有在水中或水边生活的动植物，才有很大可能留下遗骸，因为残骸保存下来的条件之一，就是迅速埋葬，而且只有在泥浆和淤泥能够接连不断沉淀的地方——海洋、河川或湖泊，动植物遗骸及其类似的东西才能被快速覆盖而保存下来。

It is animals and plants which lived in or near water whose remains are most likely to be preserved, for one of the necessary conditions of preservation is quick burial, and it is only in the seas and rivers, and sometimes lakes, where mud and silt has been continuously deposited, that bodies and the like can be rapidly covered over and preserved.

C-E Guided Translation Practice 7

1. 红海早过了,船在印度洋面上开驶着,但是太阳依然不饶人地迟落早起,侵占去大部分的夜。夜仿佛纸浸了油,变成半透明体;它给太阳拥抱住了,分不出身来,也许是给太阳陶醉了,所以夕照晚霞隐褪后的夜色也带着酡红。到红消醉醒,船舱里的睡人也一身腻汗地醒来,洗了澡赶到甲板上吹海风,又是一天开始。(节选自钱钟书《围城》,1980 年版)

2. 唐小姐妩媚端正的圆脸,有两个浅酒涡。天生着一般女人要花钱费时、调脂和粉来仿造的好脸色,新鲜得使人见了忘掉口渴而又觉嘴馋,仿佛是好水果。她眼睛并不顶大,可是灵活温柔,反衬得许多女人的大眼睛只像政治家讲的大话,大而无当。古典学者看她说笑时露出的好牙齿,会诧异为什么古今中外诗人,都甘心变成女人头插的钗,腰束的带,身体睡的席,甚至脚下践踏的鞋袜,可是从没想到化作她的牙刷。她头发没烫,眉毛不镊,口红也没有擦,似乎安心遵守天生的限止,不要弥补造化的缺陷。总而言之,唐小姐是摩登文明社会里那桩罕物——一个真正的女孩子。有许多都市女孩子已经是装模做样的早熟女人,算不得孩子;有许多女孩子只是浑沌痴顽的无性别孩子,还说不上女人。(节选自钱钟书《围城》,1980 年版)

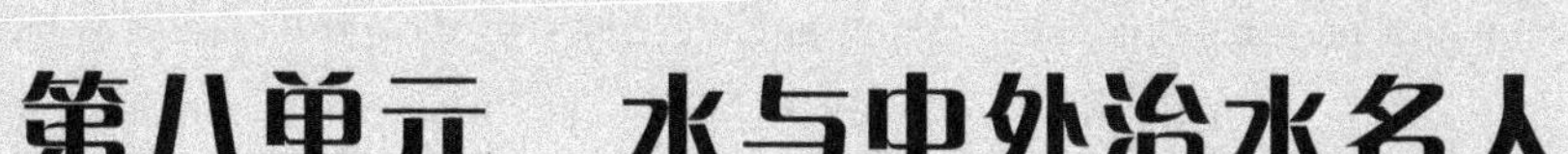

第八单元　水与中外治水名人

Unit 8　Water and Chinese and Foreign Sages and Celebrities

水是孕育生命的摇篮,也是滋养文明的源泉。早期人类在用水、治水、管水过程中,逐渐形成了民族与文明。在漫漫历史长河中,水的品格影响了无数中外圣贤。老子在《道德经》中说:"上善若水。水善利万物而不争,处众人之所恶,故几于道。"孔子曾说:"智者乐水,仁者乐山。"同样,古希腊哲学家泰勒斯认为水是万物的本源。这都体现了水对于中外圣贤思想的影响。除去对人思想的塑造,水的品格同样对人品有着重要的塑造作用。从古至今,国内外有许多与水相关的名人事迹,他们的为人与经历,无不与水的高尚品格对应。

Water is the cradle of life and the nourishing source of civilization. Early humans gradually formed nations and civilizations in the process of using water, controlling water, and managing water. In the long history, the character of water has influenced countless Chinese and foreign sages and celebrities. Lao Tzu said in the *Dao De Jing*, "The supreme good is like water, which nourishes all things without trying to. It is content with the low places that people disdain. Thus it is like the Tao." Confucius once said, "The wise are happy with water, and the benevolent are happy with mountains." Similarly, the ancient Greek philosopher Thales believed that water is the origin of all things. All these reflect the influence of water on the thinking of sages and celebrities at home and abroad. In addition to shaping people's thoughts, the character of water also plays an important role in shaping a person's character. From ancient times to the present, there have been many deeds of celebrities related to water at home and abroad, and their personalities and experiences all correspond to the noble character of water.

第一节　中国治水圣贤名人
Section A　Water and Chinese Sages and Celebrities

华夏文明的产生与发展,离不开先民对于洪水的治理。大禹是远古传说中著名的治水人物,他是夏后氏部落的首领。他在治理洪水时,吸取了父辈的治水经验,改变了治水方法,在经过实地考察后,决定利用水从高处向低处流这一特性,采用以"疏"为主,以"堙"为辅的方法来治理洪水。经过十几年的艰苦努力,终于取得了成功。古籍中大禹"三过家门而不入"的故事直到今天依然为大家津津乐道。

The emergence and development of Chinese civilization was inseparable from the ancestors' treatment of floods at that time. Yu the Great is a famous water control figure in ancient legends, and he is the leader of the Xiahoushi tribe. Legend has it that Yu the Great learned from his father's experience in water control and changed the method of water control when he was dealing with floods. After on-site investigation, he decided to take advantage of the characteristics of water flowing from high to low to control the flood. The flood control focused on "shu" (unblocking) and was supplemented by "yin" (burial). After more than ten years of hardships, it finally succeeded. In ancient books, it is documented that Yu the Great passed by his home three times but didn't set foot in because he wanted to tame the flood. This story is still widely being talked about today.

北宋时期的乔维岳，字伯周，后周陈州南顿（今项城）人。在他任淮南转运使期间，首创了二斗门复闸，成为世界上船闸最早的发明者。据《宋史》记载，两个斗门之间相距五十步，上面覆盖了房屋，有悬门来控制水位。这是我国单级船闸的最早记述，早于西方四百年，是现代船闸的前身，历史上称之为"复闸"。

Qiao Weiyue, whose courtesy name is Bozhou, was born in Nandun (now Xiangcheng City) in the Northern Song Dynasty. During his tenure as Huainan transshipment envoy, he pioneered the Erdoumen compound lock (when the first door is opened, if it is not closed, the second door will not be opened; only when the first door is closed can the second door be opened) and became the inventor of the earliest ship lock in the world. According to *Song History*, the two Erdoumen are fifty steps apart, covered with houses, and there are hanging doors controlling the water level. This is the earliest record of a single-level ship lock in our country, which is 400 years earlier than in the West. It was the predecessor of the modern ship lock and was called "multiple lock" in history.

范仲淹一生践行"先天下之忧而忧，后天下之乐而乐"的理想，他在水利建设、水旱灾害的治理方面做出了不朽的功绩。范仲淹在泰州任职时，主持了整个修堤工程。在四年努力之后，捍海堤终于修好，解除了这一带的潮水灾害，捍海堤被当地人民称为"范公堤"。

Fan Zhongyan practiced the ideal of "being the first to worry about the nation's woes and the last to share in its prosperity" throughout his life. He made immortal achievements in water conservancy construction and the management of floods and droughts. When Fan Zhongyan took office in Taizhou, he presided over the entire embankment repair project. After four years of hard work, the construction of the embankment was finally completed and the tidal disaster in this area was relieved. The embankment was hence named "Fangong Embankment (the embankment made by Fan Zhongyan)" by the local people.

王安石是北宋著名的政治家、改革家、文学家和思想家。王安石十分重视兴修水利,并将此视作"为天下理财"的途径。他撰写了《农田水利约束》,是我国第一部比较完整的农田水利法。该法实施后,大大调动了人民兴修水利的积极性。

Wang Anshi is a famous statesman, reformer, litterateur and thinker in the Northern Song Dynasty. Wang Anshi attached great importance to the construction of water conservancy and regarded this as a way to "manage money for the world". He wrote the *Irrigation and Drainage Rules of the North Song Dynasty*, which is China's first relatively complete law on farmland water conservancy. After the implementation of the law, the people's enthusiasm for water conservancy projects has been greatly aroused.

苏轼,字子瞻,号东坡居士,是北宋期间著名的文学家、政治家,同时还是一位杰出的水利专家。苏轼在徐州任职期间,洪水包围了徐州城,他亲自加入抢险队伍中,带领人民采取了有效的防洪措施。为了缅怀苏轼,后人把他在杭州西湖带领民众抢筑的长堤称为"苏堤"。

Su Shi, whose courtesy name is Zizhan and literary name is Dongpo Jushi, was a famous litterateur and statesman during the Northern Song Dynasty, as well as an outstanding water conservancy expert. During Su Shi's tenure in Xuzhou, floods surrounded Xuzhou City. Su Shi joined the rescue team and led the people to take effective flood prevention measures. In memory of him, the long dike he led the people to build in the West Lake in Hangzhou was called "Su Dike".

郏亶,字正夫,是北宋水利学家。成功考取进士后,郏亶并未上任,而是每天考察水利形势,总结前人治水的经验教训,著有《吴门水利书》四卷,提出要因地制宜来兴建农田水利。其子郏侨继承和发展了郏亶的学说,在水利建设上也颇有成就。

Jia Dan, whose courtesy name is Zhengfu, was an expert in water conservancy in the Northern Song Dynasty. After successfully being admitted as a Jinshi, Jia Dan did not take up his post. Instead, he inspected the water conservancy situation every day and summed up the experiences and lessons of predecessors in water management. He wrote four volumes of *Wu Men Water Conservancy Book*, proposing that irrigation and water conservancy showld be built according to local conditions. His son Jia Qiao inherited and developed Jia Dan's theory, and also made great achievements in water conservancy construction.

郭守敬,字若思,河北邢台人,元代杰出的科学家,十分擅长水利和天文历算。他尊重科学、因法而治,勇于担当责任,注重实地勘察,在原有水利基础上不断创新,一生在水利事业上成就斐然。

Guo Shoujing, whose courtesy name is Ruosi, was born in Xingtai in Hebei Province, and was an outstanding scientist in the Yuan Dynasty. He was very good at water conservancy and astronomical calculations. Guo Shoujing respected science, governed water by law, shouldered his responsibility courageously, paid attention to on-site surveys, innovated continuously on the basis of original water conservancy, and made remarkable achievements in water conservancy all his life.

潘季驯,字时良,浙江乌程(今湖州市)人,素有“千古治黄第一人”之誉。治黄过程中,他十分注重堤防修守,并充分吸取前人成果,全面总结了历史上治河的丰富经验,辩证地处理了黄、淮、运三者之间的关系,使得黄河近三百年没有发生改道。

Pan Jixun, whose courtesy name is Shiliang, was born in Wucheng (Huzhou City, Zhejiang Province), and is known as "the first person to govern the Yellow River through the ages". In the process of harnessing the Yellow River, he paid great attention to embankment maintenance, and fully absorbed the achievements of predecessors. He comprehensively summarized the rich experience of river governance in Chinese history, and dialectically dealt with the relationship between the Yellow River, the Huai River and the Grand Canal. Under his governance, there had been no diversion along the Yellow River within three hundred years.

林则徐,福建侯官(今福州)人,是清代后期政治家、文学家、思想家,民族英雄。在他四十年的政治生涯里,除了抵御外辱,治水也贯穿了他的一生。从北方的海河,到南方的珠江,从东南的太湖流域,到西北的伊犁河,都留下了他治水的足迹。

Lin Zexu, a native of Fujian Houguan (Fuzhou), was a statesman, writer, thinker, and national hero in the late Qing Dynasty. In his forty years of political career, in addition to resisting foreign humiliation and insult, water control ran through his lifetime. From the Haihe River in the north to the Pearl River in the south, from the Taihu Basin in the southeast to the Yili River in the northwest, were his footprints left in water management.

张謇是中国近代水利事业的先驱。在张謇七十岁生日时,荷兰驻华公使送来一副对联,称赞张謇"治水才长,功追大禹"。在治理淮河的过程中,他提出了"三分入海,七分入江"这一创新型理论,为治淮提供了思路。张謇是我国传统水利向近代水利变革中的关键人物,一生致力于水利工程的实践。

Zhang Qian is a pioneer of water conservancy in modern China. On Zhang Qian's 70th birthday, the Dutch minister in China sent him a pair of couplets, praising Zhang Qian for his "great talents in water control, and his merits are comparable to those of Yu the Great". In the process of harnessing the Huai River, the innovative theory of "three points into the sea and seven points into the river" was put forward, which provided ideas for harnessing the Huai River. Zhang Qian is a key figure in the transformation of our country's traditional water conservancy into modern water conservancy, and has devoted his lifetime to the practice of water conservancy projects.

New Words, Phrases and Expressions

countless [ˈkaʊntləs] *a.* 无数的,数不尽的

celebrity [səˈlebrəti] *n.* 名声,名望;名人,明星

benevolent [bəˈnevələnt] *a.* 仁慈的;乐善好施的;(用于慈善机构名称)慈善的,救济的

similarly [ˈsɪmələli] *adv.* 相似地;同样,也

correspond [ˌkɒrəˈspɒnd] *v.* 类似于,相当于;通信;相一致,符合

inseparable [ɪnˈseprəbl] *a.* (人)形影不离的;(东西)分不开的,不可分离的;(前缀)不可单独成词的 *n.* 不能分开的人(或事物)

supplement [ˌsʌplɪˈment] *vt.* 增补;补充

courtesy [ˈkɜːtəsi] *n.* 礼貌,彬彬有礼;礼貌的行为(言语) *a.* 免费提供的;礼节性的

compound lock 复式闸门

predecessor [ˈpriːdəsesə(r) /ˈpredəsesər] *n.* 前任,前辈;(被取代的)原有事物,前身

multiple lock 多线船闸

reign [reɪn] *n.* (君主)在位时期,统治时期;领导期,任期;支配期,极盛期 *v.* 为王;统治;支配;盛行;成为最佳,成为最重要的

immortal [ɪˈmɔːt(ə)l] *a.* 不死的，永存的；不朽的，流芳百世的，永垂千古的　*n.* 神，永生不灭者；永垂不朽的人物

preside [prɪˈzaɪd] **over** 主持；负责

embankment [ɪmˈbæŋkmənt] *n.* 路堤；堤防

relieve [rɪˈliːv] *v.* 缓解（疼痛或不快的感觉）；减轻（问题的严重性）；接替，替下；调剂，排遣；给（城镇）解围，解救；救济，救援；使某人摆脱（烦人的责任）；免去，解除；上厕所，排便

litterateur [ˌlitərəˈtəː] *n.* 文人；文学家；学者

constraint [kənˈstreɪnt] *n.* 限制，束缚；克制，拘束

implementation [ˌɪmplɪmenˈteɪʃ(ə)n] *n.* 实施，执行

astronomical [ˌæstrəˈnɒmɪk(ə)l] *a.* 天文（学）的，天体的；（数量、价格或收费）天文数字的，极其巨大的

harness [ˈhɑːnɪs] *v.* 控制并利用；（把动物）拴在一起（或拴到某物上）；给（马）套上挽具；连接，串联　*n.*（马的）挽具，马具；系带，吊带

absorb [əbˈzɔːb] *v.* 吸收；使并入，纳入；同化，汲取；消减，缓冲（外力、震动等）；理解，掌握（信息）；使全神贯注；承受（变革、影响等），承担（费用等）；花掉（大量金钱），耗费

summarize [ˈsʌməraɪz] *vt.* 总结，概述

dialectically [ˌdaɪəˈlektɪkəli] *adv.* 辩证法地

pioneer [ˌpaɪəˈnɪə(r)] *n.* 拓荒者；先锋；（苏联等社会主义国家的）少年先锋队队员；（先头部队的）工兵　*a.* 先驱的；拓荒的　*v.* 做先锋，倡导；开辟（道路）

第二节　西方治水圣贤名人
Section B　Water and Foreign Sages and Celebrities

除了中国水之圣贤，其他国家也有值得历史铭记的人物。

In addition to the sages and celebrities of water in China, other countries also have outstanding figures worth remembering in history.

古代埃及是四大文明古国之一。随着古代埃及逐步走向统一，灌溉网也逐渐覆盖到全埃及。希罗多德著作中记载了关于第一王朝创建者美尼斯为了建城而筑坝的内容："他第一个修筑了一道堤坝把孟菲斯和尼罗河隔开，……他在孟菲斯的北部和西部引出河水而挖掘了一个湖。"这些措施都大大提高了埃及的农业经济，为埃及后续的繁荣奠定了基础。

Ancient Egypt is one of the four ancient civilizations. With the gradual unification of ancient Egypt, the irrigation network gradually covered all of Egypt. Herodotus recorded that Menes, the founder of the First Dynasty, built the city through the construction of a dike: "The first one built a dam to separate Memphis from the Nile... He was in the north of Memphis. A lake was dug out to the west and led out the river." These measures have greatly improved Egypt's agricultural economy and laid the foundation for Egypt's subsequent prosperity.

日本战国时期的武田信玄注重治水,其中最具代表性的就是建筑于山梨县龙王的信玄堤。直到现在,信玄堤仍然可以算是日本土木史、治水史中一个伟大的工程。信玄治水采取非常科学的方法,他把本来和釜无川会合的御勅使川一分为二,利用逆流现象和设缓冲地带来互相牵制。筑完堤后,他下令在堤防附近开辟平原,迁徙农民去住,筑堤不仅可以防水灾,也解决了用水问题,繁荣堤下附近农田和村落。

During the Japanese Warring States Period, Takeda Shingen paid great attention to water control, and the most representative of which was the Shingen Embankment built in Ryuo, Yamanashi Prefecture. Up to now, Shingen Embankment can still be regarded as a great project in water management in the history of civil engineering in Japan. Shingen adopted a very scientific method for water management. He divided the Oteshigawa River, which had originally joined the Kamanashi River, into two by using counter-current phenomena and setting up buffering land. After the dam was built, he ordered the plains to be opened near the embankment, and the migrant farmers to go there to live. Building the embankment not only prevented water damage, but also met the water demand, which brought prosperity to the farmland and villages nearby.

日本平安时代的女作家紫式部在距离琵琶湖边不远的石山寺居住的时候,写下堪称日本历史画卷的《源氏物语》,琵琶湖是这部鸿篇巨制的灵感源泉。当年紫式部眼中的琵琶湖已成为日本文化不可分割的一部分,永远牵动着人们的心弦。琵琶湖美丽的景色浸润了紫式部的心灵,给了她创作的灵感。

The Japanese female writer Lady Murasaki, born in the Heian Period, lived in Ishiyama Temple not far from the Lake Biwa and wrote *The Tale of Genji*, a scroll of Japanese history, and the Lake Biwa was the source of inspiration for this magnum opus. The Lake Biwa in the eyes of Lady Murasaki has become an integral part of Japanese culture and will always affect people's minds. The beautiful scenery of the Lake Biwa has infiltrated the soul of Lady Murasaki and brought her creative inspiration.

经济大萧条时期,美国的社会矛盾不断加剧。富兰克林·罗斯福就任美国总统后,颁布了著名的罗斯福新政,其中国会通过的民间资源保护队计划为提供就业岗位、缓解社会矛盾,聘请身强力壮的年轻人从事防治水患、水土保持的工程建设。田纳西河流域的水利工程就是在那时建造的,该工程是一项水坝、水电站、航运、防洪功能兼有的水利系统。这些举措大大缓和了社会矛盾,把美国从经济危机的漩涡中解救出来。

During the Great Depression, social conflicts in the United States continued to intensify. After Franklin Roosevelt took office as President of the United States, he promulgated the famous New Deal. In order to provide jobs and alleviate social conflicts, the Civil Resource Protection Team approved by Congress hired able-bodied young people to engage in water and soil conservation projects. The water conservancy project to repair the Tennessee River Basin was built at that time. The project is a water conservancy system that combines dams, hydroelectric power stations, navigation, and flood control. These measures have greatly mitigated social conflicts and rescued the United States from the vortex of economic crisis.

"上善若水",是说圣人的品格同水一样,帮助万物而不与万物相争;"政善治,事善能"则是说为政要像水那样有条有理,办事要像水一样善于忍让和融通。历史上的圣贤都有着似水一般的优秀品格,不卑不亢,脚踏实地,滋养着后世的我们。

"The supreme good is like water" means that the character of a saint is the same as that of water, benefiting all things without fighting or contending with them. For statesmen, they should be organized like water and act like water, being good at tolerance and accommadation. The sages in history all have excellent characters like water, without humbling themselves or showing disrespect, but with their feet planted on solid ground, which has nourished one generation after another.

New Words, Phrases and Expressions

outstanding [aʊtˈstændɪŋ] *a.* 杰出的,优秀的;显著的,突出的;未解决或完成的;(款项)未支付或结清的

unification [ˌjuːnɪfɪˈkeɪʃ(ə)n] *n.* 联合,统一;联合的行为、实例或过程

network [ˈnetwɜːk] *n.* 网状（系统）；人际关系网，联络网；计算机网络，互联网；广播/电视网

lay the foundation for 为……奠定基础

prefecture [ˈpriːfektʃə(r)] *n.* 辖区，省，县；地方行政长官职务（或任期）；地方行政长官官邸/公署

originally [əˈrɪdʒənəli] *adv.* 起初，原来；独创地，新颖地

buffering [ˈbʌfərɪŋ] *n.* 缓冲作用；缓冲记忆装置；减震

waterproof [ˈwɔːtəpruːf] *a.* 防水的，不透水的　*v.* 使……不透水，对……做防水处理　*n.* 防水衣物，雨衣

The Tale of Genji《源氏物语》

magnum opus [ˌmæɡnəm ˈəʊpəs] 代表作；巨著；杰作

integral [ˈɪntɪɡrəl] *a.* 必需的，必要的；作为组成部分的；完整的；整的；积分的　*n.* 积分；完整

infiltrate [ˈɪnfɪltreɪt] *v.*（尤指为获取秘密情报而）渗透，渗入（组织、场所等）；（肿瘤、细胞等）浸润（组织、器官）；（液体）渗入；（某种特性缓慢地）透入，渗透　*n.*（医学）浸润物

the Great Depression 大萧条，经济大萧条

intensify [ɪnˈtensɪfaɪ] *v.* 加剧，增强；增强（底片）的阻光度，增加（底片）的厚度

take office 就职；走马上任

promulgate [ˈprɒm(ə)lɡeɪt] *v.* 传播，宣扬（思想或信仰）；发布，颁布（新法律）

New Deal 新政（美国总统罗斯福的国内政策和政府）

hydroelectric [ˌhaɪdrəʊɪˈlektrɪk] *a.* 水力发电的；水电治疗的

navigation [ˌnævɪˈɡeɪʃ(ə)n] *n.* 导航；航海/行；航运，水上运输；浏览，访问；领航/航海术；内河水道（尤指运河）

mitigate [ˈmɪtɪɡeɪt] *v.*（正式）减轻，缓和

vortex [ˈvɔːteks] *n.* 涡流；漩涡；（动乱等的）中心；旋风

omnipotent [ɒmˈnɪpətənt] *a.* 全能的，无所不能的

humble [ˈhʌmb(ə)l] *v.* 使谦卑，使感到自惭；（轻易）击败（强敌）　*a.* 谦虚的，谦卑的；（级别或地位）低下的，卑微的；简陋的，无特别之处的

disrespect [ˌdɪsrɪˈspekt] *n.* 无礼，失礼，不敬

C-E Language Disparity 8—Subjectivity vs. Objectivity 主观性与客观性

Language and Subjectivity

Language reflects people's reflections on and viewpoints of the world. As mentioned in Unit 1, it is generally agreed that language is more than a tool for expressing ourselves; it acts as a mirror to our world, reflecting back to us the way we live and think. The choice of language and new words we create reveals a lot about how we lead our lives today and how society is developing. But in a large sense, language is more often than not subjective as it usually reflects how speakers themselves look at the world. People from different countries or backgrounds may use different terms to refer to the same thing or phenomenon to show their own subjective attitudes or points of view.

Now look at the following short humorous and somewhat ironical paragraphs:

1. 爱迪生试制白炽灯泡,失败了 1200 次。一个商人讽刺他是个毫无成就的人,爱迪生哈哈大笑:"我已经有很大的成就,证明了 1200 种材料不适合做灯丝。"

2. 溥仪去故宫参观,看到墙上挂的照片,说:"这不是光绪帝,是醇亲王。"工作人员找来历史学家询问。历史学家说:"我们是专门研究历史的,是你懂还是我们懂?"溥仪说:"我是不懂历史,可我爹我还是认识的。"

Though the above two paragraphs are teasingly sarcastic, the obvious derogatory and commendatory terms reflect the speaker's attitude towards things in the world. However, the actual "world" includes both the objective world and people themselves as an object. People always subjectively separate themselves from the environment; and therefore, their ways of thinking and the language they use will take on a subjective meaning.

The most prominent characteristic of East Asian mode of thinking is regarding everything as a whole, while the most outstanding characteristic of the Western way of thinking is **analytical thinking** which stresses the dual qualities of all objective things. Philosophically, the former emphasizes the combination of two into one, while the latter stresses the division of one into two. Traditional Chinese philosophy seeks harmony between man and nature, according to which man's highest pursuit is to become an integral part of nature.

Most Chinese philosophers hold that the universe is integral and that man and nature have developed into an organic whole, while Westerners usually detach themselves from the objective world. Lao Tzu said, "Tao gave birth to the One; One gave birth successively to two, three, up to ten thousand." Both the humanizing of nature advocated by Confucianism and the naturalizing of human beings proposed by Taoism conceive of man and nature as one organic whole coming down along one continuous line, all of which reflects an integral way of thinking. Westerners, on the other hand, lay much stress on exploiting the essence of the universe, maintaining that man and nature are in constant contradiction and opposition. Rene Descartes (1596-1650), the father of modern Western philosophy, views the physical world as mechanistic, which is entirely divorced from the mind, and thinks of the contradiction of the subject and the object as the guiding principle of philosophy. This is a concentrated manifestation of analytical thinking. Traditional Western philosophy stresses rational reasoning and believes that there is a distance between the objective world and people's subjective world. As a result, the English language distinguishes objective views from subjective views, and there are more ways to express this distinction, that is the opposition or the division of one into two. Comparatively, English speakers often proceed from the objective viewpoint in their observation and description; in a philosophical term, they prefer objectification. Meanwhile, traditional Chinese philosophy emphasizes comprehensiveness so as to follow the will of Heaven (nature). The Chinese have a strong sense of participation. They think that humans and "things" are one. Both Lao Tzu and Mencius maintain a subjectively-inclined way of thinking, which indicates that the Chinese language does not pay much attention to the distinction between the subjective and the objective, comparatively showing a stronger tendency of subjectification.

It can be found that the distinction between subjectivity and objectivity is also manifested in even the daily usage of the Chinese language. In conversations, native speakers often begin statements about themselves with set phrases like "Well, you see", "You know", "You bet", etc. On the other hand, even in business talks, Chinese people often say 我们觉得,我方认为,我们希望,我们建议,etc. More often than not, Westerners would like to say "It is hoped that..." or "It is expected that...". Even when Chinese people want to emphasize their own opinions, they would use "we" instead of "I".

However, it is not enough to arrive at any convincing conclusion by merely looking at one or two aspects of the language. This issue can be seen from many perspectives: 1) subjective and objective standards, 2) description of mental activities, 3) the passive voice, and 4) inanimate subject.

Subjective and Objective Standards

The English language is well known for its richness in synonyms. Some synonyms may emphasize subjectivity while others emphasize objectivity. Synonyms such as *little* and *small* both correspond with Chinese character 小; *dear* and *expensive* match Chinese character 贵. Both *little* and *dear* show more attitudinal subjectivity while *small* and *expensive* reflect more objectivity.

In the pattern "have something done", the subject of the sentence does not necessarily perform the action itself but rather arrange for something to be done, thereby showing a sense of objectivity. Therefore, without knowing the context, it is hard to determine if the Chinese sentence 我要去照相 means "I am going to take a/some picture(s)" or "I am going to have a/some picture(s) taken".

Depiction of Mental Activities in English

The passive voice is usually used in depicting mental activities. This is shown in some causative verbs. Please look at the following examples:

She was/We were annoyed/bewildered/bored/charmed/delighted/depressed/disappointed/discouraged/disgusted/encouraged/excited/fascinated/impressed/interested/moved/obsessed/offended/panicked/pleased/relieved/satisfied/surprised/vexed/worried, etc.

The cause behind this phenomenon should be the result of believing that such mental activities are reactions to some objective situations or things. However, we Chinese people express these ideas as 她/ 我们(感到)生气/困惑/厌烦/入迷/高兴/情绪低落/失望/沮丧/讨厌/激动/收到鼓励/影响很深/有兴趣/感动/受困扰或感到痴迷/受到伤害/感到恐慌的/高兴/松了一口气/满意/惊讶/烦

心/担忧, etc. , entirely subjectively, neglecting the fact that these mental activities are reactions to objective stimulation.

In addition to verbs expressing mental activities, there are certain transitive verbs in English which take the actor as the object, often by using reflexive pronouns.

1. The baby boy is learning to dress *himself*.

2. Be seated, please! (be seated = seat yourself)

Similar verbs include words like *bathe*, which express the actions that the objective/subjective exert on the subjective/objective, obviously manifesting how English distinguishes the subjective from the objective. However, there is nothing corresponding to such transitive verbs in Chinese other than intransitive verbs expressing self-actions like 穿(衣) and 坐(下). This also proves English makes a clearer distinction between the subjective and the objective than Chinese.

The Passive Voice

Many scholars have mentioned that the passive voice itself is a way of emphasizing objectivity in one's thinking, and it is used often in scientific and technical English for this very purpose.

Compare the following Chinese sentences and their respective English translations.

1. 新婚夫妇分到了一套新房子。A new flat was allotted to the newly wed couple.

2. 他感染了新冠。He was stricken with Novel Coronavirus.

Sure, translations are usually not used as authentic language data in proving any argument or laws. It is rather difficult to translate the above two sentences by retaining their original pattern; translations will typically be "domesticated", thereby producing native-like idiomatic English. Comparisons between Chinese and English can be clearly made, with the former attaching importance to subjectivity and the latter to objectivity.

Animated and Inanimate Subjects

Many English sentences have inanimate or impersonal subjects, while the pattern is rarely found in Chinese sentences. The cause lies in the different emphasis of these two languages. In the minds of most English speakers, lifeless things, including natural and social phenomena, can be agents Chinese speakers think that can do things. Here are two examples:

1. 水太多能把有些花淹死。Too much water may kill some flowers.

2. 我没完没了地问,惹她生了气,她就没好气地回答了我。My persistent questions finally goaded her into an angry reply.

Time and place are often used as the subject of the sentence. When translated into English, inanimate subjects are often used to bring out this sense of overt objectivity.

1. 十二点了,他还躺在床上。Twelve o'clock found him still lying in bed.

2. 1949 年,中华人民共和国成立了。The year 1949 witnessed the founding of the People's Republic of China.

The large number of sentences taking subjective things or phenomena as the (animate) subject of the sentence manifests the Chinese way of thinking, which often starts from the subjective.

1. 他开始对编辑工作感到越来越乏味。The editing job began to grow increasingly tedious to him.

2. 三十年来,我至少有 5%到 10%的收入用来购买各种书籍、VCD 和 DVD。Over the past thirty years, books, VCDs and DVDs have eaten at least 5% to 10% of my earnings.

3. 一想到父亲极有可能会发现,她突然感到极度恐惧。The very thought of being probably discovered by her father suddenly filled her with great fear.

The sentences with animate subjects reveal a way of thinking that separates the subjective from the objective, while their English translations make the objective sense more prominent.

But nothing is absolute and subjectivity and objectivity can be expressed in different ways. For example:

1. 这些新设施对观光者特别有吸引力。These new facilities are especially appealing to tourists.

2. 这些新便利设施受到观光客的特别欢迎。These new facilities are especially welcomed by tourists.

Different Levels of Objectivity

Subjectivity and objectivity are relative concepts. We humans are social animals belonging to different classes with different levels of social status. The division between the subjective and objective world has certain special criteria. Using different pronouns may be a way of denoting such divisions, no matter whether in Chinese or in English.

Geographic regions, cities, working institutions, schools, classes, or even small groups and teams are all important standards for distinguishing the subjective from the objective. Such distinctions can often be seen in the use of (possessive) pronouns.

Some kinds of expressions in English may sound strange to us Chinese:

1. She is beside herself with joy on hearing the news of her being on the debate team.

听到入选辩论队时,她高兴得忘乎所以、得意忘形。

2. They lost themselves in the sophisticated design of the mobile microelectronic chip.

他们专注于这种复杂的手机微电子芯片设计。

As a matter of fact, expressions like "beside/beyond oneself", "to lose oneself", etc. take *oneself* as an objective entity different from the speaker (also oneself), or rather as an objective observer. But in Chinese we only say 忘乎所以、得意忘形(forgetting reasoning) and 不知道自己是谁 (not knowing one's own position). In these expressions, the subjective and the objective are not confused. Expressions such as "beyond oneself", which regard the self as a special objectivity, are very rare in Chinese.

C-E Translation Strategies and Skills 8—Translation Quality Assessment Criteria, Machine Translation and Post-editing 翻译质量标准与评估,机器翻译与后期编辑

A. Translation Quality Assessment Criteria

Some well-known translators or translation theorists at home and abroad have put forward their own translation quality assessment criteria.

1. Yan Fu and the triple principle of translation

信（faithfulness）：内容忠实于原文　　being faithful to the original
达（expressiveness）：通顺流畅　　being explicit and smooth
雅（elegance）：文采措辞优雅　　being elegant in diction

Yan Fu put forward this "Three-character Principle" in his preface to the translation of T. H. Huxley's book *Evolution and Ethics and Other Essays*. He thinks that translation has to do three difficult things: to be faithful, expressive, and elegant. It is difficult enough to be faithful to the original, and yet if a translation is not expressive, it is tantamount to having no translation. Hence expressiveness should be required too. Yan Fu's first two criteria of being faithful to the original text in content and being expressive in translation are generally acceptable, but his interpretation of "elegance" has aroused plenty of criticisms because, in his opinion, one has to resort to the vocabulary and syntax of pre-Han prose to achieve "elegance". Yan Fu's criteria are also controversial for his emphasis on the equal status of the three conflicting principles. Despite this, Yan's criteria are still popular in China, but the interpretation of his criteria has changed. Nowadays to many translators, "elegance" implies "the safe and sound preservation of the taste and shade of the original" or "运用读者最乐于接受的文体，使译文得以广泛流传，扩大影响".

2. Lu Xun and faithfulness and smoothness

Lu Xun thinks that translation must be exotic, that is, of foreign flavor. In fact, there is no fully naturalized translation in the world. If there is, it is seemingly in harmony but actually at variance. Strictly discriminated, it cannot be called a translation, for each translation must take into account both aspects: the first is, of course, striving to make it easy to understand; the second is preserving the beauty of the original text. This preservation is often contradictory because it is hard to get used to. But it used to be a foreign devil, and therefore no one liked it. It had to change its clothes for the sake of comparison, but it should not cut down its nose or gouge out his eyes.

3. Lin Yutang and faithfulness, smoothness and beautifulness

Lin Yutang thinks that the standard of translation should include three levels. The first is the standard of fidelity, the second is the standard of smoothness, the third is the standard of beauty. This three-level standard of translation is in general in line with Yan's "three difficulties of translation". We should also remember that the three translation difficulties include: first, the translator's problems with the original text; second, the translator's problems with the Chinese language, and third, translation and art. According to the responsibility of the translator, the first is the translator's responsibility to the original author, the second is the translator's responsibility to the Chinese readers, and the third is the translator's responsibility to art. If all three responsibilities are fulfilled, then one can qualify as a true translator.

4. Fu Lei and resemblance in spirit or spiritual resemblance

Fu Lei thinks that in terms of effect, translation should be like a painting seeking resemblance not in form but in spirit, and that the dialectical relationship between resemblance in spirit and resemblance in form is that spirit is attached to form with form as the shell of spirit, and in this sense, form and spirit are in harmony. The essence of the harmony between spiritual resemblance and formal resemblance lies in expressing not only the definite point—the manifestation of the language, but also the indefinite point—the invisibility of the language, making it both vivid and expressive.

5. Qian Zhongshu and sublimation

Qian Zhongshu thinks that the highest level of literary translation is "transformation". When a work is transformed from a language of one country to another, it can not show the traces of stiffness and far-fetchedness caused by the differences in language habits, but completely preserve the original flavor, which can be considered as a "sublimated adaptation". Some people in the seventeenth century praised this accomplished translation from the original by comparing it to "the transmigration of soul", in which the body is changed but the spirit remains the same. In other words, the translation should be true to the original so as not to read like a translation, because the work will never be read like a translation in the original.

6. Liu Zhongde and faithfulness, expressiveness and closeness

信于内容（Be **faithful** to the **content** of the original）;

达如其分（Be as **expressive** as the original）;

切合风格（Be as **close** to the original **style** as possible）.

7. Xu Yuanchong and three levels of criteria/ three aesthetic pursuits of meaning, rhyme and form

标 准	低标准	中标准	高标准
内容忠实(信)	明确	准确	精确
三似	意似	形似	神似
三化	浅化	等化	深化
三之	知之	好之	乐之
形式通顺(达)	易懂	通顺	扬长(雅或传神)

Case 1：中华儿女多奇志，不爱红装爱武装(《七绝·为女民兵题照》，毛泽东)

Most Chinese daughters have desire so strong

To face the powder and not to powder the face.

许渊冲把"红装"译为"powder the face"(涂脂抹粉)，把"武装"译为"face the powder"(面对硝烟)，恰好表现了"红"与"武"的对应和"装"的重复，滴水不漏，堪称妙绝。

Case 2：

无边落木萧萧下，

不尽长江滚滚来。

The boundless forest sheds its leaves shower by shower;

The endless river rolls its wavers hour after hour.

"草字头"用重复 sh(sheds, shower)的译法，"三点水"则用重复 r(river, rolls)的译法。音义双绝，闻者称美。

8. Alexander Fraser Tytler and three principles of translation

Alexander Fraser Tytler, eighteenth-century professor of Edinburgh University and translation theorist, put forward Three Principles of Translation in Essay on the *Principles of Translation* in 1791: 1) The translation should give a complete transcript of the ideas of the original work. 2) The style and manner of writing in the translation should be of the same character with that of the original. 3) The translation should have all the ease of the original composition. Tytler further points out that the above-said three principles are arranged and ranked according to the order of their significance, and that, when they are not simultaneously attainable, the first should be held to at the sacrifice of the third principle, then the second.

9. Eugene A. Nida and functional equivalence

Eugene A. Nida has been acclaimed as a pioneer of the linguistic approach to translation studies. His work became the basis upon which a new field of investigation in the 20th century — the "science" of translation — was founded. He believes that translating consists in reproducing in the receptor language the closest natural equivalent of the source-language message, first in terms of meaning and secondly in terms of style.

What is equivalence?

If a specific linguistic unit in one language carries the same intended meaning/message encoded in a specific linguistic medium in another, then these two units are considered to be equivalent. The domain of equivalents covers linguistic units such as morphemes, words, phrases, clauses, idioms and proverbs.

He put forward his interpretation of **functional equivalence** in his ***Language and Culture: Context in Translating***: 1) A **minimal**, **realistic** definition of functional equivalence: The readers of a translated text should be able to comprehend it to the point that they can conceive of how the original readers of the text must have understood and appreciated it. 2) A **maximal**, **ideal** definition of functional equivalence: The readers of a translated text should be able to understand and appreciate it in essentially the same manner as the original readers did.

10. Peter Newmark and "semantic translation" and "communicative translation"

Semantic translation attempts to render, as closely as the semantic and syntactic structures of the second language allow, the exact contextual meaning of the original. **Communicative translation**, on the other hand, attempts to render the exact contextual meaning of the original in such a way that both content and language are readily acceptable and comprehensible to the readership.

Case 1:"谋事在人,成事在天"

Version 1:*Man proposes, Heaven disposes.* 为语义翻译。"天"是中国古代

文化中自然界的主宰。语义翻译 Heaven 忠实地保留了原文的道教概念。

Version 2:*Man proposes*, *God disposes*. 为交际翻译。God（上帝）是西方基督教徒心目中自然界的主宰。交际翻译将道教概念转化为基督教概念,适合西方读者的宗教背景和接受心理。

Case 2:

Everything is the same, but you are not here; and I still am. In separation the one who goes away suffers less than the one who stays behind.

——拜伦致情人语

白话文:一切如常,只是你走了,而我仍在此。两人分手,远行的人总不如留下的人这么受苦。

文言文:此间百凡如故,我仍留而君已去耳。行行生别离,去者不如留者神伤之甚也。(钱钟书《谈艺录》)

其他译文:时光荏苒,伊人不在,我心依旧,痴心等待。

Case 3:

海内存知己,天涯若比邻。

Version 1:If you have a friend afar who knows your **heart**,/Distance cannot keep you two **apart**.

Version 2:As long as you live in each other's **heart**,/Distance cannot keep you **apart**.

B. Machine Translation (MT): Reasons for Using MT and Its History and Development

Reasons for Using MT

Machine translation (MT), also known as automatic translation, is the application of computers to the task of translating texts from one natural language to another. As one of the earliest pursuits in computer science, MT used to be an elusive goal, but today a number of systems are available producing output which, if not perfect, is of quality high enough to be useful in a number of specific domains. There have been many reasons behind this. The principal reason is practical: scientists, technologists, engineers, economists, agriculturalists, administrators, industrialists, businessmen, and many others have to read documents and communicate in languages they do not know; and there are just not enough translators to cope with the ever-increasing volume of materials to be translated. MT would serve to relieve the pressure. The **second reason** is that many researchers have been motivated by lofty aims: the promotion of international cooperation and peaceful development, the removal of language barriers, the transmission of technical, agricultural and medical information to the poor and developing countries of the world. The **third reason** is that by contrast, some sponsors of MT activity have sensed its importance in military and intelligence contexts. **The fourth** is purely for research: to study the basic mechanisms of language and thinking to take advantage of the computer and to find its limitations. **The final one** is just for simple commercial and economic motives: to sell a product successfully, or to maintain high standards of living in such a fiercely competitive world.

History and Development of MT

Ideas about mechanizing translation processes may be traced back to the 17th century, but realistic possibilities came only in the 20th century. In the mid-1930s, a French-Armenian Georges Artsrouni and a Russian Petr Troyanskii applied for patents for "translating machines". Of the two, Troyanskii's was the more significant, proposing not only a method for an automatic bilingual dictionary, but also a scheme for coding interlingual grammatical roles (based on Esperanto) and an outline of how analysis and synthesis might work. The earliest systems consisted primarily of large bilingual dictionaries where entries for words of the source language gave one or more equivalents in the target language, and some rules for producing the correct word order in the output. It was soon recognized that specific dictionary-driven rules for syntactic ordering were too complex and increasingly ad hoc, and the need for more systematic methods of syntactic analysis became evident.

However, disillusion increased as researchers encountered "semantic barriers" to which they saw no straightforward solutions. The 1980s witnessed the emergence of a wide variety of MT system types from a widening number of countries. There was Logos (German-English and English-French), the internally developed systems at the Pan American Health Organization (Spanish-English and English-Spanish), the Metal system (German-English), and major systems for

English-Japanese and Japanese-English translation from Japanese computer companies. Throughout the 1980s, research on more advanced methods and techniques continued. For most of the decade, the dominant strategy was that of "indirect" translation via intermediary representations, sometimes interlingual in nature, involving semantic as well as morphological and syntactic analysis, and sometimes non-linguistic "knowledge bases".

In the end of the early 1990s, the decade was a major turning point in the development of MT. A group from IBM published the results of experiments on a system (Candide) based purely on statistical methods. Then, certain Japanese groups began to use corpora-based translation examples, i. e. using the "example-based" translation approach. Both approaches differed from earlier "rule-based" methods in the exploitation of large text corpora.

Research started on speech translation, involving the integration of speech recognition, speech synthesis, and translation modules—the latter mixing rule-based and corpus-based approaches. MT activity changed its focus from theoretical research to practical applications, to the development of translator workstations for professional translators, to work on controlled language and domain-restricted systems, and to the application of translation components in multilingual information systems.

These trends have continued into the late 1990s. In particular, the use of MT and translation aids or translator workstations by large corporations has grown rapidly—a particularly impressive increase is seen in the area of software localization, i. e. the adaptation and translation of equipment and documentation for new markets. There has been a huge growth rate in the sales of MT software for personal computers (primarily for use by non-translators) and even more significantly, the availability of MT from online networked services. The demand has been met not just by new systems but also by "downsized" and improved versions of previous mainframe systems. While in these applications, reasonably good quality translation may be required, there has been even more rapid growth of automatic translation for direct Internet applications like electronic mail, Web pages, etc. With these developments, MT software is becoming a mass-market product, as familiar as word processing and desktop publishing. World-renowned translation systems include Google Translate, Baidu 翻译, Youdao 翻译, 360 翻

译, etc.

Principles of MT

The working principles of MT, based on the language database, are to establish a language database that contains the original and target languages' contradistinctions of all types of sentences. In translation, it takes out the sentences that are similar to the input sentences, then imitates examples to actualize the conversion of original language. The difficulty of this method is the construction of a huge language database. The approach of "based on language database" will improve the translation quality, though building up a perfect language database demands a great of manpower and material resources. This method is cost-effective.

Advantages and Limitations of MT

MT has the following three advantages:

1) MT is much **cheaper** than HT (Human Translation).

2) MT is much **faster** than HT.

3) MT is **easy** to operate.

Despite its obvious advantages, MT has to overcome its inevitable limitations in terms of differences in culture, grammar and context.

1. Culture

It may pose great difficulties for computers to translate from one language and culture into another, for sometimes it is almost impossible to understand cultural implications in language expressions. Please look at the following table carefully and think about differences between Baidu, Youdao and recommended versions.

	Source Text	Target Text	Recommended Version and Explanation
Baidu	There is a bit of **Old Adam** in us all.	我们每个人都有一点老亚当的气质。	我们大家都有一点干坏事的本性。
Youdao	There is a bit of **Old Adam** in us all.	我们每个人都有一点老亚当的影子。	**Old Adam** 意为"人类中固有的罪恶;未赎过罪的人"

(continued)

	Source Text	Target Text	Recommended Version and Explanation
Baidu	Whoever is **goldbricking** when I came back gets a real talking.	当我回来的时候，不管是谁在吹牛，都能得到真正的谈话。	我回来时谁要是在偷懒的话，可别怪我不客气。
Youdao	Whoever is **goldbricking** when I came back gets a real talking.	当我回来的时候，谁在说金砖，谁就得好好谈谈。	**goldbrick** 作动词，表示“欺诈；偷懒”
Baidu	狗嘴里吐不出象牙。	A dog cannot spit out ivory from its mouth.	A filthy mouth utters no decent language.
Youdao	狗嘴里吐不出象牙。	A dog's mouth emits no ivory.	出自巴金《秋》：“‘还有嘞，我替你说出来：狗嘴里吐不出象牙。’淑华调皮地笑道。”比喻坏人嘴里说不出好话来。
Baidu	天有不测风云。	The weather is unpredictable.	Anything unexpected may happen any time.
Youdao	天有不测风云。	A storm may arise from a clear sky. /Something unexpected may happen any time.	本指自然界的风云变幻难以预料。后多比喻人有难以预测的灾祸，通常与“人有旦夕祸福”连用。

2. Grammar

Eugene A. Nida pointed out that grammatical analysis is an extremely important part of the translation process. Please look at the following table carefully and think about differences between Baidu, Youdao and recommended versions.

	Source Text	Target Text	Recommended Version
Baidu	We don't read books for amusement.	我们读书不是为了娱乐。	我们读书不是为了消遣。
Youdao	We don't read books for amusement.	我们读书不是为了娱乐。	

(continued)

	Source Text	Target Text	Recommended Version
Baidu	This job gives him plenty of responsibility—he is **in charge of** several thousand of workers, and plenty of cash.	这份工作给了他足够的责任——他负责数千名工人，还有大量的现金。	这份工作给了他足够的责任——他管理着数千名工人，并掌管着大量现金。
Youdao	This job gives him plenty of responsibility—he is **in charge of** several thousand of workers, and plenty of cash.	这份工作给了他很多责任——他管理着几千名工人，而且有很多钱。	
Baidu	他有两米高。	He is two meters tall.	He is two meters tall. (high 与 tall 语法意义不同)
Youdao	他有两米高。	He has two meters high.	
Baidu	我想她了，你想去看她吗?	I missed her, do you want to go see her?	I miss her. Do you want to see her?
Youdao	我想她了，你想去看她吗?	I miss her. Do you want to see her?	

3. Context

The meaning of any word or expression relates closely to its context.

	Source Text	Target Text	Recommended Version
Baidu	Our garden is overlooked from the neighbor's balcony.	从邻居的阳台上可以俯瞰我们的花园。	从邻居家的阳台上可以俯瞰我们家的花园。
Youdao	Our garden is overlooked from the neighbor's balcony.	从邻居的阳台可以俯瞰我们的花园。	
Baidu	孔子曾说:"智者乐水，仁者乐山。"	Confucius once said, "Wise people enjoy water, benevolent people enjoy mountains."	Confucius once said that "The wise are happy with water, and the benevolent are happy with mountains."
Youdao	孔子曾说:"智者乐水，仁者乐山。"	Confucius once said, "The wise enjoy water, the benevolent enjoy mountain."	

Post-editing(PE)

MT is becoming an integral part of modern translation programs. The rapid development of MT technology—and the great sum of money companies are investing—are supportive of this enterprise. Also, MT quality is improving rapidly: the results have become increasingly fluent and accurate. But, despite technological advances, humans still need to be involved in fine-tuning MT output, particularly for high-value pieces of content. Here, we'll examine post-editing, including its definition and essence and some of the strategies you should consider when implementing a post-editing program.

Definition, Classification and Essence of PE

It is important to pause and consider the task of PE, which differs considerably from classic or traditional translation. In essence, it is actually **a special form of review**. Translators always aim to produce a translated file that is as faithful as possible to the original in terms of either meaning, grammar, culture, content, or style.

But a post-editor may work differently, depending on the purpose or readership of the text. **There are generally two types of PE**: light PE and full PE. In light of the former, the focus is on ensuring that the target text rightfully reflects the meaning of the source, so spelling or grammatical errors are of secondary importance. Even style is often overlooked unless the errors affect or distort the meaning of the source. The most important consideration is whether the translation provides readers with sufficient information. However, in the latter, the post-editor produces a translation that is at the same quality level as that of a human translation.

Here is a list of the things a post-editor would correct when performing full PE:

1. **Punctuation**. Post-editors should know differences in punctuation marks between source language and target language.

2. **Formatting/Tagging**. Ensuring that all tags used in the source text (e. g. , text formatting, cross-references, etc.) are present in the target text and in the correct locations.

3. **Terminology**. Checking for appropriate use of industry- and client-specific terminologies as well as correct use of proper names.

4. **Fluency**. Checking and establishing readability to make the text as fluent and similar to human translation as possible.

5. **Country specifics**. Adapting country-specific currencies, units of measurement, formats of dates, numbers, addresses and punctuation marks, cultural references and so on.

6. **Style**. Adapting the style for the target audience and to client- and project-specific requirements.

7. **Culture**. It is rather difficult for computers to translate overt or covert cultural meanings in languages. Post-editors must deepen their understanding of cultural elements in the original and reliably translate them into the target language.

The Evolution from MT to PE

Numerous translators may be sceptical about MT and PE. Some are afraid of losing their jobs; others dislike the nature of PE work. But there is really no reason for fear. First, the use of MT is not suitable for all types of text. For texts that have high emotional/literary weight/charge, idioms, puns, humour or complex content, MT can perform so poorly that a post-editor must be able to fix every limitation—in which case, MT actually has no value at all. Machines can substitute words and groups of words from one language to another based on patterns taught to them through training, but they cannot handle all the aspects and complexities of human language. In addition, if there are errors or ambiguities in the source content, machines lack adequate judgment required to understand them and still produce a correct translation.

PE will therefore not replace classic or traditional translation, as there are still numerous cases where it is better for professional translators to start from scratch. It is simply an additional service that will complement existing offerings.

However, the acceptance of and willingness to work with MT technology is important for success in this field. When translators are expected to learn how to post-edit, it is absolutely necessary to explain to them how machine translation works, where it can help, when it shouldn't be used, and the nature of the errors that can occur. Also, they should be provided with guidelines on the levels of quality so that they can adapt themselves to their work accordingly. In addition, post-editors should be able to work in their familiar environments, i. e. , they should be able to use the same tools as those for classic translation. For all these reasons, training alone does not make someone a great post-editor. PE skills are acquired through daily practice. Studies show that even linguists boasting hundreds of thousands of words of PE experience may be problematic post-editors if their experiences were gained merely through very random tasks and over very long periods of time. Also, linguists who have experiences of more than two to three years might not have the right understanding of the actual quality of today's MT outputs.

In summary, translators can learn PE as an additional offering and skill set that may make them more marketable and available for more types of work.

How to Become a Qualified Post-editor

Becoming qualified and efficient post-editors takes more than attending free webinars that are usually offered by many colleges/universities and translation companies. Some language service providers offer a series of sessions of offline/online training for their employees or freelance translators. Also, some universities offer seminars on the topic. **Critical PE training** should include: 1) a technical introduction to MT; 2) the history of machine translation; 3) possible applications of MT and the associated decision criteria; 4) the differences between PE for **statistics-based MT** (SMT) and **neural MT** (NMT); 5) practical PE exercises in both light and full PE techniques. The last point, guided practice, is very important. All these aspects will give prospective post-editors opportunities to ask questions and learn the nuances between the two types of PE first-hand. In any case, training or other continuing education to become post-editors is an investment in both the career of translators and the future of enterprise MT development and deployment. The increase in the use of MT will lead to a greater demand for PE.

C-E Guided Translation Practice 8

1. 水池中，几许荷叶托着晶莹的露珠，一支细长的花枝，洁白的花瓣腼腆地伸向湖面，随着微风吹拂，宛如少女揽镜自照，欲语还羞。一阵轻风，湖边的柳絮飘飞，如仙女散花旋转飞舞。（节选自《天乳》第四章）

2. 毛泽东出生于山水相依的韶山冲，就连他的名字都充满着水的润泽。“仁者乐山，智者乐水”，毛泽东是仁者，也是智者。毛泽东迷恋山岭峰峦，也钟情江河湖海。水赋予他跃动的灵感和才思、澎湃的激情和斗志、敏锐的诗情和智慧。对毛泽东而言，水是历史馆，水是风物志；水是思想库，水是教科书；水是比武台，水是运动场，包含了深邃的人生感悟、悠长的历史积淀和厚重的文化底蕴。毛泽东吟咏的江河湖海气韵生动，或湍急、或流深、或汹涌、或壮阔；要么纪实叙事，要么写景抒情，要么明志喻理。这些作品气势恢宏，想象丰富，思想深刻，意境高远。（节选自《毛泽东诗词中的江河湖海》）

3. 优秀的山水诗大都具有“诗中有画，画中有诗”的特征。所谓“诗中有画”，就是用画笔把山水风物中精深微妙的蕴涵点染出来，使读者获得直接的审美感受。如孟浩然《秋登万山寄张五》，把登高的“怡悦”之情抒发得淋漓尽致：“北山白云里，隐者自怡悦。相望始登高，心随雁飞灭。愁因薄暮起，兴是清秋发。时见归村人，平沙渡头歇。天边树若荠，江畔洲如月。何当载酒来，共醉重阳节。”其中有诗人自己登山的身影，有想象中北山隐者张五的怡悦之情，还有阔远的视野以及闪烁于其间的种种景物。它的突出特点就是表现在一个“远”字上，用远景烘托远意。“远意”没有明说，只是影影绰绰地表现在“心随雁飞灭”的描摹上。勾画远景的笔墨也不多，却很有层次，显示出和谐的韵律与虚静阔远的美，像“天边树若荠，江畔洲如月”，清新淡远，与隐者（包括诗人自身）恬淡高远的情趣相为表里，几乎达到天然淡泊的完美境界。

参考文献
References

[1] CAO X Q,GAO E. A Dream of Red Mansions [M]. Translated by Yang Xianyi and Gladys Yang. Beijing:Foreign Languages Press, 2005.

[2] VENUTI L. The translator's invisibility: a history of translation [M]. London; New York:Routledge, 1994.

[3] 许渊冲. 道德经:汉英对照[M]. 北京:海豚出版社,2013.

[4] 艾柯. 别停下生命的脚步[M]. 天津:天津教育出版社,2006.

[5] 艾学山,李万红. 水科学若干领域研究前沿[J]. 水利学报,2002(7):125-128.

[6] 蔡基刚. 英语写作与抽象名词表达[M]. 上海:复旦大学出版社,2003.

[7] 陈德彰. 汉英对比语言学[M]. 北京:外语教学与研究出版社,2010.

[8] 董增川. 科学合理配置区域水资源[J]. 山西水利,2006,22(6):10.

[9] 董哲仁. 探索生态水利工程学[EB/OL]. (2007-02-08)[2023-03-10]. http://gjkj. mwr. gov. cn/slkj1/zslt/200702/t20070208_621910. html.

[10] 冯庆华,陈科芳. 汉英翻译基础教程[M]. 北京:高等教育出版社,2008.

[11] 光善万. 大型水利工程的哲学思考[D/OL]. 成都:成都理工大学,2010[2023-03-10]. https://wenku. so. com/d/718219a226e92b576cc0bb30b0260691.

[12] 胡敏. 论语(中英双语·诵读版)[M]. 保罗·怀特,译. 北京:外文出版社, 2019.

[13] 金迪. 音乐与水文化[J]. 时代教育(教育教学版), 2012 (4):12.

[14] 金惠康. 跨文化交际翻译[M]. 北京:中国对外翻译出版公司,2003.

[15] 李扬. 听谭盾《永恒的水》[J]. 人民音乐, 2002(3): 31-33.

[16] 李宗新. 浅议加强水文化建设的主要任务及措施[J]. 华北水利水电学院学报(社会科学版),2008(5):18-21.

[17] 刘白羽. 长江三日[R/OL]. (2020-03-10)[2023-01-15]. https://www. vrrw. net/wx/8783. html.

[18] 刘宓庆, 章艳. 翻译美学教程[M]. 北京:中译出版社,2016.

[19] 敬正书. 加强水文化建设 为水利的可持续发展提供支撑[N]. 中国水利报,2006-11-30(2).
[20] 马吉刚,包婷. 人工自然是实现人与自然和谐的直接手段——谈如何从传统治水中吸取经验创造绿色治水环境[J]. 山东水利,1999(Z2):42-43.
[21] 梅明玉. 英汉语言对比分析与翻译[M]. 杭州:浙江大学出版社,2020.
[22] 钱钟书. 围城[M]. 北京:人民文学出版社,1980.
[23] 沈振中. 水利工程概论[M]. 北京:中国水利水电出版社,2011.
[24] 仝益民. 说词解句英汉语言对比与翻译[M]. 大连:大连理工大学出版社,2009.
[25] 王亚华. 中国治水转型:背景、挑战与前瞻[J]. 水利发展研究,2007,7(9):4-9.
[26] 王亚华,黄译萱. 中国水利现代化进程的评价和展望[J]. 中国人口·资源与环境,2012,22(6):120-127.
[27] 王金霞. 资源节约型社会建设中的水资源管理问题[J]. 中国科学院院刊,2012,27(4):447-454.
[28] 尉天骄. 乐水之旅——水文化探索与思考[M]. 北京:中国水利水电出版社,2020.
[28] 吴志才. 汉英水科学词典[M]. 南京:河海大学出版社,2015.
[29] 谢静波. 音乐艺术与水的交融对身心健康的作用积极——评《水与音乐》[J]. 给水排水, 2021(9):38.
[30] 徐钧. 可持续发展与水文化[C]//《鄂尔多斯学研究成果丛书》生态研究,2012.
[31] 徐莉萍. 水与绘画艺术[J]. 齐齐哈尔大学学报(哲学社会科学版),2005(3):125-127.
[32] 应丹. 国外治水的经验及启示[N]. 浙江日报,2014-02-10(6).
[33] 曾诚. 实用汉英翻译教程[M]. 北京:外语教学与研究出版社,2002.
[34] 张宇. 上善若水任方圆 厚德如霖泽九州——浅析谭盾《水乐》的音乐特征及文化价值[J]. 中国水利,2015(12):61-64.
[35] 郑炜东. 创新管理体制和运行机制 全面推进依法治水进程[J]. 山东水利,2007(4):20-21.
[36] 中国社会科学院语言研究所词典编写室. 现代汉语词典(汉英双语)[M]. 北京:外语教学与研究出版社,2002.

[37] 祝吉芳. 英汉翻译:方法与试笔[M]. 北京:北京大学出版社,2004.

[38] 左其亭. 水科学的学科体系及研究框架探讨[J]. 南水北调与水利科技,2011,9(1):113-129.

[39] 王磊,解华顶,张裕童. 水文化遗产生存状态及解决办法初探[J]. 中国水利,2019(12):59-61.

[40] 朱纯深翻译的《荷塘月色》赏析[EB/OL]. (2020-12-04)[2023-02-10]. https://zhuanlan. zhihu. com/p/330364942.

[41] 朱自清荷塘月色英语全文[EB/OL]. (2023-03-06)[2023-5-30]. https://www. ruiwen. com/wenxue/zhuziqing/28019. html.

[42] 品味中国文字之美:莎翁诗歌《你说你多爱雨》多版本翻译[EB/OL]. (2021-12-05)[2023-5-10]. http://news. sohu. com/a/505621631_121124407. https://tieba. baidu. com/p/6633583494

[43] 东晋故事:山水诗鼻祖谢灵运[EB/OL]. (2018-02-24)[2023-5-10]. http://www. doc88. com/p-7763888144885. html.

[44] 黎越常艺术. 立象以尽意:山水画中的写意精神[EB/OL]. (2019-10-20)[2023-5-20]. https://baijiahao. baidu. com/s? id=1647885606451153914.

[45] 现代汉语中表示动态的几种方法[EB/OL]. (2017-01-06)[2023-4-20]. https://wenda. so. com/q/1484673635722922.

参考译文
Guided Practice Reference Versions

C-E Guided Translation Practice 1

Water culture is an important part of the cultural system and a new form of culture that exists objectively. It is the sum of the material, behavioral and institutional achievements with spiritual achievements as the core, created by people in the process of human history and civilization in dealing with the relationship between man and nature and embodying a social state of the relationship between man and water, the essence of which is the culture of the relationship between man and water. The emergence, formation and development of water culture has its profound historical origins, natural factors, social environment, cultural elements and even the background of the water conservancy industry. It originates from the crystallization and sublimation of the understanding of the relationship between human and water in the process of dealing with water. The understanding of water has risen to "the source of life, the foundation of ecology, and the essentials of production". The status of water conservancy in national economic and social development and the role of civilization in the progress of civilization have become increasingly important. Water culture is an important source and support that unites man and water. Therefore, strengthening the construction of water culture is the need of the times for economic and social development, and an important part of the prosperity of advanced socialist culture.

C-E Guided Translation Practice 2

The originator of landscape poetry is Xie Lingyun of the Eastern Jin Dynasty. The landscape poetry pioneered by Xie Lingyun brought the beauty of the natural world in poems, making it an independent aesthetic object. His creation not only liberated poetry from the metaphysics of "indifference", but also strengthened the artistic skills and expressiveness of poetry, and influenced a generation of new style of poetry. The emergence of landscape poetry not only made landscape an independent aesthetic object, adding a new theme to Chinese poetry, but also opened a new poetry style of the Southern Dynasty generation. Following Tao Yuanming's idyllic poems, landscape poetry marked the further communication and harmony between man and nature, and signified the emergence of a new natural aesthetic concept and taste. A large number of landscape poems emerged in the Eastern Jin Dynasty, mainly because of the chaotic national conditions.

C-E Guided Translation Practice 3

A Brief Introduction to Landscape Painting: Before the Wei, Jin, Southern and Northern dynasties, landscape painting is not an independent type of painting; the economic prosperity of the Sui and Tang dynasties promoted the development of culture and broadened the range of painting subjects. The development of landscape painting had begun to take shape. During the Five Dynasties period, dyeing method of landscape painting was developed. With different landscape factions, a large number of famous people emerged at this stage. All kinds of paintings were fully developed in the Song Dynasty and came in fashion during that time. Underlying philosophies and techniques also varied. Landscape painting had thus reached its peak. With the development of literati painting in the Yuan Dynasty, the mutual integration of calligraphy and painting while focusing on the depiction of the natural scenery, and with more emphasis on the expression of subjective emotions, landscape painting tends to be freehand brushwork. There were many factions of landscape painting in the Ming and Qing dynasties. With variable styles and hundreds of flowers blooming in the painting world, Eastern and Western art began to communicate and landscape painting has developed into a new style. Up till the present, landscape painting has not stopped developing.

C-E Guided Translation Practice 4

1. China has a profound water culture. Water culture heritages as important historical precipitations of water culture are of particular significance. In the face of severe surviving situations of water culture heritages, solutions should be explored. For important water culture heritages, cultural relics and corresponding cultural departments should actively work together to apply to the national,

provincial and municipal levels of cultural relic protection units and national and provincial intangible cultural heritages to carry out graded protection, erect cultural relic preservation monuments in front of important water culture heritages, and introduce relevant information about the heritages and their importance. For different water culture heritages in specific heritage concentration areas, targeted research and discussion should be carried out as a whole, and corresponding plans formulated, so as to implement the protection of water culture heritages by combining the three aspects of point, line and surface into one in large regional scopes across river basins and provinces.

2. Water culture heritage is the remains of human water activities and the witness to the history of human's water control and social development. Therefore, historicity is its significant characteristic. Different historical times, regions and nationalities present different historical and cultural characteristics. Water culture heritage is of important historical and cultural value, which is manifested in three aspects. First, it records history and culture. Many of the intangible cultural heritages record human water activities and describe the relationship between human beings and water. The myths, legends, epics, songs, literature and stories widely spread in the folk contain a large number of historical themes concerning water affairs, which is an important content of water cultural heritage. Second, it represents the level of social development, and the historicity and timeliness of water culture. It can also represent the overall level of social and economic development in ancient times. On the one hand, water activities can reflect the ancient social and economic conditions and agricultural production level; on the other hand, through the coordinating relationship between human and water, social politics, culture, art and philosophy can be viewed from the deeper perspective. Third, we will carry forward fine cultural achievements and engage ourselves in spiritual thinking. Water culture is the mother culture of Chinese national culture, which integrates and gathers the excellent cultural achievements derived from laborious creation of Chinese sons and daughters, and is the essence of Chinese national culture. "Those who govern the country must first control the water." The idea of water control can be refined and sublimated into the idea of governing the country, and can even develop into the philosophical thought, and have a profound impact on religious beliefs, moral culture and life philosophy.

3. The Grand Canal is the longest artificial river that extends all the way from Beijing in the north to Hangzhou in the south, and one of the greatest projects in Chinese history. It was first built for grain transportation and later also for transportation of other commodities. The areas along the canal have gradually developed into the industrial and commercial centers of China. For a long period of time, the canal has been playing a significant role in the development of Chinese economy, greatly enhancing the personnel exchange and cultural communication between northern and southern regions.

4. Dujiangyan, whose construction was started in the third century BC, is located across the Minjiang River in west Chengdu Plain, approximately 50 kilometers away from Chengdu. What impresses people most is its damless water control. For more than 2,000 years, it has been playing an effective role in flood prevention and irrigation, turning the Chengdu Plain into a fertile land guaranteed for harvest against droughts or floods and one of the most significant grain production areas in China. Dujiangyan serves as the oldest water conservancy project in the world, which is still used to control water without the help of dams, embodying the Chinese wisdom that human and nature co-exist in harmony.

5. Karez is a water conservancy system found in the dry region of Xinjiang, in which underground channels join wells together. The system collects a large amount of rainwater and melted snow water that seeps into underground, and drains the water to the ground by the natural mountain slope for the irrigation of fields and daily use. Karez reduces the evaporation on the ground and does little harm to the surface, thus effectively protecting natural resources and the ecological environment. The system embodies the Chinese wisdom that human and nature co-exist in harmony, and is well recognized as a major contribution to human civilization.

6. Ecological progress is an important component of our overall approach to building socialism with Chinese characteristics and the Four-pronged comprehensive Strategy. All regions and departments should diligently implement the new development concepts, be fully aware that "clear water and green mountains are invaluable assets", and make every effort to usher in a new era of ecological development under the socialist system.

Reform for ecological progress should be driven to a new level, and a pertinent institutional framework should be set up as soon as possible, providing functional mechanisms buttressed by the rule of law. By introducing supply-side structural reform, we will speed up China's development in a green, circular, and low-carbon fashion, and make our work and our daily life less resource-reliant and more environment-friendly. Emphasis will be put on the supervision of environmental crimes and violations of Party discipline and the law in relation to environmental protection will be handled accordingly. We will focus on our strength on pressing environmental problems, so that the public will see noticeable improvement in the ecological environment. Party committees and governments at all levels, along with other relevant bodies, must treat ecological progress as an important task, take solid steps to tackle difficult issues, and be persistent and pragmatic to achieve concrete results. They must make sure that the decisions and plans of the Party Central Committee on ecological development are thoroughly implemented and strive to contribute to a better environment for a beautiful China and to global ecological safety. (Clear Waters and Green Mountains Are Invaluable Assets November 28, 2016: 426-427)

C-E Guided Translation Practice 5

1. The Swiss writer and Nobel laureate Hermann Hesse stressed the importance of serving "not war and destruction but peace and reconciliation". Countries should foster partnerships based on dialogue, non-confrontation and non-alliance. Major powers should respect each other's core interests and major concerns, keep their differences under control and build a new model of relations featuring non-conflict, non-confrontation, mutual respect and win-win cooperation. As long as we maintain communication and treat each other with sincerity, the "Thucydides trap" can be avoided. Big countries should treat smaller ones as equals instead of acting as a hegemony imposing their will on others. No country should open the Pandora's box by willfully waging wars or undermining the international rule of law. Nuclear weapons, the Sword of Damocles that hangs over mankind, should be completely prohibited and thoroughly destroyed over time to make the world free of nuclear weapons. Guided by the principle of peace, sovereignty, inclusiveness and shared governance, we should turn the deep sea, the polar regions, the outer space and the Internet into new frontiers for

cooperation rather than a wrestling ground for competition.

2. The Three Gorges Hydropower Station, namely the Three Gorges Project on the Yangtze River, is also known as the Three Gorges Project. The Xiling Gorge section of the Yangtze River in Yichang City, Hubei Province, China and the Gezhouba Hydropower Station downstream form a cascade power station. The Three Gorges Hydropower Station is currently the world's largest hydropower station and clean energy production base, and is also the largest engineering project ever constructed in China. The Three Gorges Hydropower Station has more than ten functions, including shipping, power generation, planting and so on. The Three Gorges Hydropower Station was approved by the National People's Congress of China in 1992, and officially started construction in 1994, began storage and power generation on the afternoon of June 1, 2003, and was completed in 2009. The unit equipment is mainly provided by the joint venture co-founded by the German VOITH, the United States General Electric (GE) and the German SIEMENS VGS and the joint venture by the French ALSTOM and the Swiss ABB.

With an elevation of 185 meters and a storage elevation of 175 meters, the reservoir is 2,335 meters long. With a total investment of 95.46 billion yuan, 32 hydropower units with a capacity of 700,000 kilowatts are installed. The last hydropower unit of the Three Gorges Power Station was put into operation on July 4, 2012, which means that the Three Gorges Hydropower Station with an installed capacity of 22.4 million kilowatts has become the world's largest hydropower station and clean energy production base ever since the day.

C-E Guided Translation Practice 6

1. As oil is found deep in the ground, its presence cannot be determined only by a study of the surface. Consequently, a geological survey of the underground rock structure must be carried out. If it is thought that the rocks in a certain area contain oil, a "drilling rig" is assembled, the most obvious part of which is called "a derrick". It is used to lift sections of a pipe which are lowered into the hole made by the drill. As the hole is being drilled, a steel pipe is pushed down to prevent the sides from falling in. If oil is struck, a cover is firmly fixed to the top of the pipe and the oil is allowed to escape through a series of valves.

2. She is very charming when singing *Hand in Hand* in a duet with her life-

long companion. White-haired and wrinkled, she may be one of our grannies, a perfect image of kindness as she is often described. The furrows ploughed by time deny replenishment with cosmetics, for they are fertile soil radiating the fragrance of history.

3. A female is most beautiful when she is in tears, which reveals her innermost love. Tears are gifts bestowed by God to all living things of sensitivity, especially a woman, for they serve as an outlet to her pent-up feelings. When crystallized, love turns into tears to convey messages of the heart.

4. As the birthplace of dragon boat races, Dongting Lake is very famous in the Chinese culture. It is said that dragon boat races started on the eastern side of the lake, in order to look for the body of Qu Yuan, a country-loving poet in the State of Chu. Dragon boat races and the beautiful scenery around Dongting Lake attract thousands of tourists from all over China and the world every year.

5. Qinghai Lake is at the crossing point of several bird migration paths across Asia. Many birds take Qinghai Lake as a place to rest during their migration. To the west of the lake, are the famous "Bird Islands", attracting birdwatchers from all over the world. Every summer, visitors also come here to watch the Qinghai Lake international cycling race.

6. Water is one of the three natural elements of human survival besides sunlight and air. Water gives birth to life. In general, water accounts for 70% of body weight in infants, 52% in adult women, and 61% in adult men. An adult needs about two litres of water a day to survive normally, and will die within a few days without water.

7. Three-quarters of the earth's surface is covered by the ocean of water, so water is one of the important external environments for human beings. Water is also an important part of the human internal environment, because water is the medium of human metabolism. The human body needs to constantly absorb water and nutrients from the outside world to transport various nutrients to various parts of the body and expel metabolites through water. And the water also contains a variety of trace elements. If the water quality is poor, or it is polluted halfway, its health consequences can be unimaginable.

8. Natural water is colorless, odorless, tasteless and transparent. A river, for example, is like this from its source. However, after flowing through a long river,

flowing through large and small factory areas and towns, bringing together industrial wastewater and domestic sewage from all directions, the originally clear river will have had a large number of pathogens, chemicals and suspended substances, and the river will have been seriously polluted. The causes of pollution are both natural and man-made. Polluted water is absolutely undrinkable. If the contaminated water without sanitation treatment is drunk by people, depending on the pollution situation, a variety of diseases caused by viruses, bacteria, parasites, and insects can occur. Acute and chronic poisoning can be caused by the toxic metals contained in the water. Cancer can result from carcinogens contained in water. Of course, the application of such kinds of polluted water will also affect the normal progress of industrial and agricultural production.

C-E Guided Translation Practice 7

1. The Red Sea had long since been crossed, and the ship was now on its way over the Indian Ocean; but as always the sun mercilessly rose early and set late, encroaching upon the better part of the night. The night, like paper soaked in oil, had become translucent. Locked in the embrace of the sun, the night's own form was indiscernible. Perhaps it had become intoxicated by the sun, which would explain why the night sky remained flushed long after the gradual fading of the rosy sunset. By the time the ruddiness dissipated and the night itself awoke from its stupor, the passengers in their cabins had awakened, glistening with sweat; after bathing, they hurried out on deck to catch the ocean breeze. Another day had begun. (Translated by Jeanne Kelly and Nathan K. Mao)

2. On Miss Tang's charming, well-proportioned, round face were two shallow dimples; one look at her fresh and natural complexion, which most girls would have had to spend time and money to imitate, was enough to make one drool and forget his thirst, as though her skin were a piece of delicious fruit. Not especially large, her eyes were lively and gentle, making the big eyes of many women seem like the big talk of politicians — big and useless. A classics scholar, upon seeing her lovely teeth when she smiled, might wonder why both Chinese and Western traditional and modern poets would want to turn into the pin in a woman's hair, the belt around her waist, the mat on which she slept, or even the shoes and socks, that she wore, and not think of transforming themselves into her toothbrush. Her

hair unwaved, her eyebrows unplucked, and her lips unadorned by lipstick, she appeared to allow nature to take its own course with regard to her looks and had no wish to amend it in any way. In short, she was one of those rarities of modern civilized society — a genuine girl. Many city girls who put on all the precocious airs cannot be considered as girls; then there are just as many others who are confused, silly, and sexless, and they too don't deserve to be called women. (Translated by Jeanne Kelly and Nathan K. Mao)

C-E Guided Translation Practice 8

1. In the pool were a few lotus leaves holding some sparkling dewdrops and a slender flower branch with white petals stretching out over the lake. With the gentle breeze blowing, it was like a shy girl looking into a mirror, intending to talk but daring not because of her timidity. A gentle breeze fluttered the willow catkins by the lake, making them spin and dance like a fairy scattering flowers.

2. Mao Zedong was born in Shaoshan Chong, where mountains and rivers are intertwined, and even his name is filled with the radiance of water. "The wise are happy with water; and the benevolent are happy with mountains." Mao Zedong is a benevolent and wise person and infatuated with mountains and peaks, as well as rivers, lakes, and seas. Water has endowed him with vibrant inspiration and talent, surging passion and fighting spirit, sharp poetry and wisdom. For Mao Zedong, water is a museum of history, and a record of scenery. Water is a think tank; water is a textbook; water is a martial arts platform; water is a sports field, containing profound insights into life, longtime historical accumulation, and rich cultural heritage. Mao Zedong's chants of rivers, lakes, and seas are vivid, either turbulent, deep, or magnificent; they are either narratives based on facts, lyrics through scenery depiction, or metaphors imbued with clear aspirations. All these works are magnificent in momentum, rich in imagination, profound in thought, and lofty in artistic conception.

3. Most of the excellent landscape poems have the characteristics of "painting in poetry, and poetry in painting". The so-called "painting in poetry" is to use the brush to dye out the profound and subtle connotations in the landscape, so that the reader can obtain a direct aesthetic feeling. For example, Meng Haoran's "To Zhang Wu on Climbing Mount Wan in Autumn" vividly expresses the "pleasant

joy" of climbing: "This mountain is hidden amongst white clouds. The recluse is complacently pleased being alone. Looking at each other, the heart flies with the geese. Sorrow rises because of thin twilight, and happiness rises because it's early autumn. When seeing the people of the village, Pingsha Ferry rested I. The tree on the edge of the sky is like a buckwheat, and the riverside bottomland is like the moon. Why not bring wine and get drunk with the festival?" Among these verses are the figure of the poet himself climbing the mountain, the pleasant feeling of Zhang Wu, the hermit in the North Mountain, and the broad vision and various scenes that flicker in between. Its outstanding feature is that it is expressed in the word "far", which uses the vision to set off the distant meaning. "Far meaning" is not explicitly stated, but is only vaguely depicted in "the heart flies with the geese". There are not many brushstrokes and inks to sketch the vista, but they are very layered, showing a harmonious rhythm and the beauty of the void and vastness, like "the tree on the edge of the sky is like a buckwheat, the riverside bottomland is like the moon", fresh and distant, and the hermits' (including the poet himself) idyllic and lofty taste, almost reaching the perfect realm of natural indifference.